ISBN 978-1-331-78466-1
PIBN 10234309

1 MONTH OF
FREE
READING

at
www.ForgottenBooks.com

By purchasing this book you are eligible for one month membership to ForgottenBooks.com, giving you unlimited access to our entire collection of over 700,000 titles via our web site and mobile apps.

To claim your free month visit:

www.forgottenbooks.com/free234309

Lady Blane
from
Lord Swansea.
Christmas 1916.

Great calling names /
H. Walpole '9-57-59-73 (90)
Parish house (good) 11-12
Dress 15=16   101-104
Devonshire House Set 19, 137
Devonshire house   20, 22
+ George II Old Squarters, 23
5 Duke, 48, 24 yrs in 1772 - 62 [90-91]
Romance of Fox's mother 51—
2 beautiful Gunnings 57-59
  Fox, (51)
  Almack, 60.
  Bury June 87 - 107
  Social life 105

Fox as Speaker 1776, 107 +129
  verses, 127, character 127-129, Georgiana, 129
Dorset 107 <u>III</u>
gaily Derby 109 (Betty Hamilton 61
Dr Johnson 115, 121
Tunbridge 117
Sheridan, 131, 141, 3
Anne of Anspach
  Burke 137,

(married 1774) 62 - 63 - 64 . 67, 69 &
138,
) 1775, Venn censorship 88,) 93. vid
93 - 98, character 99 . 101, Mrs Delanne
Fears 101, feathers, 101 - 102 head dress &
married life 107 - 9 - 110. character 1
on uniform 114. Camp life 117, For
Burneys description (good 119

THE DEVONSHIRE
HOUSE CIRCLE

The Duchess of Devonshire

From an engraving by F. Bartolozzi after a portrait by Downman

THE DEVONSHIRE HOUSE CIRCLE

BY HUGH STOKES
WITH ·· ILLUSTRATIONS

HERBERT JENKINS LIMITED
ARUNDEL PLACE, HAYMARKET
LONDON, S.W. ⌗ ⌗ MCMXVII

THE DEVONSHIRE HOUSE CIRCLE

BY HUGH STOKES
WITH 17 ILLUSTRATIONS

HERBERT JENKINS LIMITED
ARUNDEL PLACE, HAYMARKET
LONDON, S.W. ✿ ✿ MCMXVII

THE LONDON AND NORWICH PRESS LIMITED, LONDON AND NORWICH, ENGLAND

CONTENTS

vii

CHAPTER X

CHAPTER XI

CHAPTER XII

CHAPTER XIII

CHAPTER XIV

CHAPTER XV

CHAPTER XVI

CHAPTER XVII

CHAPTER XVIII

CHAPTER XIX

CHAPTER XX

CONTENTS

CHAPTER XXI

CHAPTER XXII

CHAPTER XXIII

ILLUSTRATIONS

THE DEVONSHIRE
HOUSE CIRCLE

THE DEVONSHIRE HOUSE CIRCLE

INTRODUCTION

Talleyrand and the sweetness of life—the " good old days "—the charm of the late eighteenth century—the *ton*—the Duchess of Devonshire and Lady Holland—the French Revolution and the doctrines of Rousseau—George II. and George III.—an unsocial Court—the Whig aristocracy and the royal struggle for power—political animosities—sinecures and place-hunters—the lax clergy—coarse manners—privilege and fine clothes—an age of individuality.

"THEY who did not live before 1789 knew not the sweetness of life," once remarked Talleyrand, with an air of melancholy regret. Men who agreed with the former Bishop of Autun on no other subject were at one with him in this judgment upon a cherished past. Horne Tooke, also a clerical failure, who belonged to a slightly earlier generation (he was eighteen years older than the French diplomatist), said that the middle of the eighteenth century was England's happiest time. Edmund Burke remembered his youth with joy, and could find no pleasure in the contemplation of the future. " If I shall live much longer," he wrote in 1797, " I shall see the end of all that is worth living for in this world."

Man is invariably a pessimist when he compares the present with the past. The few exceptions to so general a rule hardly need consideration, for such attitude is profoundly human. We mourn our dead days as we mourn our dead friends. They return to our memory enshrined in a sunshine which seldom illuminates the present. " 'Tis a maxim with me to be as young as long as one can," cried Lady Mary Wortley Montagu. " There is nothing can pay one for that

B   I

unavailable ignorance which is the companion of youth ; those sanguine, groundless hopes, and that lively vanity which makes all the happiness of life." The " good old days " are, in reality, the " good young days," before a youth of frolics has faded into " an old age of cards." In regretting the past we are offering unconscious homage to our own lost youth. The verdict of Talleyrand and his contemporaries is repeated whenever one generation criticises the rise of its successor.

Yet in the second half of the eighteenth century there was indubitably a charm which has vanished. To discover the secret of its fascination is difficult, but it was probably the charm and interest which often surround strongly-marked individualities. London during those years reached an intellectual and fashionable brilliance which has never since been equalled. The social life of the metropolis blazed with an extraordinary number of curious personalities who bubbled over with egotistical wisdom and eccentric wit. Around them gathered crowds of eager listeners. These varying circles were interlinked by a community of excitement. Thanks to the patient genius of James Boswell, the table-talk of Samuel Johnson and his friends has been preserved to us almost without a gap. We know their names, what they thought, what they said, how they disagreed. But there were other *coteries* as interesting, if not quite so brilliant, of which we can collect but a few scattered fragments. The " blue-stockings," Mrs. Montagu, Mrs. Vesey, and a dozen rivals, held salons which were far from contemptible. The musical circle presided over by Dr. Burney has been preserved to a slight extent in the diaries of his daughter. Mrs. Thrale's drawing-room gave hospitality to fashion, commerce, and the arts. The portraits of her friends which decorated the library at Streatham included those of Lords Sandys and Lyttelton, Johnson, Burke, Goldsmith, Murphy, Garrick, Baretti, Chambers, and Reynolds. Mr. Thrale himself, " obliging to nobody, and confers a favour less pleasingly than many a man refuses to confer one," and that blithe spirit his wife, were as attractive personally as the men who sat round their board.[1] The green-rooms of the theatres, Drury Lane, Covent Garden, the Haymarket ; the coffee-houses skirting the Temple, the stone flags of Westminster Hall and the peaceful squares of the Inns of Court ; the officers' messes in the Horse Guards and St. James's Palace ; the studios of the great painters, Reynolds in Leicester Square, Gainsborough in Pall Mall ; other well-known, not to say notorious houses around Piccadilly and on the road to Marylebone, which sheltered less reputable but not less entertaining company—each centre of mirth and gossip might have lived for ever had it been blessed with a Boswell.

From this enumeration have been omitted the names of those high-born ladies who reigned as queens of the *ton*. They sparkled across the town like a string of diamonds. If they had beauty without intelligence, as Lady Coventry, for example, they were freely forgiven their lack of wit. If they had wit alone, and Lady Mary Wortley Montagu will in such case be at once remembered, no rude scribe referred to the plainness of their features. But more often they were as clever and good as they were beautiful. They, too, were the centres of vast circles, fashionable, artistic, and political. The bitter Lady Mary Coke, the fascinating Duchess of Argyll and Hamilton, the wicked Elizabeth Chudleigh, Duchess of Kingston, belonged to an older generation, the age of George II. rather than that of George III. They could not aspire to the same social importance as their successors, because society in itself was so much smaller. At the accession of George III. there were only 174 British peers. Within the first ten years of his reign the number was increased by forty-two. And society, as a

---

[1] Mrs. Piozzi (Hester Thrale) gives a far better picture of her first husband than of her second. Thrale was a man of character, Piozzi simply an amiability and therefore characterless. Thrale, according to his wife, was " a most exemplary brother . . . When the house of his favourite sister was on fire, and we were all alarmed with the account of it in the night, I well remember that he never rose, but bidding the servant who called us to go to her assistance, quietly turned about and slept to his usual hour." A classical example of " brotherliness."

whole, was not so rich, for commerce had not been yet admitted (never was, in fact, fully recognised until the early nineteenth century), whilst nabobs from the Indies were making, and not spending, their wealth.

Georgiana, Duchess of Devonshire, was favoured by fortune. She was not the most beautiful, nor the most intellectual of her class, but she was the most soft-hearted and the most susceptible to outside influence. Her supremacy was never really threatened until the end of the century. To the power of Devonshire House succeeded the power of Holland House. Lady Holland was a cleverer woman, but the essentially acrid humour of her temperament does not contrast favourably with the easy grace and good-will of the Duchess of Devonshire.

Lady Holland belonged to another world, for the eighteenth century and all its charm had passed. Many of the problems which beset the Duchess of Devonshire had been solved. Her age was one of many curiously-opposed characteristics. Weak sentimentalism was matched by callous brutality ; hot enthusiasm dashed itself unavailingly against the rocks of sober common-sense ; loyalty towards the sovereign mingled with a sincere belief in the virtues of a triumphant democracy ; appalling ignorance was rendered blacker still by contrasting heights of education and learning ; sensuality and debauchery, so widespread and universal as to be almost unnoticed, were associated with a refinement which tended towards effeminacy.

The tremendous upheaval in France shook the social fabric like an earthquake. Even philosophers and idealists began to tremble, and wondered whether the wreck of the old order was not a precursor of graver disasters. Rousseau had been carefully read in England, particularly in the higher circles. There is that famous outburst in Boswell's *Life* which shows the state of the wind. Boswell was a convert ; " had read many of Rousseau's animated writings with great pleasure and edification." In 1763 Johnson and several others were supping in Boswell's chambers, Inner Temple Lane. " Rousseau's treatise on the equality of mankind was at this time a fashionable topic," wrote Boswell, and a chance observation from a Mr. Dempster brought down the storm. In 1766 Johnson was even more violent upon the subject. Rousseau was " one of the worst of men ; a rascal who ought to be hunted out of society. . . . I would sooner sign a sentence for his transportation than that of any felon who has gone from the Old Bailey these many years." Johnson did not believe for a moment in the doctrine of the equality of men, and reflected the opinion of a large class of fellow-citizens when he asserted that " mankind are happier in a state of inequality and of subordination." Georgiana Cavendish belonged to a circle which admitted Rousseau's logic and could not deny Samuel Johnson's common-sense.

The reign of George III., coinciding almost exactly with the period covered by the subject of this volume, was an age of privilege and pleasure. It might almost be distinguished as the Age of Privilege. Pleasure will always remain the chief preoccupation of every wealthy civilization. But privilege was doomed when the gates of the Bastille were battered down on July 14, 1789. " The taking of the Bastille,' said Charles James Fox, " was the greatest event and the best in the world." With his brain obscured by party politics and a desire for Whig advantage, Fox did not fully comprehend the terrific nature of the change. The fall of the Bastille foreshadowed the ultimate extinction of those privileges of rank which had formed so large a part of the sweetness of life that Talleyrand lamented. Fox himself, who posed as the friend of the people and the upholder of liberty, was essentially a child of privilege. There is no place for another Fox in the modern democracy.

The older England, which had altered little since the days of the Restoration, ended abruptly at the death of George II. That monarch belonged to a discredited tradition as well as to an alien race. " He had the haughtiness of Henry the Eighth, without his spirit ; the avarice of Henry the Seventh, without his exactions ; the indignities of Charles the First, without his bigotry for his prerogative ; the vexations of King William, with as little skill in the management of parties; and the gross gallantry of his father, without his good nature or his honesty—he might, perhaps, have been honest if he had never hated his father, or had ever loved his son." Walpole's censure was sweeping, but not untrue in substance. George II. was the unloved head of an unsympathetic family, as the doggerel verse-maker endeavoured to suggest at the death of Frederick, Prince of Wales.

> " Here lies Fred,
> Who was alive and is dead.
> Had it been his father,
> I had much rather.
> Had it been his sister,
> No one would have missed her ;
> Had it been his brother,
> 'T would have been better than any other."

The children of George II. were described by their niece as " the best-humoured asses that ever were born." Other members of the circle could not even be described as good humoured. A medley of selfish men and women who lacked force of character, they failed to influence a society they were unable to govern, and certainly did not adorn.

George III. was but twenty-two when he ascended the throne, his Queen only seventeen when she arrived in Great Britain. In knowledge of the world they were both little more than children, and the obstinacy and tactlessness of children marked their actions until the end of their career. " Great kings have always been social," said Dr. Johnson in 1763, and George III. was not a social king. For half a century he and his consort remained almost completely out of touch with the brilliant life around them. " As private individuals," wrote a critic, " they were blameless and exemplary, but they seem to have considered public business and public representation as a heavy tax imposed on their station, instead of their being the first and inalienable duties of it. This tax duly paid in two weekly Drawing-Rooms and two yearly balls, the rest of their time was spent in a retirement which few of their opulent subjects were disposed to share with them. The Court, instead of being looked up to by the young as a source of gaiety, by the handsome as a scene of triumph, and by the fashionable as necessary to the confirmation of their pretensions, was soon voted by all as a duty, which was performed with a sort of contemptuous reluctance. No fashions emanated from a Court itself an enemy to show and avoiding all occasions of representation. To be distinguished by the sovereign, and to form a part of their small domestic circle, was considered a sort of superannuation in the gay society of the metropolis."

To some extent the reason was political. Young as he was, the new monarch quickly realised that he was under the thumb of a Whig oligarchy. The English aristocracy, as a whole, was liberal in its tendencies. The King, scion of a petty German principality, was reactionary. The Whig peerage had been responsible for the Revolution which dethroned James II. and placed William of Orange on the British throne. In the words of a recent historian, the Whigs affected to monopolize, by a kind of divine right of permanent tenure, the trusteeship of the Revolution settlement. The government of the country was practically in the hands of the great Whig families, the Cavendishes, Russells, Bentincks, Temples, Fitzroys, Pelhams, Wentworths, Lennoxes, and Conways.

After the long dominion of Sir Robert Walpole the Tories gradually disintegrated until they practically ceased to exist as a party. George III. determined to make a bid for untrammelled power, and looked to the old Jacobites for support against their traditional foes. For seven years he intrigued to gain their goodwill and assistance. At last, in 1770, he was successful. A ministry was formed which acknowledged his will. Throughout the years that followed the names remained unaltered. But the two opposing parties were, in reality, " King's men " and " Anti-court." The Tories did not invariably support the King ; the Whigs were sometimes to be found in the royal circle. Lord North, for example, who led the attack upon the supremacy of the Whig families, considered himself a Whig. The royal secret service funds attracted every greedy spirit. Statesmen

" ratted " from standard to standard according to the nature of the prospective reward, and although they lost the respect of every honest man they never appeared to lose a particle of their political power.

The intricate ebb and flow of party government, its coalitions, shifts and bids for place, concern this volume only indirectly. A period which included the loss of the American colonies, the fall of the French monarchy and the rise of a new spirit of freedom, could hardly fail to colour its social life with politics. In 1775 Mrs. Delany wrote to a friend : " The world is in a bother about the American affairs, but I am no politician and don't enter into these matters. Women lose all dignity when they enter into subjects that don't belong to them ; their own sphere affords them opportunities eno' to show their own consequence." That may have been the measured opinion of an older generation, although English women of the seventeenth century did not hold aloof when their country was threatened. But during the reign of George III. the younger women " entered into these matters " without a care for their dignity, and became most ardent politicians. " I wish there were any other topic of discourse than politics," wrote Horace Walpole despairingly in 1792, " but one can hear, one can talk nor think on anything else. It has pervaded all ranks and ages. A miss, not fourteen, asked Miss Agnes Berry lately whether she was aristocrat or democrat."

Extreme bitterness marked the party warfare, an animosity which probably would not have been so intense had not the ladies worked actively for their respective causes. Dr. Johnson, whose Jacobite youth was succeeded by an old age of rabid Toryism, surmised that " the first Whig was the Devil."[1] At another time he asserted that " Whiggism is a negation of all principle," and one evening when Charles James Fox occupied the presidential chair at " The

[1] The enemy was equally emphatic in its views. " Mama," asked the daughter of a famous Whig, " are Tories born wicked, or do they grow wicked afterwards ? " " They are born wicked, and grow worse," was the reply.

Club," Johnson rudely and emphatically declared every Whig to be a scoundrel. Nearly half a century later, towards the close of the period, Charles Kirkpatrick Sharpe wrote in a letter that " a Whig, properly such, always shows a complete ignorance of history as well as of human nature."[1] In the heat of his criticism, Sharpe overstepped the truth. There was a good deal of human nature in a party which could boast of such adherents as Georgiana, Duchess of Devonshire, Lady Elizabeth Foster, Mrs. Crewe, Mrs. Bouverie, and their followers.

Whig or Tory, King's friends or King's enemies, the labels were different, but the men and women remained the same. Politics became an engrossing game of skill, enjoyable for its own sake, but worth playing because the rewards were high. The Government of the country, whether nominally Whig or Tory, remained the monopoly of the governing classes, an exceedingly valuable monopoly, for no man was so rich that he deemed it unnecessary to extract what he could from the public funds. When we read of the sinecures held by Horace Walpole, George Selwyn and their associates, we are able to appreciate the fact that the complicated system was in reality extremely simple, and clearly designed by Heaven for the benefit of younger sons, penniless brothers, or any desolate relation of a minister who could so far pull himself together to appoint a deputy and sign a receipt for a quarterly salary. Walpole, at the age of twenty-one, was inspector of imports and exports in the custom-house, a post soon resigned for the more lucrative ushership of the exchequer. Later he was given " two other little patent offices," a comptrollership of the pipe and a clerkship of the estreats. The three were worth about £1,300 a year. George Selwyn enjoyed a brace of sinecures before he was of age, having been appointed clerk of the irons and surveyor of the meltings of the mint. They were not valuable, but they more

---

[1] This bitterness of political feeling continued well into the Victorian age. Coke of Norfolk, who was created Earl of Leicester in 1837, referred to George III., in a public speech delivered at Lynn during 1830, as " that wretch covered with blood."

than paid him for his sole official duty, which was to dine weekly at the public expense. When in after years he owned the two pocket boroughs of Gloucester and Ludgershall his devotion to the Court was rewarded by a registrarship of the Court of Chancery in Barbadoes and Paymaster of the Works. Pitt abolished the last sinecure in 1782, but Selwyn and his two votes were too important to be forgotten, and he was advanced to the vacant office of Surveyor-General of the Crown Works.

In the world of politics, as in the ordinary everyday world of people who have to work for their living, some men were less greedy than others. But the purest patriot and the noblest idealist differed little from the most venial place hunter. Few could resist the overpowering attraction of a dip into the chests of the Treasury. Even Burke did not neglect to profit from his position, finding money for himself and rich sinecures for the various members of his family. Wilkes, despite his protestations, was not clean-handed. Others, less famous, but not more public-spirited, did not trouble to ascend a pedestal. They lined their pockets with an energy which would excite our admiration if directed in some other manner. A Paymaster of the Forces, after a few years' enjoyment of his office, was able to leave his heirs an estate of half a million. One peer, a member of the Grenville clan, held sinecures worth £25,000 per annum, whilst a commoner who combined the offices of Secretary to the Treasury, Clerk to the House of Lords, and Master of the Pleas, drew an income of £10,000.

Political opponents were not to be gained over by argument, nor were political friends to be kept by conviction. Sir Robert Walpole, who bribed indiscriminately from the King downwards, said that he was obliged to bribe members not to vote against, but for their conscience. "My dear Madam," said Goldsmith's Lofty in the *Good-natured Man*, "all this is but a mere exchange. We do greater things for one another every day. Let me suppose you the First Lord of the Treasury; you have an employment in you that I want; I have a place in me that you want; do me here ; do you there ; interest on both sides, few words, flat, done and done, and it's over." Pit and boxes laughed at a sarcasm which was truth itself. In 1790 the common price of a seat in the House of Commons was £4,500 to £5,000, and the King, as well as public departments like the Admiralty and the Treasury, secured as many boroughs as they could pay for. The electorate was demoralised. " You need not ask me, my lord, who I votes for," said a free and independent elector in 1805, " I always votes for Mister Most."

Interest ruled the Church as it ruled the Parliament. Dr. Johnson confessed that in his day few of the clergy were raised to the episcopal bench for learning or piety, their only chance of promotion being a connection with some one who possessed parliamentary interest.[1] Whilst the inferior clergy starved upon stipends of £25 to £50 a year, the greater men scrambled for every gift they could extort from their privileged friends. Dr. Cornwallis held, in 1750, the rectory of Chelmondiston, in Suffolk, Tittleshall St. Mary, in Norfolk, a chaplaincy in ordinary to the King, a canonry at Windsor, and a prebendal stall at Lincoln. When elevated to the See of Lichfield he retained the Deanery of St. Paul's. A nephew combined the rectories of Boughton Malherbe and Wrotham in Kent, the incumbencies of Ickham and Adesham in the same county, the rectory of Newington in Oxfordshire, and then became prebendary of Westminster and Dean of Salisbury, when he relinquished the living of Adesham only. Paley was another notorious pluralist. Cowper described a parish priest as

"Loose in morals, and in manners vain,
In conversation frivolous, in dress
Extreme ; at once rapacious and profuse,
Frequent in park with lady at his side,
Ambling and prattling scandal as he goes,
But rare at home and never at his books."

[1] Yet no man had a greater respect for a bishop. " Mrs. Seward saw him presented to the Archbishop of York, and described his bow to an Archbishop as such a studied elaboration of homage, such an extension of limb, such a flexion of body, as have seldom or ever been equalled. The lay nobility were not equally grateful, although his deference for the peerage was extreme."—*Mrs. Piozzi.*

Hannah More, in her *Estimate of the Religion of the Fashionable World* (published in 1787), wrote : " Those who are able to make a fair comparison must allow that, however the present age may be improved in other important and valuable advantages, there is but little appearance remaining among the great and the powerful of that righteousness which exalteth a nation. They must confess that there has been a moral revolution in the national manners and principles very little analogous to that great political one which we hear so much and so justly extolled ; that our public virtue bears little proportion to our religious blessings, and that our religion has decreased in a pretty exact proportion to our having secured the means of enjoying it." With the exception of the Methodists there was a general indifference towards religion, and even a good Churchman like Dr. Johnson despised and disliked the Revivalists.

" I had a walk in New Inn Hall Garden with Dr. Johnson, Sir Robert Chambers, and some other gentlemen," runs a story in the Life of Lord Eldon. " Sir Robert was gathering snails and throwing them over the wall into his neighbour's garden. The Doctor reproached him very roughly, and stated to him that this was unmannerly and unneighbourly. ' Sir,' said Sir Robert, ' my neighbour is a Dissenter.' ' Oh ! ' said the Doctor, ' if so, Chambers, toss away, toss away, as hard as you can.' "

The incident was trifling, but characteristic of the lack of estimation in which Dissenters were held. But the clergy of the Established Church had as mean a sense of duty as the politicians. Arthur Young, referring to the French priests in 1789, does not praise his own countrymen. " The French clergy preserved, what is not always preserved in England, an exterior decency of behaviour. One did not find among them poachers or fox hunters, who having spent the morning scampering after the hounds, dedicate the evening to the bottle, and reel from inebriety to the pulpit. Such advertisements were never seen in France as I have heard of in England. ' Wanted, a curacy in a good sporting country, where the duty is light and the neighbourhood convivial.'"

Yet, on the whole, the public work of the country was not ill done, despite a financial code which was utterly corrupt and unscrupulous, and a social morality which left much to be desired. The art of management, wrote Lecky, whether applied to public business or to assemblies, lies strictly within the limits of education, and what is required is much less transcendent abilities than early practice, tact, courage, good temper, courtesy, and industry.

The giants of the Georgian age did not always possess such a string of estimable qualities. Fox cannot be praised for his industry, except over the faro table. Burke may have been sublime ; he was assuredly not courteous.

" When I forsake my King, may my God forsake me," cried the insincere Thurlow with a rhetorical outburst.

" He'll see you d—d first ! " added Wilkes.

" The sooner the better," was Burke's interpolation.[1] This was polished repartee in comparison with some flights of abuse. A prudish age is always coarse beneath the skin, and the late eighteenth century was extremely prudish and excessively coarse. Miss Burney's *Evelina* reeks of prudery as the novels of Smollett are tainted by coarseness. In this respect the great ladies were no different from the fishwives. Lavinia, Lady Spencer, described by Gibbon soon after her marriage in 1781 as " a charming woman who, with sense and spirit, has the wit and simplicity of a child,' swore with a wealth of vituperative adjective which shocked her younger relations. Ladies of the highest rank could use the argot of Seven Dials and Billingsgate. Lady Northumberland's reply to Lady Talbot at a crowded reception at

---

[1] Thurlow, who " avowed a disbelief in all public virtues," was, according to Lord Holland, a " morose and unamiable nature . . . an ill-natured and unfriendly man." Mrs. Piozzi told a story that he was one day storming at his old valet, who thought little of a violence with which he had been long familiar. " Go to the devil, *do*," cried the enraged master. " Go, I say, to the devil." " Give me a character, my lord," replied the fellow drily. " People like, you know, to have characters from their acquaintance."

Marlborough House must be searched for in Horace Walpole's correspondence. The same author reproduces the remark of an angry lady at Court in these terms : " This is not the place to be indecent, and therefore I shall *only* tell you that you are a rascal and a villain, and that if ever you dare to put your head into my house, I will kick you downstairs myself." Lady Mary Wortley Montagu, who never minced her words, told a friend that " fig leaves are as necessary for our minds as our bodies, and 'tis as indecent to show all we think as all we have." The later Georgian period was an age of social fig leaves which hid nothing.

" Qui n'a pas vécu avant 1789, ne connait pas la douceur de vivre." Ernest, King of Hanover, had been born within the charmed century—and lamented it. He remembered " the time when all peers never attended the House but dressed like gentlemen and peers," when " no minister came down to the House, having announced a motion, without being full dressed, with his sword by his side." A man might behave like a blackguard as long as he dressed like a gentleman. The same royal pessimist had no doubt when decay set in. " I maintain that the first change and shock in the ecclesiastical habits was the bishops being allowed to lay aside their wigs, their purple coats, short cassocks and stockings and cocked hats when appearing in public; for I can remember when Bishop Heard of Worcester, Courtenay of Exeter, and Markham, Archbishop of York, resided in Kew and its vicinity, that as a boy, I met them frequently walking about, dressed as I now tell you, in the fields and walks in the neighbourhood, and their male servants appeared equally all dressed in purple, which was the custom. The present Bishop of Oxford was the first who persuaded George IV. to be allowed to lay aside his wig, because his wife found him better-looking without it. I recollect full well that the Bishop of London who succeeded Bishop Porteous [Bishop Randolph, 1809-13] coming to St. James' to do homage to my father, which is the custom in the closet prior to the levée. Then Lord Sidmouth was Secretary of State, and he came into the closet, where I was at the time, and informed his Majesty that the bishop was there, but that he had refused to introduce him, as he had not a wig. Upon which I remember full well, as if it were to-day, that the King replied : ' You were perfectly right, my lord, and tell the bishop from me that until he has shaven his head, and has provided himself with a wig suitable to his garb, I shall not admit him into my presence,' and he was forced to go home, and could not be admitted until the week following, when he appeared *en costume*." [1]

Privilege and dress could not well be dissociated. " In civilized society," said Dr. Johnson, who touched upon everything concerning humankind, " external advantage make us more respected. A man with a good coat upon his back meets with a better reception than he who has a bad one. Sir, you may analyse this, and say what is there in it ? But that will avail you nothing, for it is a part of a general system." [2] The system was pushed to its fullest extent when the Duchess of Devonshire reigned. The clergy wore cassocks, black stockings, knee breeches, gown and bands. A doctor usually sported a tie wig, a scarlet cloak, a black velvet coat, a gold headed cane, deep ruffles, a sword, a snuff box, and to carry his hat under his arm was to denote his profession without possible question. Horne Tooke, who was not proud of his clerical garb and tried to escape from his ecclesiastical function, possessed a wardrobe which included suits of scarlet and gold, white and silver cloth, blue and silver camlet, and flowered silk. Wilkes dressed

[1] " No innovations ! no innovations ! " was the answer George III. made to Lord Eldon, when the Chancellor asked permission to sit without wearing a heavy wig which always made his head ache. This cry against innovation is almost pathetic in its intensity. Dr. Johnson said to Lord Stowell (Sir William Scott) : " The age is running mad after innovation ; all the business of the world is to be done in a new way ; men are to be hanged in a new way ; Tyburn itself is not safe from the fury of innovation."

[2] Whilst visiting the Thrales at Brighton, Dr. Johnson met Lord Bolingbroke, and deliberately turned his back upon the peer. The brewer was annoyed. Said Johnson : " I am not obliged, sir, to find reasons for respecting the rank of him who will not condescend to declare it by his dress and some other visible mark. What are stars and other signs of superiority made for ? "

in scarlet or green, edged with gold. Oliver Goldsmith, ever ready to masquerade as a man of the world, swaggered in " Tyrian bloom satin grain and garter blue silk breeches," and did not scruple to pay, or to owe, for suits worth twenty guineas.

Horace Walpole's visiting-dress has been described as " a lavender suit, the waistcoat embroidered with a little silver ; or of white silk worked on the tambour, partridge silk stockings and gold buckles, ruffles and frill, generally lace. In summer no powder, but his wig combed straight, and showing his very pale forehead, and queued behind ; in winter, powder." In 1773 Lord Villiers appeared at Court in a coat of pale velvet turned up with lemon colour, embroidered all over with SS's of pearls as big as peas, and in all the spaces little medallions in beaten gold—real gold —in various figures of cupids and the like. At the opening of Parliament in 1783 the Prince of Wales wore "a black velvet, mostly richly embroidered with gold and pink spangles, and lined with pink satin. His shoes had pink heels; his hair was pressed much at the sides, and very full frizzed, with two very small curls at the bottom." Peers wore their stars upon every occasion, and thus privilege was easy to distinguish.

When Georgiana Cavendish held court at Devonshire House the costume of men as well as of women reached an extreme. Its decadence was one of the results of the political movements of 1789. In 1759 Horace Walpole attended a wedding in a suit of white, purple, and green. Thirty years later he was at another wedding feast. Simplicity was now the only vogue. " Our wedding is over, very properly, though with little ceremony, for the men were in frocks and white waistcoats, most of the women in white, and no diamonds." Within a few months the Bastille had fallen, and the sweetness of life had gone for those who could look upon the past. In the same year, 1789, Walpole wrote to an old friend : " I live so little in the world that I do not know the present generation by sight ; for though I pass by them in the streets, the hats with valences, the folds above the chins of the ladies, and the dirty shirts and shaggy hair of the young men, who have levelled nobility almost as much as· the mobility in France have, have confounded all individuality."

And thus, all unconsciously, Horace Walpole revealed the secret of that time. It was an age of privilege ; it was also an age of individuality. The French revolution confounded both. Before 1789 every man and woman, no matter to what class of society they belonged, if they hoped to succeed even moderately in the world had to exert the whole force of their character. The doctrine of equality of opportunity gave an easier chance for the feeble to rise at the expense of the strong ; for the poor to flourish at the cost of the rich. The process was one of levelling down rather than of banking up, with the natural result of uniformity of mediocre effort rather than concentrated but intermittent feats of strength.

Individuality and character were the keynotes of that vigorous age. Mrs. Piozzi, in her eightieth year, recognised a change. " I love to see individuality of character, and abhor sameness, especially in what is feeble and flimsy." When Lord Thurlow damned his valet he showed irritability, but the servant in his quick answer displayed coolness of mind, resource, independence, in a word, individuality. Men were self-confident because they were neither afraid of their fellow-men nor of themselves. Topham Beauclerk found Fox intently engaged in reading a Greek *Herodotus*. " What would you have me do ? " said he. " I have lost my last shilling."

Wraxall seeks to explain the remark as indicative of Fox's elasticity, suavity, and equality of disposition. In reality, it was based upon Fox's conviction that the sweetness of the day for Charles James Fox had not yet ended.

Such a spirit of independence—the independence of the few ready and able to grasp the prize for themselves, and not the independence of the crowd, querulously demanding freedom as their unearned right—could not fail to result in picturesque and richly-coloured social history.

The period was complex. Its beginning was mirrored in the coarse brutalities of Smollett, its close in the purring gentilities of Jane Austen. " The habits of fifty years ago were," wrote Dr. Croly in 1830, " beyond all comparison those of a more prominent, showy and popular system. The English nobleman sustained the honours of his rank with a larger display ; the Englishman of fashionable life was more conspicuous in his establishment, in his appearance, and even in his eccentricities : the phaeton, his favourite equipage, was not more unlike the cabriolet, that miserable and creeping contrivance of our day, than his rich dress and cultivated manners were like the wretched costume and low fooleries that make the vapid lounger of modern society. The women of rank, if not wiser or better than their successors, at least aimed at nobler objects : they threw open their mansions to the intelligent and accomplished minds of their time, and instead of *fêteing* every foreign coxcomb who came with no better title to respect than his grimace and his guitar, surrounded themselves with the wits, orators and scholars of England."

> " Bliss was it in that dawn to be alive,
> But to be young was very heaven ! "

CHAPTER I

Devonshire House and its circle—the palaces of London—William
Kent—the early Georgians—comfort and security—the outer
wall of Devonshire House—London thieves and housebreakers
—Hogarth and Tyburn—the rise of the Cavendishes—" Building Bess of Hardwicke "—the " pretty red-haired wench "—the
first Duke—his successors—a house-party at Chatsworth in 1760.

> " Piccadilly ! Shops, palaces, bustle and breeze,
> The whirring of wheels, and the murmur of trees ;
> By night or by day, whether noisy or silly,
> Whatever my mood is, I love Piccadilly."

IN the centre of Mayfair stands an old mansion typical
of the century in which it was built, and of the
illustrious men and women who have made it their
home for nearly two hundred years. From its drawing-room the illustrious Georgiana, Duchess of Devonshire,
reigned undisputed queen of the Whigs during one of the
most momentous periods in the political history of Europe.
Under her sway Devonshire House opened its doors to
politicians, princes, poets, artists, authors, gentlemen of wit,
ladies of fashion, all the thousand personalities who, by
reason of wealth or talent, gave added brilliancy to the life
of that time. Fox, Burke, Sheridan, Walpole, Gibbon,
Johnson, Reynolds, Gainsborough, and a hundred others,
met here on common ground. The list of names is inexhaustible, and makes us long to recapture the faintest echo
which may still linger in such haunted walls.

The house in Piccadilly is the scene of our story. Its
master and mistresses, their families, and the friends they
attracted across their threshold, are the characters in a
curious but very human tragedy. When men and women
of keen intellect and strong individuality refuse to cloud

their lives by starving their passions, the result can only be disaster. Good and evil were strangely mixed in the Devonshire House Circle. Although the good predominated, unhappiness is the keynote of the history.

Step by step we will trace the drama to its end. The task is not easy. To divide the events of fifty years into a sequence of acts, to bring the curtain down upon climax and anti-climax, are impossible feats. Life never conforms to the unities. And because we have to deal with flesh and blood, and not with the marionettes of imaginative romance, our pages must be discursive. People will cross the boards who have little concern with the action of the play. Does not the same thing happen every moment to all of us ? We meet fascinating creatures who brighten the passing hour before they vanish. They remain a pleasant memory, but they are for nothing in the main current of our existence.

Yet they cannot be left out of the representation. They are local colour, atmosphere, in many cases formative influence. And they are the comedy of life, for they have gone before we are wearied. It is the people we see every day, the environment we cannot escape from, which make the tragedy.

Whilst in some respects Time has dealt kindly with Devonshire House, for the ducal palace has lost little of its ancient importance, Fate has played many strange tricks with the surroundings. Formerly the last house on the western border of the town, amidst fragrant hayfields and pastures, its square windows commanding unbroken views of the Hampstead hills and the towers and pinnacles of Westminster, the advancing tide of bricks and mortar swept up to the tiny demesne and time after time seemed likely to engulf it. Threatened houses, like threatened men, live long, and the doom of this pleasant oasis has happily not yet been pronounced.

To-day, unaltered,[1] it marks one of the busiest quarters

---

[1] In 1840 the external double flight of stairs, which led to the first floor, was removed, and the original principal entrance replaced by

DEVONSHIRE HOUSE, SOUTH FRONT

of the West End. Giant hotels dwarf its squat proportions. A street of palaces has gradually changed into a street of clubhouses. Yet, within its courtyard, there still reigns an atmosphere of peace and brooding reminiscence, a contrast and a reproof to the restless, unceasing race of the life without its gates.

Devonshire House is not only the most interesting building in Piccadilly, it is also one of the landmarks of a great city. The private palaces of London are secluded from the public gaze. Lansdowne House modestly hides between Piccadilly and Berkeley Square with good reason, for its builder, Lord Bute, was no favourite with the mob which cursed his power. Few Londoners could name offhand the row of palaces bordering the Green Park from Piccadilly to St. James's. A search for Marlborough House, Duchess Sarah's mansion in Pall Mall, may prove unsuccessful if the trees are in full foliage. How many men who profess to know their London could unhesitatingly locate Crewe House, Chesterfield House, Chandos House, Norfolk House, Ashburn-ham House ? Devonshire House, however, boldly faces the broad highway to the west. Its very lack of beauty challenges attention. Despite its ugliness, Londoners love the grimy pile, a relic of the past they can ill afford to lose.

As London buildings go, Devonshire House can boast no lengthy tradition. It cannot be compared in age with the Tudor palace at the foot of St James's Street, or the quiet home of William and Mary on the further side of Hyde Park. There are many rambling houses in Soho which claim precedence. Lincoln's Inn Fields has not been robbed of all the work of Inigo Jones, and Westminster still contains one or two tottering shells dating from the days of the Commonwealth and the Restoration.

For grace Devonshire House can certainly ask for no privilege. Critics have always reserved their keenest

---

a window. Before 1897 the brick wall was unbroken. In that year the exquisite iron gates were brought from Lord Burlington's villa at Chiswick, a house " not large enough to live in, but too big to hang on one's watch-chain."

criticisms for its unimpressive façade. Until a few years ago the wall of the courtyard facing Piccadilly formed an impenetrable screen, and the house itself could only be seen from the roof of a mail coach or the top of an omnibus. "The public has nothing to regret in losing the sight of Devonshire House," wrote one topographer. "It is spacious, and so are the East India Company's warehouses : and both are equally deserving of praise." Yet, with a grumbling insistence, illogical but perfectly natural, there was a general complaint that the palace, admittedly not worth seeing, remained hidden from view.

The first Devonshire House was burnt to the ground in 1733. The third Duke determined to erect a mansion more fitting to his position. Personally he was "plain in his manners, negligent in his dress," but his unassuming modesty did not extend to his housing arrangements. An old house is not so comfortable as an old coat. The Duke accordingly commissioned William Kent [1] to build a palace, and Devonshire House is characteristic of its period. Dull and ungraceful in its lines it was made to last rather than to please.

Whilst Georgiana Spencer was being educated in the schoolrooms of Althorp and Wimbledon, the English world was passing through a vast social change. She was reared by people whose memories could go back to the Revolution.

---

[1] William Kent (1684-1748) started life as a coachpainter, tried to paint, and finally ended as the fashionable architect and landscape gardener of the early eighteenth century. He was a clever man, but lacked the talent of Sir John Vanbrugh or James Gibbs. Hogarth made fun of his pictures and lost all chances of success as a court painter, for Kent, in revenge, diverted a royal commission from the artist who dared to make fun of him. Horace Walpole was in a safer position to criticise. " He was not only consulted for furniture, as frames of pictures, glasses, tables, chairs, etc., but for plate, for a barge, for a cradle. And so impetuous was fashion that two great ladies prevailed on him to make designs for their birthday gowns. The one he dressed in a petticoat decorated with columns of the five orders : the other like a bronze, in a copper-coloured satin with ornaments of gold." Kent's craftmanship as a decorator can be studied in his additions to Kensington Palace. His best work in London is the Horse Guards in Whitehall. The Palladian palace for the Duke of Devonshire cost over £20,000 (about £70,000 at present value) and the result hardly justified the expense.

The animosities of the "forty-five" were by no means ended.[1]   She was born during an age of transition.

George II., "old Squaretoes," sat upon a throne which could not yet be called secure.   Although he cared for Hanover more than Great Britain, he was nervously afraid of losing his English heritage.   His Queen and his Prime Minister enabled him to hand the crown to his grandson, but his subjects had no misapprehension as to his ability as a statesman.

> "You may strut, dapper George, but 'twill all be in vain;
> We know 'tis Queen Caroline, not you that reign."

Sir Robert Walpole and the Queen were not creatures of romance.   Commonsense is never romantic, and Caroline of Anspach and "Bluff Bob" were two of the most severely practical persons in the three kingdoms.   Romance they left to the Jacobites, for their aim was the consolidation of a new nation.

The reign of George II. was coloured by the feeling— or rather the lack of feeling—of these two strong personalities.   It was a constructive age which had little leisure or inclination for the more pleasant graces of life.   Great Britain was in the making, and, despite the genius of Handel or Hogarth, the dilettanteism of connoisseurs, such as the Earl of Burlington, there was no real call for the arts of peace. Sir Robert Walpole was a coarse-minded sentimentalist. The very fact of the existence of Maria Skerritt, his mistress, proves that he was a sentimentalist.   The Queen was a coarse-tongued virago with a soft heart.   Walpole belongs to the type of man who grows sentimental as he grows old. The Queen was not sentimental.

The early Georgians asked for comfort, and when that desirable ideal was attained they were content.   Beauty was not their conscious aim, although they sometimes reached

[1] Their final home was in the nursery.   Frances, Lady Shelley, speaks in her diary of her early years at Preston, 1787-1795.   "We were at that time all strong Jacobites. . . . Many were the quarrels I had with my Whig cousins, the Hornbys, on the respective merits of the Stuarts and Queen Mary."

it through simplicity and lack of affectation. Devonshire House was built for comfort and security.

In 1783, when the Duchess was at the height of her power, the transition was over. Ideas had altered, and the walls of Devonshire House itself marked the change. An author was writing about the London houses of the nobility: "The Duke of Devonshire's is one of those which present a horrid blank of wall, cheerless and unsocial by day, and terrible by night. . . . Would it be credible that any man of taste, fashion, and figure would prefer the solitary grandeur of enclosing himself in a jail, to the enjoyment of the first view in Britain, which he might possess by throwing down this execrable brick screen ? "

There was good reason for the enclosure. In the eighteenth century the thieves and housebreakers of the metropolis were daring to the verge of madness. No door, even in the humblest dwelling, was safe unironed, no window free from night attack when unprotected by a grill. Every yard was fortified by high walls and stout gates. The great mansions of London were prisons. Harcourt House, similar in type to Devonshire House, has disappeared within the last few years, but the present generation can easily remember the waste of brickwork which disfigured almost the whole of the west side of Cavendish Square. Under the shadow of St. Paul's, in Dean's Court, can still be seen the Deanery, defended by a wall no burglar could hope to scale. Yet the Deanery is almost within call of the Lord Mayor himself, and not a stone's throw from Newgate and the Old Bailey, with all their dread paraphernalia of the law.

The brick wall of Devonshire House marks an epoch, and remains an object lesson to those who study the social history of London. It was built in an age when gentlemen of the road did not confine their activities to Hounslow Heath or Finchley Common, but often—like birds driven in by foul weather—came closer to the haunts of humankind. When Dr. Johnson wrote his poem, entitled, *London*, he observed with perfect truth :

" Prepare for death if here at night you roam,
And sign your will before you sup from home."

A Lord Chancellor was deprived of his cash and what Mr.
Wemmick was pleased to call " portable property," whilst
driven in his coach across the fields now covered by Lowndes
Square. A woman could hardly journey from Charing
Cross to Knightsbridge in safety. Lady Mary Coke, who
lived in Aubrey House, a mansion still to be found on the
heights between Notting Hill and Kensington, wrote in her
journal in 1774 : " I expect every night to be robbed :
my neighbour, Mrs. Lahoop, was robbed last night at the
bottom of my ground in the Acton road, within a hundred
yards of her own house, at a little after nine o'clock. The
two men who robbed her remained in the neighbourhood
all night, and early this morning stopped a poor woman,
who, having no money, they would have stript of her clothes,
but somebody coming on, they made off." Lady Mary
went to dine with the Princess Amelia at Gunnersbury.[1]
" I stayed with her Royal Highness till near nine, and came
home with only one servant behind the chaise. 'Tis extraordinary that I am never robbed, when there are robberies
every night in all the roads about me. One of the Princess's
bed-chamber women, Mrs. Howard, was robbed in that road
the other night by three footpads : one on each side of the
coach open'd the doors and got into the coach to her :
very disagreeable company I shou'd have thought, but she

---

[1] The Princess Amelia Sophia was the second daughter of George
II. Her sister, the Princess Caroline, lived hopelessly in love with
Lord Hervey, but Princess Amelia was a creature of less sentiment
and greater passion. The Dukes of Newcastle and Grafton were
rivals for her good will, and Grafton has the credit of being the
favoured man. A mysterious " little Miss Ashe " is often referred
to by Horace Walpole, who was an intimate member of the Princess's
circle at her house in Cavendish Square. " Detraction, in every
age, from Elizabeth down to the present times, has not spared the
most illustrious females," wrote Wraxall, and the Princess was
generally thought to be Miss Ashe's mother. Her father was said to
be Lord Rodney. Miss Ashe married a Captain Falkner in the
Navy. Princess Amelia, an ardent gambler, as Lady Mary Coke
knew to her cost, and an old gossip, for Walpole has chronicled her
small talk, died in 1786 at the age of seventy-six.

said she was not at all frighted." Highwaymen stopped
and searched coaches travelling to and from town with the
regularity of ticket collectors. Servants took to the road
between their engagements. The chaplain at Gunnersbury
was robbed of his watch and eighteenpence—the minor
clergy were far from rich in 1774. When the thief was
caught he proved to be Lord Palmerston's coachman. Six
years earlier the same journal describes how the Bishop of
Landaff's carriage was stopped in Upper Grosvenor Street.
There were frequent robberies in Park Lane. Horace Walpole relates that he was sitting one Sunday evening in his
dining-room in Arlington Street : " The clock had not
struck eleven, when I heard a loud cry of ' stop thief ! '
a highwayman had attacked a post-chaise in Piccadilly,
within fifty yards of this house : the fellow was pursued,
rode over the watchman, almost killed him, and escaped."
There is a story, famous amongst Londoners, of one follower
of Captain Macheath, who was pursued so hotly along Curzon
Street that he could only escape by spurring his horse
through the narrow walled passage dividing the gardens of
Devonshire House and Lansdowne House, and was able to
gallop unchecked to Berkeley Square and liberty.

" Robbing is the only thing that goes on with any vivacity,"
cried Walpole to Mann. Within a mile of Piccadilly were
the rookeries of Seven Dials, crowded with keen-witted
pupils of Jonathan Wild. Hogarth, who knew every aspect
of the city, limns their vicious and hardened faces in " The
Idle Apprentice," and other plates. He shows them dicing
on the square tombs of Old Marylebone Church, sharing
their disreputable pleasures with their doxies in the thieves'
kitchens of Saffron Hill and Clare Market, standing their
trial in the loathsome dock of the Old Bailey, and finally
travelling to their doom at Tyburn.

> " Scarce can our fields, such crowds at Tyburn die,
> With hemp the gallows and the fleet supply."

" How could you live in such a dull spot ? " asked a friend of
one who had recently moved out of town to the rural soli-
tudes of Westbourne Grove. " Dull ? " cried the fair lady.

" Dull ? Why we have hangings every week at Tyburn just across the fields."[1]

The strife between Law and Crime was in reality a civil war between two classes of the community. No mercy was given or expected. But the courage of the adventurers excited an unhealthy admiration, and, when Gentleman M'Lean was doomed three thousand people went to see him in Newgate the Sunday after his condemnation. " He fainted away twice with the heat of his cell," wrote Horace Walpole. Newgate had become a pleasure resort, whilst Tyburn had lost its terrors. Newspapers chronicled week by week the houses recently broken into. This systematic looting was accepted as a matter of course. The brick walls of Devonshire House had their reason. During the life-time of the Duchess that reason to a great extent vanished. But the walls remained, for the Cavendishes were ever indifferent to public ways and outside criticism.

There is no more honourable name in the British peerage than that of Cavendish. " Think of what the Cavendishes have done in days gone by," said John Bright. " Think of their services to the State." From the sixteenth century the family shouldered its share of the responsibilities of government, and each succeeding generation lived up to ideals which have not distinguished every ducal line. Their origin is uncertain, but the surname came into use when the younger son of a Norman house married a Suffolk heiress, and called himself " de Cavendish " after his wife's lands. This was in the reign of Edward II., and the family prospered. Sir John Cavendish was Chief Justice in 1366, 1373, and 1377, and by marriage with another heiress of the eastern counties acquired a territorial influence which brought him the Chancellorship of Cambridge University. During the troubles which ushered in the reign of Richard II., the Lord Chief Justice fell into the hands of Jack Straw and the Suffolk

[1] The lady exaggerated. Executions took place every six weeks. But the little hamlet of Westbourne Grove was often busy on these occasions. When a wealthy criminal was cut down from the gallows his friends would hurry the hearse to the inn at Westbourne Green, and make a generally unavailing attempt to restore life to the corpse.

rebels, and was beheaded in the Market-square of Bury St. Edmunds. The murder was in many respects an act of revenge, for Sir John's son and heir, an esquire to the King, assisted Walworth in the slaughter of Wat Tyler at Smithfield. For this deed of butchery he was immediately knighted and granted a pension of £40, but his father's life was forfeit before a year had run.

The Cavendishes were still a Suffolk family when Thomas Cavendish, the Clerk of the Pipe, died in 1523. His elder son entered the household of Cardinal Wolsey. He abandoned, to quote Wolsey's own words, " his own country, wife, and children, his own house and family, rest and quietness, only to serve me." After attending his master through his disgrace until his death at Leicester, George Cavendish retired to his Suffolk home, and wrote the famous Memoir of his dead lord. Henry VIII. recognised his faithful service by giving him six of the Cardinal's cart-horses, a farm-cart, £10 on account of unpaid wages, and £20 as a gift of peace.

Sir William Cavendish, the younger brother, went to Court, and, with a more accommodating conscience, remained a favourite through three reigns. After his knighthood he was created Treasurer of the Chamber to Henry VIII., and retained the office under Edward VI. and Mary. As early as 1530 he was a Royal Commissioner employed in the lucrative task of the dissolution of the monasteries. But his most successful achievement was his third marriage. His first and second wives gave him daughters, but no sons. Then he married the daughter of John Hardwick, of Hardwick in Derbyshire, a widow of thirty who brought great estates. When Sir William died in 1557 he left a family of three sons and three daughters. His widow married a third husband, William St. Loe, then a fourth, dying at the age of eighty-seven as Countess of Shrewsbury. Of her Horace Walpole wrote :

> " Four times the nuptial bed she warm'd,
> And every time so well perform'd,
> That when death spoil'd each Husband's billing,
> He left the Widow ev'ry shilling.

Sad was the Dame : but not dejected ;
Five stately Mansions she erected
With more than Royal pomp, to vary
The prison of her captive Mary.
When Hardwicke's towers shall bow their head,
Nor Mass be more in Worksop said,
When Bolsover's fair frame shall tend,
Like Oldcoates, to its destined end,
When Chatsworth knows no Cavendish bounties,
Let Fame forget this costly Countess."

" Building Bess of Hardwick," rather than her second husband, was the true founder of the Cavendish family. Only by Sir William had she children, and these boys and girls inherited the wealth of her four husbands. The eldest son died early in life without legitimate heirs. The second son, William, became the first Earl of Devonshire, the third, Charles, was the father of the first Marquis and Duke of Newcastle.[1] One of the daughters was mother to the unhappy Lady Arabella Stuart. Elizabeth Hardwicke has been well described as a great general and a great financier. She was also a great builder. Hardwicke Hall, which she bought from her bankrupt brother, remains in much the same state as she left it. Then she erected Oldcotes, and finally turned her attention to Chatsworth. It was predicted that when she ceased to build she would cease to live. A severe frost stopped building operations at Chatsworth, and " Building Bess of Hardwicke ' died.

She was the first of three women of this noble house who played a leading part in the social and political history of their times. " Bess of Hardwicke " defied Queen Elizabeth ; Christian Bruce, the wife of the second Earl, was one of the boldest supporters of Charles I. The first Earl, heir to Chatsworth, Oldcotes, and Hardwicke, had been created Baron Cavendish of Hardwicke in 1605, and then advanced to the Earldom of Devonshire in 1618 by James I., it is said for a payment of £10,000. Another story suggests that he had actually selected Derbyshire as his title, but Devonshire was written in the patent by error. The

---

[1] Now represented (through a descent in the female line) by the Cavendish-Bentincks, Dukes of Portland.

fact remains that the Dukes of Devonshire, with all their 200,000 acres, have never possessed an acre in the county from which they take their name.

The first Earl married his son to a daughter of the Bruces of Elgin. She was twelve years and three months at the date of her marriage. " A pretty red-headed wench ; her portion is £7,000 ; the youth at first refused her, but Lord Cavendish (his father) told him Kinloss was well-favoured by the Queen, and if he refused it he would make him the worse by £100,000. The King made up her portion to £10,000."

The youth himself, educated by Hobbes the philosopher, was a strange mixture of intelligence and folly. " For his own study," wrote his tutor, "it was bestowed for the most part in that kind of learning which best deserved the pains and hours of great persons, history and civil knowledge, and directed not to the ostentation of his reading, but to the government of his life and the public good." During the thirty-eight years of his short career he earned the reputation of a polished gentleman of more than ordinary gifts. Though he did not display his reading with ostentation he lived upon a scale of profuse magnificence, and died " from indulgence in good living," bequeathing heavily embarrassed estates for his widow to disentangle.

The " pretty red-haired wench " was thirty-two. Her widowhood lasted over forty years. Christian Bruce was the second of the great ladies of the House of Cavendish. The " White King " found in her one of his most zealous supporters. A son was killed in a skirmish with Cromwell's cavalry. His mother and elder brother afterwards retired to their house at Latimer, in Bucks, and here they gave hospitality for the last time to the doomed monarch. She lived to see Charles Stuart restored to his father's throne, and Charles II., when he visited her in her retirement at Roehampton, never forgot to show his respect for one who truly had been more royalist than the King.

The fourth Earl died in 1684. His father had been interested in literature ; he became engrossed in science. Both strains reappear in the family. The fifth Earl, under

DEVONSHIRE HOUSE, NORTH FRONT

T. H. Shepherd delt.

James II., took a different attitude towards the Crown from that assumed by his father and grandmother. He opposed the Catholic party, quarrelled with the Tory supporters of James II., and led the movement which placed William of Orange on the throne. These actions were bitterly criticized by the party he had left, which inculcated a blind obedience to the Crown. As a boy he carried the King's train at the Coronation of Charles II. He was Cupbearer to the Queen at the Coronation of James II. But, with a bold and hot temper, he never allowed his party feeling to blind his senses of what was best for the State. His great-grandmother, Bess of Hardwicke, had refused to follow Queen Elizabeth in every action, although she never lost the Maiden Queen's confidence. His father, a devoted adherent of Charles I., voted in the open house against the attainder of Strafford. He, despite the influences of his youth, was a keen critic of his grandmother's idol, Charles II., and, although he fought as a volunteer under the Duke of York, he became one of the chiefs of the opposition when that prince succeeded to the throne.

For the third time he assisted at a coronation when William and Mary stood before the people in Westminster Abbey. As Lord High Steward of England he bore the crown, and his services were rewarded when he was created Duke of Devonshire, Marquis of Hartington, and Knight of the Garter, being one of the nine dukes created by William III. within six years.

He had but recently passed middle-age when he thus became the most important man after the king. Bishop Burnet called him " the finest and handsomest gentleman of his time ; loves the ladies and plays ; keeps a noble house and equipage ; is tall, well-made, and of a princely behaviour ; of nice honour in everything but the paying of his tradesmen." He wrote verse, he completed Chatsworth, and he made love. " A patriot among men," said one contemporary, " a Corydon amongst ladies." The victims admitted the fascinations of this nobleman :

" Whose awful sweetness challenged our esteem,
Our sex's wonder and our sex's theme ;
Whose soft commanding looks our breasts assailed.
He came and saw, and at first sight prevailed."

His interests were many. As a young man he was a reckless gambler. One night at the rooms of the Duchesse de Mazarin in Whitehall palace, he lost at cards £1000, all his horses, and all his plate, and was so impoverished that he was compelled to postpone an intended journey to France. He was an enthusiastic supporter of horse-racing and cock-fighting, patronized poets and artists, gave away many gifts in charity, and was a duellist of reputation. When he died, in 1707, the social world lost one of the most interesting links which joined the careless rapture of the cavalier spirit to a heavier and more sedate age.

His son, the second Duke, had been educated to politics almost from his cradle. His marriage had a political complexion, for Rachel Russell was the daughter of that Lord Russell whose punishment on the scaffold the first Duke had vainly endeavoured to avert. Directly the boy came of age he was elected to the House of Commons, and he was Lord President of the Council to George I. and George II. The third Duke was, according to Dr. Johnson, " distinguished before all men for a dogged veracity. . . . If for instance he had promised you an acorn, and none had grown that year in his woods, he would not have contented himself with that excuse. He would have sent to Denmark for it. So unconditional was he in keeping his word ; so high as to the point of honour. '

Johnson, an unbending Tory, commended the chief of the Whigs for " a dogged veracity," and in an age of the fiercest party warfare no praise could have been higher. Sir Nathaniel Wraxall, in memoirs which do not tend towards an exaggerated estimate of the better side of his friends, talks about " the hereditary probity of the Cavendish family." Horace Walpole, another man of bitter tongue, spoke of the Duke's " conscientious idea of honesty." The Cavendishes seldom rose to the supreme heights of political genius, and they suffered from the very fact of their exalted social position. But they never shirked their duty, and they never acted in opposition to the dictates of their conscience.

During his short career the fourth Duke was a useful minister in the Whig Cabinets which succeeded each other after the death of Sir Robert Walpole. He acted as Lord Lieutenant of Ireland, as first Lord of the Treasury, and for seven months, in 1756—1757, he was Prime Minister, the only Cavendish to fill that office. Like many of his ancestors he made a brilliant marriage, for his wife was daughter of the Earl of Burlington, Baroness Clifford in her own right, and heiress to large estates in Yorkshire and Ireland which were added to the Cavendish patrimony. She died at the age of twenty-three in 1754, and the Duke lived but ten years longer. Life was too wearisome a struggle. " The letters yesterday from Spa give a melancholy account of the poor Duke of Devonshire," wrote Horace Walpole in October, 1764. " As he cannot drink the waters they think of removing him, I suppose to the baths at Aix-la-Chapelle ; but I look on his case as a lost one. There's a chapter for moralizing ! but five and forty, with forty thousand pounds a year, and happiness wherever he turned him ! My reflection is, that it is folly to be unhappy at anything, when felicity itself is such a phantom ! "

The character of the fourth Duke is difficult to disinter from the multitude of journals and letters which chronicle the political history of George II. He was staid and reserved like most of his house, and he laboured conscientiously at the affairs of the State. His mother was of different clay. Caroline Hoskins was the heiress of a Middlesex commoner, and when she married the third Duke in 1718, brought a large dowry. In later years she was the source of continual amusement to Horace Walpole. In 1752 he wrote that " she was more delightfully vulgar than you can imagine ; complained of the wet night, and how the members of the party would dirty the room with their shoes ; called out at supper to the Duke, " Good God ! my lord, don't cut the ham, nobody will eat any ! " In 1760 she was still active.

D

A house-party at Chatsworth included Lady Mary Coke, Lord Bessborough and his daughters, Lord Thomond, Mr. Bonfoy, the fourth Duke, his daughter, Lady Dorothy Cavendish, who married the third Duke of Portland, his mother the old Duchess, and the critical Horace Walpole. " Would you believe that nothing was ever better humoured than the ancient Grace ! " wrote the last named. " She stayed every evening till it was dark, in the skittle-ground, keeping the score : and one night that the servants had a ball for Lady Dorothy's birthday, we fetched the fiddles into the drawing-room, and the Dowager herself danced with us ! "

In the story of this noble house the women have always played a leading part. Three stand forth pre-eminently. " Bess of Hardwicke " founded the family, and dared to defy Queen Elizabeth. Christian Bruce guided the fortunes of the Cavendishes during one of its most troublous periods. Lastly Georgiana Spencer raised it to a supreme position of political and social influence and opened Devonshire House to the most brilliant circle of men and women London has ever boasted.

CHAPTER II

O F the childhood of Georgiana Spencer, the future Duchess of Devonshire, there is little to be said. Together with a brother and a sister, she was educated at the home of the Spencers, Althorp, near Northampton, and upon the estate her father had inherited from the Marlboroughs at Wimbledon, in Surrey. She was carefully reared, although her mother was never credited with the possession of more than average learning, and was sometimes described as being " silly." But Lady Spencer was certainly good-hearted, and her daughter resembled her in that respect.

Lineally descended from Sarah Jennings, the masterful wife of the great Duke of Marlborough, the child Georgiana was said to have inherited her features from that extraordinary woman. Perhaps she inherited some of her quick wit, and desire for power, from the same source. She had other relations, not so well known to-day, though famous enough in their own time. Her mother was a Poyntz, and, if we can judge from her interest in after life in her mother's family, she was more interested in them than in the Churchills. Besides, the history of the marriage of her father and mother was one of the many romantic stories of the eighteenth century

35

About the year 1750 had died the Right Honourable
Stephen Poyntz, a gentleman of considerable reputation
in the world of diplomacy.   The heralds asserted that his
house had been founded by Drogo Fitz Pons, a nebulous hero
who reputedly came over with the Conqueror.   They proved
their statement with a flawless genealogical table which
was worth all the money it must have cost.   Despite the
Norman blood vouched for by the College of Arms, the Pons
or Poyntz family fell on evil days.   In the late seventeenth
century its head was an upholsterer in Cornhill, and its
heir a boy at Cambridge known as Stephen.

He was ambitious and did not miss a chance.   After
acting as bear-leader to the third Duke of Devonshire,
when that nobleman made the grand tour necessary to
complete his education, Stephen Poyntz became tutor to
the sons of Lord Townshend whilst that diplomatist was
resident at the Hague.   Imperceptibly he became a diplomatist himself, one of those serviceable men who are content
to devote their lives to the State for a small consideration
and a Privy Councillorship.   Poyntz was given his Privy
Councillorship, and not much else.   He was made Governor
and Steward of the Household to the Duke of Cumberland,
and he had apartments over the archway of St. James's
Palace.   " Mr. Poyntz was called a very great man," said
Horace Walpole when he told Mann of his death, " but few
knew anything of his talents, for he was timorous to child-
ishness.   .   .   .   (He) was ruined in his circumstances by
a devout brother, whom he trusted, and by a simple wife,
who had a devotion of marrying dozens of her poor cousins
at his expense.   You know she was the ' fair Circassian.' "

To us the title means nothing.   In the eighteenth century
it was recognised as the most popular poem of the age.
Edition succeeded edition for nearly half-a-century.   The
earlier editions announced that the author was a young
gentleman at Oxford, who had fallen so deeply in love
with the subject of his verse as to die of his passion.   This
Grub Street dodge was as unnecessary as it was untrue.
The author was a clergyman who was determined to succeed

in a difficult world. Instead of dedicating his very free (and very loose) rhyming version of Solomon's " Song of Songs " to a wealthy nobleman, he offered his work to a reigning beauty. " When I saw you, like the Star which is Harbinger of the Day, dart thro' the Gloom and glow with charms too bright to be beheld, good Gods ! how astonished, how chang'd I was ! . . . To you I owe my Creation as a Lover, and in the Beams of your Beauty only I live and move and exist. If there should be a total Suspension of your Charms, I must fall to nothing."

Anna Maria Mordaunt did not suspend her charms, and the wealthy author ultimately became a Prebendary. If he preached as he wrote, his sermons would bear redelivering. His great poem told the story of Solomon's glories anew, with an oriental warmth of emotion.

> " Unnumber'd females, of a form divine,
> The soft seraglio's private walls confine ;
> Where blooming virgins ripen to desire,
> And bright Sultanas glow with practis'd fire."

The heroine was a Circassian beauty, Saphira by name. " She's a magazine of charms alone," cried the excited poet, who left nothing to the imagination. " Her well-turned legs . .. charm by degrees," he wrote, as if drawing up a furniture catalogue. His dedication plainly suggested that Saphira was no other than Mistress Anna Mordaunt, one of those angelic beings,

> " For grandeur, and for glorious fame design'd,
> To awe the vulgar, and amuse mankind."

And, when Saphira yearned for Solomon, a chorus of virgins took the stage, and solemnly chanted,

> " How blest, how more than blest the happy swain !
> For whom so fine a creature can complain."

The public of Pope, Addison, Steele, and Defoe bought edition after edition of this erotic nonsense, and Miss Anna Maria Mordaunt remained the " fair Circassian ' until her death.

She was the daughter of a brigadier-general, the grand-daughter of the Earl of Peterborough, and a maid of honour to Queen Caroline.   The Mordaunts were an energetic race, and she did not find a good match in Stephen Poyntz. When he died the Duke of Cumberland, " Butcher " Cumberland, George II.'s son, sent the two sons abroad and allowed them a generous income.   The two daughters remained with their mother.   The elder, Margaret Georgiana, inherited all the " fair Circassian's " beauty, which she passed on to the child who became Duchess of Devonshire ; the younger, Louisa, was described as a hoyden.

Old Mrs. Poyntz may have been as simple as Horace Walpole would have us believe.   Edward Gibbon liked her, though he thought her a chatterbox.   Yet she had sufficient intelligence to arrange a marriage between her daughter and the richest young man of the period.

The heir of Althorp had been born, December 19, 1734, under a fortunate star.   He was the great-grandson of Sarah, Duchess of Marlborough, and, at the death of his father in 1746, inherited the greater part of the vast Marlborough wealth, his uncle being Charles, fifth Earl of Sunderland, who was created Duke of Marlborough in 1733.[1] Despite all the honours which came in after life, Mr. John Spencer was a man of amiability rather than of ability. Only once did he display any outstanding strength of character, and that was in relation to his marriage.

Some chroniclers assert that even Mrs. Poyntz was not sure of his intentions.   The " fair Circassian " was an old campaigner, the widow of a diplomatist, and reared in the atmosphere of courts.   Perhaps the simplest explanation is after all the truest.   Mr. John Spencer fell in love with Miss Margaret Poyntz.   Mrs. Delany, the gossip of St. James's Place, took an early interest in the affair, for Mrs. Poyntz was an old friend.   In November, 1754, there is a

[1] The two grandsons of the Duchess were notorious in their day. Lord Wharncliffe relates that " Jack Spencer and the Duke " had a rule " never to dirty their fingers with silver." When they appeared in the street the chairmen used to fight for the honour of carrying them, in the hopes of picking up the guinea sure to be flung down instead of the usual fare, a shilling.

cryptic reference in a letter. " I hope little Cupid will keep his ground." The following February Mr. Spencer took his inamorata to the oratorio. " Matters go on very well there," reports Mrs. Delany. The music was by Handel, but Mr. Spencer was " on duty and had no attention for anything but the lady." When a woman can no longer hope for love affairs of her own she becomes keenly and sympathetically interested in the loves of the younger generation, and Mrs. Delany was no exception to the universal rule.

In March, 1755, Mrs. Delany reported progress. Mrs. Dawes had asked her influence upon behalf of a *protégé*. Application had been made to Mr. Spencer's mother, who, by a second marriage, was now Lady Cowper. " I have written to Lady Cowper to lay in (against Mr. Spencer comes of age) for some agency. There must be several in such a vast estate. I heartily wish *that* poor young man may live to enjoy it, and to fulfil his engagement with his present passion." It is difficult to understand why Mr. Spencer should have been spoken of with such pity. Poverty was the last vice to accuse him of. With regard to the girl, Mrs. Delany, like all gossips, evidently feared the worst. " She is too worthy a young woman to be trifled with, and he has not been won by any arts on her side, but attached by the strong bent of his inclination, and a happier choice he could not have made. She was born a gentlewoman, greatly allied by her mother's side, well-educated, a most sensible, generous, delicate mind, and I think a very agreeable person. He has rank and an immense fortune, and I hope good qualities—I have never heard of any bad ones. Thus summed up, which I really believe is the true state of the case, it is evident where the advantage lies most."

Mr. Spencer and Miss Poyntz had clearly made their own arrangements, but the plot was kept secret, for the future heir was not yet a free agent. The mothers, Lady Cowper and Mrs. Poyntz, must have known, for early in December Mrs. Delany was shown the wedding clothes. At Christmas a great house-party was held at Althorp to celebrate Mr. John's coming of age, and accession to his property. For ten years the estates had been nursed. Amongst the five hundred guests were Mrs. Poyntz and her daughter. Mrs. Delany must be left to tell the romantic tale. " There were magnificent doings at Althorp, and nobody could have acquitted themselves with more dignity and given more universal content than Mr. Spencer did. When his birthday came, he told Mrs. Poyntz it was his firm resolution to make Miss Poyntz his wife, as soon as he was master of himself ; that now he was, he entreated her leave that he might be married the next day. You may believe the request was granted, and it was so managed that nobody in the house, though near five hundred people, knew anything of the matter but Lord and Lady Cowper, Mrs. Poyntz, and her eldest son ; and it was not declared until the Saturday after. On the 20th December, after tea, the parties necessary for the wedding stole by degrees from the company into Lady Cowper's dressing-room, where the ceremony was performed, and they returned different ways to the company again, who had begun dancing, and they joined with them."

The social history of the eighteenth century contains many other instances of romantic love. At one and the same time it was an age of frankness and of sentiment, the first probably a reaction from the second. Swift told Stella that love is " a ridiculous passion, which has no being but in playbooks and romances," but Stella knew that the bitter and disappointed satirist was himself a scarred victim. In the Georgian Age no man or woman was afraid to show their feelings. Men wept and women swooned without provocation, and were admired for their weakness. There were two separate and distinct methods of wooing. Men bullied, like Lovelace, most objectionable of heroes, or they dribbled like Sir Charles Grandison. A heroine describes the courtship of Sir Charles Grandison. " In a soothing, tender and respectful manner, he put his arm round me, and taking my own handkerchief, unresisted, wiped away the tears as they fell on my cheek. Sweet humanity !

Charming sensibility! Check not the kindly gush. Dew-drops of heaven! (wiping away my tears and kissing the handkerchief), dewdrops of heaven, from a mind like that heaven, mild and gracious." With all his absurdities Samuel Richardson caught faithfully some of the charac-teristics of the life around him. Had it been otherwise, strong-minded old women, such as Lady Mary Wortley Montagu could not have written : " I was such an old fool as to weep over *Clarissa Harlowe* like any milkmaid of six-teen over the ballad of the " Lady's Fall." . . . I sob over his (Richardson's) works in a most scandalous manner." [1] The " dewdrops of heaven " were plentifully shed by Mrs. Poyntz and Lady Cowper as Mr. John and Mistress Margaret stood in front of Lady Cowper's dressing-table and were made man and wife.

The Spencer marriage was a happy one. Years later, in 1776, Lady Spencer wrote to David Garrick : " It will to-morrow be one-and-twenty years since Lord Spencer married me, and I verily believe that we have neither of us for one instant repented our lot from that time to this."

The former Miss Poyntz, the girl who had left the lodgings in St. James's with little more than the clothes she stood in, returned to town with a husband, who, in Lady Cowper's words, could spend near £30,000 a year " without hurting himself." Her jointure was £4,000 per annum, with pin-money in proportion. She succeeded to the Marlborough diamonds, and her trousseau was a nine days' wonder. Mrs. Delany described it with unction. " If I had sooner known all the particulars relating to our new cousin, Mrs. Spencer, you should not have been so long ignorant of them. She had four negligées, four nightgowns, four mantuas, and

---

[1] In fairness to Lady Mary it must be said that she considered Richardson had little knowledge of " the manners of high life ; his old Lord M. talks in the style of a country justice, and his virtuous young ladies romp like the wenches round a maypole. Such liberties as pass between Mr. Lovelace and his cousin are not to be excused by the relation. I should have been much astonished if Lord Den-bigh should have offered to kiss me ; and I dare swear Lord Trentham never attempted such an impertinence to you."

petticoats. She was married in a white and silver trimmed. I cannot remember the rest, only a pink satin with embroidered facings and robings in silver done by Mrs. Glegg. Her first suit she went to Court in was white and silver, as fine as brocade and trimming could make it ; the second, blue and silver ; the third, white and gold and colours, six pounds a yard ; the fourth, plain pink-coloured satin. The diamonds worth twelve thousand pounds ; her earrings, three drops, all diamonds, *no paltry scrolls of silver*. Her necklace most perfect brilliants, the middle stone worth a thousand pounds, set at the edge with small brilliants, the large diamonds meet in this manner. Her cap, all brilliants (made in the fashion of a small butterfly-skeleton), had a very good effect with a pompon ; and behind, where you may suppose the bottom of the caul, a knot of diamonds, with two little puffs of diamonds where the lappets are fastened, and two shaking sprigs of brilliants for her hair ; six roses, all brilliants, for her stays."

Yet Mrs. Spencer was not overwhelmed by her sudden greatness. " All these things I have just seen at Mrs. Spencer's, who looked at them with the utmost unconcern, though not insensible to their merit as fine of their kind, and pretty things, but as the *least part* of her happiness. A begging letter was given her at the same time which brought tears into her eyes and made her appear with much more lustre than the diamonds." Only that touch was needed to complete the picture.

The marriage at Althorp was unassuming in its simplicity. The journey to London was a processional triumph. Lady Hervey described it, with evident pique, as " all vanity and folly," only to be explained by the fact that Mr. Spencer's mother, Lady Cowper, was a daughter of the Granvilles. The bridal party travelled in three coaches, each with six horses. Two hundred horsemen surrounded them. Such a guard was not altogether foolishness, for the coaches must have contained a rich booty of jewels.

The villages rose in alarm as the cavalcade passed. With a general cry of " The invasion has come " the countryfolk fled to their cottages and barricaded the doors, whilst the farmers and their labourers came forth armed with pitchforks and spades. From mouth to mouth the rumour spread that this was the advance party of a fresh descent upon England, and that the Pretender and the King of France were on their way to attack London. To the surprise of Hodge the coaches and the escort clattered by without murdering his family or burning his house.

Mrs. Spencer was presented at Court the following Sunday after Church. George II. was in residence at St. James's Palace, and another quieter procession proceeded through Pall Mall. It consisted of two coaches and a sedan chair. In the first coach sat the bridegroom, Mr. Spencer, and his stepfather, Lord Cowper. Three footmen held on to the straps behind. The second coach contained Mrs. Poyntz and her younger daughter, Louisa, also with three footmen in attendance. Lastly followed a new sedan chair lined with white satin. A black page walked in front, and three footmen behind, all clad in superb liveries. Inside the chair could be seen the bride, bespangled with the Marlborough diamonds reputed to be worth some £100,000. The bridegroom's shoe buckles alone were valued at £30,000. Rarely had Londoners witnessed such a display of wealth.

Within the first five weeks of her residence in town, Mrs. Spencer was visited by six hundred people, " pulled to pieces about visiting " is the exact description. Her success was curiously repeated in all its details when her daughter Georgiana was married some twenty years later.

Her sweetness of disposition conquered society. Twice was she confined to her room with a cold. " It is the only fault laid to her charge, so she is well off," was the complacent criticism. Then, in the early summer, the whole family moved to Spa.

The popularity of Spa in the eighteenth century as an inland watering-place is hard to account for. We are told that the prevailing English desire to travel abroad is a fancy of comparatively recent growth, whereas English society has always been anxious to spend its leisure on the Continent. The discomforts and perils of such journeys were never allowed to bar the path. A trip to Paris was thought little of when the sea was open, yet frequently the crossing from Dover to Calais was a longer torment than suffices nowadays from capital to capital.

The chief towns of Europe were visited not only by young men like Philip Stanhope for the sake of education and social polish, but ladies travelled far afield with no other escort than their servants. Lady Mary Coke went to Vienna more than once. Adventurous spirits, such as Lady Mary Wortley Montagu, penetrated the Balkans, and wrote boastingly from Adrianople : " I have now, madam, past a journey that has not been undertaken by any Christian since the time of the Greek emperors."

Italy was crowded with travelling English families. Lady Mary kept a watchful eye upon the young Englishmen who were with their governors in Rome. " Whilst I stayed, there was neither gaming or any sort of extravagance. I used to preach to them very freely, and they all thanked me for it." They came back speaking a bastard language which Fielding satirised in *Joseph Andrews*, when the traveller from Italy, meeting Parson Adams at the inn, described the reverend pastor as " *uno insipidio del nullo senso. Damnato di me*, if I have ever seen such a *spectaculo* in my way from Viterbo." [1]

---

[1] These youths, with their foreign airs and graces, were a real annoyance to their friends and relations. Edward Gibbon described one in a letter to his stepmother dated March 21, 1772. " Sir Richard Worsley is just come home. I am sorry to see many alterations, and little improvement. From an honest wild English buck, he is grown a *philosopher*. Lord Petersfield displeases everybody by the affectation of consequence : the young baronet disgusts no less by the affectation of wisdom. He speaks in short sentences, quotes Montaigne, seldom smiles, never laughs, drinks only water, professes to command his passions, and intends to marry in five months. The two lords, his uncle as well as Jemmy, attempt to show him that such behaviour, even were it reasonable, does not suit this country. He remains incorrigible, and is every day losing ground in the good opinion of the public, which at his first arrival ran strongly in his favour " (*Private Letters of Edward Gibbon*).

For health, there were half-a-dozen towns in the south
of France. Smollett went to Montpellier. Wealthy con-
sumptives were sent to Nice or the Italian riviera. Avignon
had given hospitality to a Jacobite court, and a visit to Spa
was a convenient excuse for meeting friends who found it
inconvenient to live under Hanoverian rule. Those who
had been taking the cure at Aix-la-Chapelle usually travelled
to Spa for the after-cure. But those who agreed with Lady
Mary Wortley Montagu that the best cure was " not the
drinking of nasty water, but galloping all day, and a moderate
glass of champagne at night in good company " formed the
majority. A season at Spa meant change of air and scene,
a period of pleasant idleness, and a succession of nights in
the ballroom or over the faro table.

Spa always remained one of the favourite Continental
resorts of Georgiana Cavendish. It was not easy to reach.
" We got a coach and went all to Spa, but such roads I
never saw for a coach," complained Mrs. Calderwood in her
diary (1784). " By the time we arrived my head was like
to split with perfect fear. It is about seven hours' journey
[from Liége] through a moorish and woody country. . . .
Spa lies in a very pretty bottom, the banks are steep to the
one hand, but a gradual ascent to the other ; the meadows
have a very fine verdure, and there are walks cut upon the
high banks, which make it easy to get up, and a very pretty
prospect of a wild woody country from it, not very populous.
There are two or three very good streets in it, and burns
running through, with bridges over them to join the streets,
which keeps it clean."

The company was drawn from every class of society.
Many Scottish and Irish exiles, victims of the " forty-five,"
and faithful adherents to a dead cause, found the little
town a peaceful refuge. Ladies of super-birth were able to
exist upon infinitesimal pensions without loss of dignity.
French and Austrian officers spent their convalescence here,
and, whilst recovering from their wounds, met former
enemies in friendship. Tempers were uncertain, particularly
in the assembly room, scandal and gossip lessened the

tedium, new-comers were open to bitter criticism. Life was more free but less orderly than at Bath.

Mrs. Calderwood gives a picture of the Spencers too quaint to be omitted. " As for the English, who are the most regarded because they stay the longest, there was Mr. Spencer, his wife, her sister, her mother, a cousin, her two brothers, a chaplain, and one Major Barton, who was Spencer's governor, and such a following of other attendants that they had one pacquet boat for themselves, and another for their servants and baggage. I suppose they would have three going back, for they bought up everything they could lay their hands on, as did their servants. . . . Mrs. Spencer is a very sweet-like girl, her sister is a great hoyden. Miss Collier, the cousin, is a well-looked little lassie, and several little sparkies were in love with her."

In those early days the Spencers were not liked. " The mother Poyntz commands the party, and she is a deaf, short-sighted, loud-spoken, hackney-headed wife, and played at cards from morning to night. Because she had been at Court she imagined she was the resident at Spa, and kept very little company with her own country-folks, because some were Jacobites, others in opposition." Evidently the lady who had once acted as Maid of Honour to Queen Caroline refused to be friendly with the lady whose father had been out in the " forty-five."

" After the Spencers had gone, the English became more sociable," wrote the Scottish dame. In the same letter she told her relations at home that " there are few or none of the English who are not troubled with low spirits and vapours of which they speak very freely ; they will tell you they are quite over-run with the hip, or that they are quite ' hipa-condryick.' That is the name they give to low spirits or nerves."

Year after year the family returned to the same pleasure spot. In 1757 their first child was born, and named Georgiana after its grandmother, Mrs. Poyntz. In 1758 a son and heir was christened George John. The third and last child was a daughter, Henrietta Frances.

From Spa the Spencers went regularly to Paris and Brussels. The child Georgiana was soon introduced to the most fashionable life of the two capitals. As a girl she mixed with the many extraordinary characters who crowded the *salle-de-jeu*. Perhaps she was allowed to dance in the Redoute, which could boast on one night thirty princes, blazing in jewels and decorations, and more than thirty of the rogues and adventurers of Europe. It was not the best or the sweetest life for a young girl to study, however carefully she was guarded by Mrs. Spencer and Mrs. Poyntz.

A *Liste des Seigneurs et Dames*, published at Spa, in 1763, contains the names of Milord Althorp (John Spencer had been raised to the peerage) and Lady Henriette Spencer. They lodged at the Cornet, the chief inn in the town, kept by a Scotsman named Alexander Hay. Ten years later, in 1773, the *Liste* includes the names of Lady Georgiana Spencer and the Duke of Devonshire. Their marriage was probably arranged during this holiday at Spa.

CHAPTER III

IN 1772 William Cavendish, fifth Duke of Devonshire, was twenty-four years of age. Horace Walpole's all-embracing pen did not forget to include his name in the correspondence to Sir Horace Mann. The Duke, he said, was a very handsome young man, even better looking than Sir Watkin Williams Wynne,[1] and quite equal to the letter-writer's nephew by marriage, Lord Villiers.[2] But Walpole's standard of male beauty varied from time to time, and did not invariably agree with that of his contemporaries. For example, Mrs. Delany, a shrewd enough judge, considered Lord Villiers " a poor weak-looking soul." This description could by no means be applied to the head of the House of Cavendish.

William Cavendish's character was contradictory. By temperament he was apathetic, listless, and cold. It is seldom that we find him taking any energetic step, or displaying the slightest activity. In the political world he could have asserted a right to the highest offices of the state. That he was interested in the government of his country seems clear, but he was a silent member of the House of Lords, and spoke only twice. Yet his intellectual powers were generally recognised by his friends, and his taste as a classical scholar admitted in an age of classical learning.

[1] The fourth baronet, who died in 1789. A leader of fashion during his short life.

[2] Afterwards second Earl of Grandison. He died in 1800, when the title became extinct.

Sir Joshua Reynolds pinxt.   J. R. Smith sculpt.

WILLIAM, FIFTH DUKE OF DEVONSHIRE

Lady Holland must have had the fifth Duke of Devonshire in her thoughts many years later at an evening gathering at Holland House. It was agreed, runs the story as told by Sir William Fraser, that everyone should write secretly on a piece of paper what would be the most miserable being to create. The papers were then handed to Lady Holland to read out. Most forms of ultra misery were suggested. Lady Holland was asked as to what the being of her creation should be. She gave it at once and obtained the prize.

" A handsome Duke."

Her philosophical mind convinced her that a man born into the world where he has nothing to gain would soon find life a burden to him. If she had added the word " learned," the nadir of Despair would have been reached, added Sir William.

William Cavendish was a duke, handsome—if we are to believe Reynolds' portrait—and undoubtedly learned. How could he be happy ? When he came of age and entered the great world he found it a ball asking to be kicked. The son of a father who had been termed " head of the Whigs," the party were ready to elect him to the succession. He could not wholly refuse the dignities and responsibilities thrust upon him, but he preferred to stand in the shadow. His uncles, Lord Frederick and Lord John Cavendish, shouldered their share of the duties the State demands from men of rank. Lord Frederick was an enthusiastic soldier, Lord John a statesman of conspicuous ability. The first became a Field-Marshal, the second, as Chancellor of the Exchequer, earned the praise of Edmund Burke for perfect disinterestedness and simplicity of manner. Their nephew was equally gifted, disinterested, and simple. But he refused the position to which he was entitled by rank and intellect, and left no mark upon the history of his period.

His father, the fourth Duke, died in 1764. His mother, Charlotte, Baroness Clifford of Lanesborough in her own right, and heir of Richard Boyle, Earl of Burlington and Cork, pre-deceased her husband by more than ten years.

E

Their child passed his schooldays at Chatsworth, and then made the " grand tour." He was presented at Court in 1765, at the age of seventeen, and at once became the target of every match-making dowager who had daughters to provide for.

The marriage of daughters has always remained a problem for mothers since the world became civilised. " Marry your daughter betimes, for fear she should marry herself," has been a proverb of sinister meaning to many noble families. In the eighteenth century mothers and daughters agreed for the most part that marriage was the aim of a woman's life. They did not, however, agree in the choice of the man, and the argument led to innumerable family quarrels and public scandals.

Children were taught to obey their parents blindly. Affection was blended into obedience until it became impossible to separate one quality from the other.[1] Mothers betrothed their children in the cradle ; fathers treated their daughters as convenient and valuable gambling-counters. A well-known example was quoted at the time. The first Earl of Cadogan, having contracted a debt at cards to the first Duke of Richmond which he could not satisfy, saved his honour by agreeing to marry his daughter and co-heiress, Lady Sarah Cadogan, to the Duke's eldest son, Lord March. The bride was thirteen, the bridegroom slightly older. They mutually disliked each other. She was gloomy and silent during the wedding ; he made the single remark : " Surely you are not going to marry me to that dowdy ! " Married they were, without mercy from their respective fathers. The boy was taken to the Continent by his tutor, and the girl went back to the schoolroom. Three years later Lord March returned to England, and, with unpleasant memories of the girl he had seen for an hour, was in no hurry to meet his wife. On the night of his arrival in London

---

[1] Lady Mary Wortley Montagu was of different mind. She wrote to her daughter : " You are no more obliged to me for bringing you into the world than I am to you for coming into it, and I never make use of that commonplace (and, like most commonplaces, false) argument as exacting any return of affection."

he visited the theatre. A beautiful young woman in one of the boxes attracted the attention of the audience. " Who is she ? " asked the traveller. " The reigning toast, Lady March ! " was the astounding reply. He lost no time in making himself known, and, as in all good fairy tales, they lived happily ever after. Unlike most fairy tales, which end abruptly at this point, history tells us that they had twelve children, and one of their daughters, Lady Caroline Lennox, was the mother of Charles James Fox.

This was a comedy of marriage which did not end in tragedy. Sheridan summed up the situation in four lines :

" If a daughter you have, she's the plague of your life,
No peace shall you know, though you've buried your wife !
At twenty she mocks at the duty you taught her ;
Oh, what a plague is an obstinate daughter."

The problem was too serious for humour. Daughters had to be married. There was no alternative. " For after all," said Jenny Warburton, the strong-minded wife of the second Duke of Argyll, " if you had a pack of daughters—if you were so unlucky—what on earth could you do with them but find husbands to take them off your hands ? "

What dangers the young Duke had to guard himself against can be discovered in the correspondence of his age. Mrs. Delany referred to the matrons, beating the ballrooms through and through for possible sons-in-law, as " the harpies." " I hope he will escape the harpies, both as to his purse and his person," she wrote when once speaking of a young Marquess of Carmarthen. " I make no doubt deep schemes are laid for both." Mrs. Delany blamed the mothers. The moral Richardson censured the daughters. " When I read those *Spectators* which took notice of the misbehaviour of young women at church, by which they vainly hope to attract admirers, I used to pronounce such forward young women SEEKERS, in order to distinguish them by a mark of infamy from those who had patience and decency to stay till they were sought.'

For eight years the young Duke eluded " harpies " and " seekers." He travelled and had his share of the gaieties and dissipations of the town. A reputation for eccentricity attached itself to his name. Horace Walpole, writing to the Countess of Upper Ossory, in 1773, from his retreat at Strawberry Hill, incidentally remarks that, " His Grace of Devonshire seems to be buying the character of singularity very dear. . . . May not his passion for antiques bring forth more dresses after old pictures ? "

The phrase has some cryptic meaning hard to unravel. Most possibly it referred to rumours of an approaching match. Mrs. Delany hinted at an early date that a duchess might be found in the schoolroom at Althorp. On January 7, 1772, she told her cousin John Dewes that " many weddings are talked of, but so often contradicted. I am afraid of naming them : it is ' thought there is a future scheme under consideration for a union between the Duke of Devonshire and Lady Georgiana Spencer.' I think that paragraph would make a figure in a newspaper, and just in that style ! " The paragraph indeed would have made a sensation, for, if Mrs. Delany was correctly voicing the aspirations of her friends Lady Spencer and old Mrs. Poyntz, the suggested engagement was probably news to the chief person concerned.

A few streets north of Mrs. Delany's apartments in St. James's Place lived another lady of mature age who also was writing long letters to her friends and entering copious notes in her journals. Lady Mary Coke,[1] a daughter

---

[1] She was the youngest daughter of the Duke of Argyll and Greenwich, and at the age of twenty-one, in 1747, was married by her parents and against her will, to Edward, Viscount Coke, only son of the Earl of Leicester. She had never hidden her dislike of Edward Coke, and he resolved to take his revenge. Upon the evening of the marriage (to quote Lady Louisa Stuart) the bridegroom found her ladyship " in the mood of King Solomon's Egyptian captive :—

' Darting scorn and sorrow from her eyes ; '

prepared to become the wretched victim of abhorred compulsion. Therefore, coolly assuring her she was quite mistaken in apprehending any violence from him, he begged she would make herself easy, and wished her a very good-night."

of the Duke of Argyll and that " Jenny " Warburton already referred to, was a celebrated if not notorious member of society. In her diary she chronicled with secret complacency every event which troubled the serenity of her acquaintances. " Poll ' Coke watched the ups and downs of her contemporaries with a peevish equanimity. She suffered from a combination of misfortunes. Had she been

---

This was the preliminary to two years of incessant wrangling. At first the Earl of Leicester took the part of his daughter-in-law, then, upon the refusal of Lady Mary to live with his son, he became her bitter opponent. Virulent warfare raged between the Argylls and the Cokes, and finally she was locked up in the old house at Holkham, and for seven months an attempt was made to starve her into submission. The Duchess of Argyll journeyed to Holkham and was refused access to her daughter. She returned to London and moved the King's Bench to issue a writ of Habeas Corpus enjoining Lord Coke to produce his wife. Lady Mary attended the court in tatters, although the Cokes asserted that her pin money had never been withheld. The public interest in the suit was so keen that the crowd, pressing to gain a sight of her as she went to Westminster Hall, smashed the glass of her sedan chair. She irritated her own attornies so severely that one of them remarked after a trying interview, "Well, if her husband did thrash her, he was not without excuse."

The trial ended in a drawn battle. But she did not return to her husband, whose mode of life resulted in his early death. At six-and-twenty she was a free woman with an income of £2,500 a year. To the bitter disappointment of her father-in-law there could now be no heir to the earldom, and the Coke estates passed to a remote cousin. Lady Mary had triumphed over her enemies in a peculiarly feminine manner. Love, it was said, was " the only passion that had no place in her composition," and she refused to marry a second time.

> " She sometimes laughs, but never loud ;
> She's handsome, too, but somewhat proud :
> At court she bears away the bell,
> She dresses fine and figures well :
> With decency she's gay and airy ;
> Who can this be but Lady Mary ? "

" Poll " Coke went through life with a succession of grievances, and although her eccentricity never degenerated into actual madness there was undoubtedly a slight mental twist in her character. Yet, after studying the four volumes of her journal, the reader cannot refrain from a feeling of sympathy with this stout-hearted, lonely old woman, whose bitter tongue must have been more than once felt by the young Duchess of Devonshire.

a boy she would have succeeded her father as Duke of Argyll, and she acted throughout her life as if her family were responsible for an error which really should have been laid at the door of Dame Nature. From the point of view of happiness, her life was not a success, and although (like many other unsuccessful lives) the fault was chiefly due to her own uncertain temper, it must be allowed that fate had treated her shabbily.[1]

In 1772 Lady Mary was at Vienna. Amongst the letters she received from London was one written by Lady Elizabeth Hamilton, daughter of the sixth Duke of Hamilton and his wife Miss Elizabeth Gunning, who had married *en secondes noces* the Duke of Argyll. The letter itself has been lost, but its contents can be judged from Lady Mary's comments in her journal. " I begin to think," she wrote, " that the Duke of Devonshire will certainly marry Lady Betty Hamilton. After there has been so much talk about it, if he did not intend it, he would undoubtedly not chose to go constantly to the Duchess of Argyll's box at the Opera, nor do I think, as a Man of Honour, it would be consistent to give her so much reason to flatter herself, if he did not intend it."

Was Lady Betty engineering a surprise which would overturn the careful plans of Lady Spencer and Mrs. Poyntz ? Although documentary corroboration is difficult to trace in the papers of that period, Lady Mary's reference to the " talk " about the expected engagement is too definite to be disregarded. As a highly critical and somewhat hostile member of the family, Lady Mary Coke was in a position to collect the earliest news. The Duke, too, was involved in a very different quarter. A certain Mrs. Oliver, probably the wife of an Alderman Oliver of the City of London, was asking the peer to state definitely whether or no he intended to marry her daughter.

---

[1] Horace Walpole put the truth of the matter in a letter to Sir Horace Mann. " I have regard and esteem for her good qualities, which are many, but I doubt her genius will ever suffer her to be quite happy."

Lady Elizabeth Hamilton and Lady Georgiana Spencer were at this time unconscious rivals. They both made brilliant matches, they both were extremely unhappy. One life ended in open disaster, the sorrows of the Duchess were lamented in private. The interest taken in the matrimonial future of Lady Elizabeth was partly accounted for by the history of her mother, whose position as the head of English society was only equalled in later years by Georgiana, Duchess of Devonshire. In fact, the story of the one is a necessary preface to the history of the other.

CHAPTER IV

ELIZABETH, Duchess of Argyll and Hamilton, was
a romantic figure in an age of romance and sentiment. She was one of the three beautiful Miss
Gunnings, and, in Ireland, the "luck of the
Gunnings" had passed into a proverb.

She was the second of the three most beautiful women
who had ever conquered English society. The Gunnings
were of mixed Cornish and Irish descent. The father of
"the beauties," a barrister of the Middle Temple, who had
married a charming Irishwoman, the daughter of Viscount
Bourke, lived near St. Ives, in Huntingdonshire. Here
were born Maria, Elizabeth, and Kitty. The first became
Lady Coventry. The second was successively Duchess of
Hamilton and then of Argyll. The third married a wealthy
commoner of Lombard Street.

The popular appreciation of female beauty is not so keen
in the twentieth century as it was in the middle of the
eighteenth. It would be heresy to suggest that female
beauty is itself in process of deterioration, although Horace
Walpole had fears on the subject when he promised "a
thousand years hence, if that can ever be . . . I shall
tell the young people how much handsomer the women of
my time were than they will be then."

The three Miss Gunnings, whenever they appeared in
public, created a sensation. When the Duchess of Hamilton
was presented at Court "the noble mob in the drawing-room
clambered upon chairs and tables to look at her." When

she travelled north with her husband crowds sat up all night at the inns so that they might see the Duchess as she stepped into her chariot in the morning.   When her sister married the sixth Earl of Coventry, a Worcester shoemaker earned two guineas and a half by exhibiting a shoe he was making for the Countess at a penny ahead.[1] From the moment they stepped into the world, the penniless daughters of an Irish barrister, they had received the same adulation. Horace Walpole was captious in his criticism, but he was compelled to admit their success. " The handsomest women alive," was his verdict. " I think their being so handsome too, and both such perfect figures, is their chief excellence, for singly I have seen much handsomer then either ;   however they can't walk in the Park, or go to Vauxhall, but such mobs follow them that they are generally driven away.'   No wonder Lady Coventry was able to tell George II., deaf, blind in one eye, almost in the grave, that, " As for sights, I am quite sick of them.   There is only one I am eager to see—a coronation." [2]

Elizabeth Gunning had not the perfect features of her elder sister, although she was of surpassing loveliness, captivating   manners,   and   irreproachable   character.   A

[1] Now that every village boasts its cinema, we are able to smile at the simple joys of our forefathers. Who would care to look at a beautiful woman, or pay a penny to gaze at her shoe, when for threepence we can blink in the evil-smelling gloom of a cinema palace at the preposterous absurdities which flicker across the screen.   And we are losing much of an earlier interest in the peerage.   When the Duchess of Gordon (one of the Duchess of Devonshire's rivals) died suddenly in an hotel, the waiter made a small fortune by allowing visitors into the funeral chamber at a shilling a head—at least so says C. K. Sharpe.   Creevey tells us that when Lady Olivia Fitzgerald (who married Lord Kinnaird) and her sister, Lady Foley, entered the Dublin theatre, the whole house would rise and applaud, " in admiration of their beauty, and not of their rank, for they did so to no others of the Leinster family."

[2] This is the earliest of several well-known anecdotes, and one other must follow.   George III.'s coronation was badly stage-managed. The young king, he was only twenty-three, criticised the arrangement.   Lord Effingham, nervous and discomposed, could only stutter : " Your Majesty, the next time it shall be performed in perfect order."

critic described her as " too tall to be genteel, and her face
out of proportion to her height." She admitted to her
daughter, Lady Charlotte Campbell, that " her sister Maria
exceeded her in beauty." The Duchess of Hamilton and
Argyll was " without the aid of heels, at least five foot
seven, but Lady Coventry's form was faultless, and her
dark eyes and the jet black of her eyelashes, with that
animation which conscious beauty gave, rendered her more
dazzlingly attractive than her younger sister, whose mild,
dignified air characterised her beauty. Grand and majestic,
her manners checked the passion her charms inspired, and
I have always heard that the soft beams of her blue eyes
never were known to give one glance in favour of coquetry."

The Duke of Hamilton proposed to her at a masquerade
ball held in the house still standing at the corner of South
Audley Street and Curzon Street, the house built by Lord
Chesterfield and destined for the son who never developed
into " the perfect gentleman." Hamilton was eight and
twenty, and had already been entangled with the notorious
Elizabeth Chudleigh, whose bigamous career as the wife of
Augustus Hervey (afterwards Earl of Bristol, and uncle to
the second wife of the fifth Duke of Devonshire) and then
of the Duke of Kingston was the chief scandal and humour
of a later year. But Elizabeth Chudleigh did not become
Duchess of Hamilton, and the young nobleman was able
to offer his hand as a bachelor to the girl of eighteen. The
wedding quickly followed, on February 14, 1752, at midnight, in the ill-famed " marriage shop," known as Mayfair
Chapel, kept by Alexander Keith.[1] As the Duke had

[1] The Chapel stood in Curzon Street. Keith was said " to have
made a ' very bishopric of revenue ' by clandestine marriages, and
the expression can hardly be exaggerated if it be true, as was asserted
in Parliament, that he married on an average 6,000 couples every
year. He himself stated that he had married many thousands,
the great majority of whom had not known each other more than a
week, and many only a day or half a day. Young and inexperienced
heirs fresh from college, or even from school, were thus continually
entrapped. A passing frolic, the excitement of drink, an almost
momentary passion, the deception or intimidation of a few unprincipled
confederates, were often sufficient to drive or inveigle them into

forgotten a ring a curtain ring was used. Naturally such actions increased the public excitement. " The world is still mad about the Gunnings,'' wrote Horace Walpole. " There are mobs at their doors to see them get into their chairs, and people go early to get places at the theatre when it is known that they will be there.''

Lady Coventry soon died of the curse of the Gunnings— consumption. The Duchess of Hamilton found that her lover was no ideal husband. His death at Great Tew, in Oxfordshire, six years after the marriage, solved a difficult situation. With her three children, Lady Elizabeth and two tiny sons, she came up to town. Within a year she refused one duke, the Duke of Bridgewater, and became the wife of a good-looking colonel in the dragoons whose father was heir-apparent to his first cousin the Duke of Argyll. Elizabeth Campbell became Duchess of Argyll in 1770.

From that moment her position was beyond question, and was only challenged when Georgiana, Duchess of Devonshire, the first of a younger generation, entered into her own. But Georgiana Cavendish was never so beautiful as Elizabeth Hamilton. When the two Duchesses of Ancaster and Hamilton met the Princess Charlotte of Mecklenburg-Strelitz at Stade to escort her to Great Britain and a throne, the royal bride burst into tears, and cried, " Are all the women of England as beautiful as you ? " The Duchess of Hamilton might well have been a serious rival, for the princess, bred in the close atmosphere of a minor German court, had her mind full of the stories of morganatic marriages, and marriages that were not marriages at all. The Duchess of Hamilton was at that time " almost in possession of her greatest beauty ' (to quote Horace Walpole), whilst the Queen's unfortunate looks actually " exasperated " the English nobility.

sudden marriages which blasted all the prospects of their lives '' (Lecky). That a woman of so stainless a character should consent to be married in such a den is strange, and a sufficient indication of the freedom of life and lack of restraint and order in the eighteenth century.

The Duchess of Hamilton became Lady of the Bed-chamber to Queen Charlotte, a position she continued to occupy as Duchess of Argyll. There could have been little sympathy between the two women. Elizabeth Hamilton was by nature of kind-hearted temperament, but she described Queen Charlotte on the day of her marriage with an exactness hardly flattering. "Niggardly endowed by Nature with any charms to render her desirable, the stiff German stays added formality to Her Majesty's already stiff figure, and her hair, which was black and greasy, being drawn tight from the head in an erect dry frizz, betrayed the oilyness of the bare skin between every black pin that supported." Then followed an amusing touch of malice. "At night she insisted on sleeping in her stiff stays—a German piece of prudery to which, I imagine, the king had no objection." The attitude of the Duchess of Argyll and Hamilton towards the Queen was that of all the beautiful and quick-witted Englishwomen during the latter part of the century. And Queen Charlotte's later refusal to receive Lady Betty Hamilton, and her censure of her indiscretions as a wife, may well have been inspired by a long slumbering jealousy towards her mother.

The Duchess of Argyll and Hamilton occupied another post which was quite as important as that of Lady of the Bedchamber. She was the founder and patroness of that most select *coterie* known as Almack's. Mackal, a Scots-man, married the Duchess's maid, and borrowed sufficient money from the Duke of Argyll (then Lord Lorne) to open the assembly-room in King Street, St. James's. By revers-ing the syllables of his name he became Almack. " Almack's Scotch face in a bag wig, waiting at supper, would divert you as much as would his lady in a sack, making tea and curtseying to our Duchesses." The subscription to Almack's was ten guineas, which entitled the members to a weekly ball and supper.[1] The greater attraction was the oppor-

---

[1] " You may imagine by the sum, the company is chosen," wrote Selwyn to Gilly Williams, " though, refined as it is, it will scarce put old Soho out of countenance," a reference to Mrs. Cornelys and

tunity afforded for card playing with heavy stakes. Almack's was difficult to enter, and gave its noble patrons an irresistible influence upon society. But this Duchess hardly needed more power. In the north her position was unique. As Mrs. Montagu observed, between the interests of her son, the Duke of Hamilton, and her husband, the Duke of Argyll, she was Queen of Scotland.

This was the woman whose daughter entered the world of fashion at the same time as Georgiana Spencer. Lady Elizabeth Hamilton was never actually one of the Devonshire House Circle. She was too much a rival to be admitted into the intimacy, although she knew the same people, and belonged to the same set. She was then nineteen. " Though far from a beauty (wrote Lady Charlotte Campbell), my sister Betty had the figure of a sylph, the air and step of a Hebe, with all the *éclat* of natural rosy red and lily white, together with a sweetness of disposition and manners that won every heart, and which time, sorrow, and sickness never deprived her of ; but a natural want of solidity of character, joined to a tender and artless disposition, left her an easy prey to folly and vice."

Lady Mary Coke discussed the girl and her future with Princess Amelia, aunt to George III. The conversation was methodically entered in the journal. They had been talking of the Duchess of Argyll. Then they gossiped about the daughter. " Speaking of her puts me in mind of the Duke of Devonshire, who I am told is as assiduous in that quarter as ever. He sat with her Grace [of Argyll] and Lady Betty Hamilton almost the whole night at the opera. It is a point of perfect indifference to me who the Duke marries,[1] but I cannot help supposing it will be Lady Betty. If it is not so, his Grace most certainly does not behave properly."

her notorious assemblies in Soho Square. " The men's tickets are not transferable, so if the ladies do not like us, they have no opportunity of changing us, but must see the same persons for ever."

[1] Lady Mary Coke, it must be remembered, was for many years on bad terms with the Duchess of Argyll, and Lady Betty's bitterest judge during the troubles of her after life.

Within six months the situation changed abruptly. The Duchess of Argyll asked for leave of absence from Court. Preparations for a journey to Scotland were quickly completed. Lady Mary Coke met Lady Betty Hamilton at the house of a common friend, Lady Gower (Lady Susan Stewart), who was a cousin to the Hamiltons. The girl was evidently troubled. " She told me they were going to set out that evening ; did not seem in very good spirits, and appears to have given up all hopes of the Duke of Devonshire."

Only faint indications of the reason for her anxiety can be extracted from the tangle of contemporary letters and journals. Lady Mary Coke doubtless ferretted out every detail, but she wrote no more in her diary. There was undoubtedly a personal disagreement between the young Duke and the girl he loved, who had other strings to her bow. She had lost her heart to the Duke of Dorset, who had been paying her much attention. He was called abroad upon a foreign mission, and forgot his obligations, to the despair of Lady Betty. " The pride of youth and of woman enabled her to bury her mortification in dissipation and admiration." A Mr. Nisbet went to Inverary " to stay a couple of days, but love riveted him to the spot for I know not how long—long enough, however, for prayers, entreaties, and ardent passion so far to get the better of Lady Betty's reluctance as to allow Mr. Nisbet strong hopes of success." But he went to Italy to gain her brother's consent. " L'amour est en absence ce qu'un feu est au vent : il éteint le petit, il ranime le grand." Lady Betty was fickle and forgot Mr. Nisbet as the Duke of Dorset had forgotten her.

There was reason enough for the vacillation of the Duke of Devonshire. He found himself in competition with a Duke and a commoner. The sequel was rapid. In 1773, as we have already related, he visited Spa and met the Spencer family. Early in the season of 1774 the Duke of Devonshire married Lady Spencer's eldest daughter. A week later, almost to a day, Lady Betty Hamilton was

married to Lord Stanley, who soon succeeded his grandfather as Earl of Derby.

These two marriages were the chief sensations of the
London season of 1774. The events which led up to them
form a part of the history of the respective families which
explains much. They were both *mariages de convenance.*
They were both failures.

Lady Georgiana Spencer had also been the object of
much adoration before she was betrothed to the Duke of
Devonshire. Alexander, Lord Polwarth, a " precious only
son, grew up very like his mother in face, with the same
regular refined features, a pale, handsome man with
powdered hair and dark melancholy eyes. Lady Marchmont's ambition was even greater than her affection for
him. Though she attained her desire she broke her son's
heart. The romance of his life was Georgiana Spencer ;
but in his mother's eyes no one less than the greatest fortune
of the day was worthy to mate with the heir of Marchmont.
She married him when barely twenty-two to Lady Annabel
Yorke, Lord Chancellor Hardwicke's daughter." Lord
Polwarth lived long enough to see Georgiana Cavendish
the leader of the gayest set in London society. He died of
a rapid decline in 1781. She probably had long since
forgotten the melancholy young man who had worshipped
the girl of fifteen.

"THE great wedding is over, and at last a surprise, for this was the expected day ; but they managed very cleverly, as they were all at the birthday, and the Duke and Duchess danced at the ball. It was as great a secret to Lady Georgiana Spencer as to the world. Sunday morning she was told her doom ; she went out of town to Wimbledon, early on Sunday, and they were married at Wimbledon church, between church and church, as quietly and uncrowded as if John and Joan had tied the Gordian knot. . . Nobody was at the wedding but the Duchess of Portland and Lady Cowper."

Thus wrote Mrs. Delany, June 7, 1774, and her account is another instance of how difficult it is to arrive at the true facts of history even in respect to the simplest actions. Mrs. Delany was an intimate friend of the Spencers. She was writing within two days of the event, and living amidst the people of whom she wrote. Yet her account disagrees with all other contemporary versions.

Undoubtedly the marriage was hurried, and conducted with much of the traditional reserve of the House of Cavendish. During the first week of June a London newspaper announced that " the most splendid preparations are now making at Wimbledon, the seat of the Right Honourable Earl Spencer, for the nuptials of his eldest daughter, Lady Georgiana Spencer, with His Grace the Duke of Devonshire. A grand masque is to be performed on the occasion, in which

64

several of the young nobility of both sexes are to perform ;
the music of which is now composing by Dr. Arne. To
conclude with a grand ballet by Mr. Slingsby, who takes
down with him above twenty of the opera figure dancers." [1]

These elaborate preparations are difficult to reconcile
with Mrs. Delany's " Sunday morning she was told her
doom."

On Saturday, June 4, 1774, George III. celebrated his
thirty-seventh birthday, and the ducal marriage was to
follow that festival. There was a good reason for selecting
a day after and not before the royal *fête*. In the eighteenth
century the King's Birthday marked the close of the London
season.

The anniversary was celebrated according to tradition.
In the morning Mr. William Whitehead, Poet Laureate,
attended the Court with his annual royal ode. It was set
to music by Dr. Boyce, Master of the King's Band of
Musicians, and solemnly performed before the Monarch in
St. James's Palace. This painful duty having been disposed
of their Majesties received the compliments of the ambassadors and nobility. In the evening a ball was held.
King and Queen entered the ballroom at a quarter to nine,
and on this Saturday night the ball was opened by the
Duke of Devonshire and the daughter of the Duke of
Grafton. Minuets occupied the evening until eleven, then
followed the more enjoyable country dances.

The gloomy Tudor palace was illuminated by hundreds of
flickering wax candles, which cast an uncertain light upon
the velvet habits of the men and the gorgeous brocades
of the women. Every movement made the long wicks
quiver and tremble in the wind. The King was dressed
in half-mourning, the diamonds of his star scintillating
as they caught the rays from the sconces. By his side stood
the Prime Minister, Lord North, who, it was whispered,

[1] Wimbledon must have been a joyous and high-spirited household. One correspondent of the period, an elderly and nervous
lady, complained that she dreaded visiting the Spencers at Wimbledon, for the servants always made her coachman drunk, and she
expected to be killed on one of the homeward journeys.

would allow no political opponent to talk with his master. The members of the Court wore their most wonderful clothes and all their jewels. Queen Charlotte's dress was covered with diamonds worth more than £300,000.

The conversation was carried on in low tones. The thoughts were perhaps not deep or conspicuously witty, but the words would sound quaint to the modern ear. A lady would be " much obleeged " to the partner who led her into the ballroom. He, in a coat of " goold and yaller," would admire her " laylock " robes. The music was thin and feeble in volume. The grave melodies of Corelli or Handel floated from the violins and along the corridors like ghosts uncertain of their path.

At half-past eleven the royal couple retired. Then the court separated. There must have been a considerable crowd in the yards of the palace as they tried to find their servants, their sedans, and their coaches. One lady had her pocket cut out and lost nine guineas. Another dropped three guineas in the gutter which she did not find again. An officer in the Guards missed his gold watch. Such mishaps occasionally happened on red-letter days even in the rooms of the palace itself.[1] Before midnight the gaily apparelled throng had melted away. At the last stroke of twelve on the cracked bell in the turret there was none left but the redcoated sentry to usher in a peaceful Sabbath and the coming dawn of a summer's morning.

The Duke of Devonshire was carried in his chair, surrounded by footmen and torches, up St. James's Street and round the corner into Piccadilly and his own mansion. His marriage, if we accept the usual account, was solemnized that same evening in the drawing-room of Devonshire House. But again discrepancies creep in. One newspaper referred to " a splendid appearance of nobility." Another informed

---

[1] A few years later (January 20, 1777) the Duchess wrote to Lady Spencer : " The Birthday was extremely full, but not compos'd of the best company, for Sir George Warren had his order cut off and stole." This audacity created some sensation, for Horace Walpole also noticed it : " Sir George Warren lost his diamond order in the Council Chamber at the Birthday in the crowd of loyal subjects."

its readers that very few witnesses were present, which seems more likely.

A suggestion has been recently made that Lady Georgiana Spencer was married against her will, and that her affection had been already given to the young Duke of Hamilton, brother to Lady Betty Hamilton.[1] Compelled by her parents to marry the Duke of Devonshire, " the result of this unfortunate alliance was that the Duke of Hamilton retired to Scotland, let his beard grow, and died of despair not long after, whilst the young Duchess of Devonshire refused to live with her husband, although she did the honours of his house." The slightest critical examination destroys the tale. The eighth Duke of Hamilton succeeded his elder brother in 1769 at the age of thirteen. He was thus one year older than Lady Georgiana Spencer, certainly knew her, and might have fallen a victim to her charms. But, owing to ill-health, he was on the Continent from 1771 to 1777. Whatever his state of mind at the marriage of the Duke of Devonshire in 1774, history does not record a long beard or a broken heart. He married Elizabeth, the youngest of the four Burrell sisters,[2] in 1778, lived a wild life, was divorced in 1794, and died in 1799.

Tradition appears to have confused the broken engagement of the Duke of Devonshire and Lady Elizabeth Hamilton, which was hardly public knowledge at the time, and a problematical *affaire de cœur* between the Duke of Hamilton and Lady Georgiana Spencer. Many years later Lady " Caro " Lamb told Lady Morgan that " Lady Georgiana's marriage was one *de convenance*. Her delight was hunting butterflies. The Housekeeper, breaking a lath over

---

[1] In an article entitled " Spa and its English Associations," by Mrs. Walter Creyke, *Nineteenth Century*, vol. 52, p. 656, based upon Ferdinand Christin's letter in the *Archives Russes*.

[2] " Never were any women less endowed with uncommon attractions of external form," wrote Wraxall. But they were " modest, amiable, and virtuous." The only good-looking sister of the three married a commoner, but a special providence intervened for the ugly ones, who became respectively the wives of the Earl of Beverley, the Duke of Northumberland, and the Duke of Hamilton. After her divorce the Duchess of Hamilton married the Marquess of Exeter.

her head, reconciled her to the match (to become Duchess of Devonshire)." But Georgiana Cavendish, if she had no deep affection for her husband, had no regrets for the Duke of Hamilton or Lord Polwarth. She was undoubtedly happy during the early days of her marriage. Lady Mary Coke attended St. James's Palace to see the bride presented. " The drawing-room was fuller than ever I saw it, excepting of a Birthday, owing, as I suppose, to the curiosity to see the Duchess of Devonshire. She look'd very pretty, and happiness was never more marked in a countenance than in hers. She was properly fine for the time of the year, and her diamonds are very magnificent : the girdle is a piece of finery so uncommon it made it the more admired. The Duke of Devonshire had very near been too late : it was nearly four o'clock when he came into the drawing-room. I made no doubt but His Grace is as happy as his Duchess, but his countenance does not mark it so strongly."[1]

The Duke preserved a characteristic lack of interest in his new companion, as other observers were not slow to notice. At the moment Lady Mary Coke was writing in her journal, the Hon. Mrs. Boscawen was composing a letter to Mrs. Delany. " The Duchess of Devonshire was to be presented to-day, but I have not seen anybody that was at Court. The Duke was at the levée yesterday ; and at night at Ranelagh, leaving his fair bride l " That, within two weeks of the marriage, was an action incomprehensible to the old lady. On June 23, Lady Mary Coke made another entry in her journal. " The Duchess of Devonshire was again at Court : never had anybody such general approbation as her Grace. I was told the Queen said She admired her more every time She saw her ; everybody remarks what I mention'd, that happiness was never so painted in any countenance as hers."

That happiness was of brief duration. Misfortune

[1] The *Public Advertiser*, June 15, 1774, announced that at a levée held at St. James's Palace on the previous day, " the Duke of Devonshire was introduced to His Majesty on account of his late marriage, and graciously received, and this day his newly married Duchess was introduced to Her Majesty on the said occasion."

pursued every woman who attracted the interest of the fifth Duke of Devonshire. On the same page of the journal in which Lady Mary Coke chronicled the appearance at Court of the new Duchess there is a short reference to Lady Betty Hamilton. That the two names were coupled together is in itself significant. " Lady Betty Hamilton was married to-day to Lord Stanley, quite privately, very few people at the wedding." Lady Mary Coke added no comment, although the news must have profoundly interested her.

A stern-minded aunt, Lady Charlotte Edwin, had taken the unfortunate Lady Betty in hand. The girl was still dreaming of the far-away Duke of Dorset, who possessed all the easy grace and fascinating manners which distinguished the Sackville family. Lady Charlotte decided that the girl had got to settle down. The Duke of Devonshire had married, the Duke of Dorset had disappeared, Mr. Nisbet was nursing a broken heart in the background. Further coquetries were out of the question. Lady Charlotte arranged a marriage between her niece and Lord Stanley, heir to the Earl of Derby, who, if not a duke, would be probably wealthier. Lady Charlotte Campbell, in her memoirs, tells the story of the sacrifice. " My mother [the Duchess of Argyll and Hamilton], imagining that wealth, title, and splendour would suffice the demands of her daughter's heart, gave in to the plan, and though she did not command, yet used every argument and set forth every circumstance likely to win upon my sister's will. Many were the means employed till Lord Derby's constant and assiduous care veiled the ugliness of his person before the idol he worshipped. Time and despair made Lady Betty give a hasty and undigested consent. After a day of persecutions from every quarter, while a hairdresser was adorning her unhappy head, she traced the consent with a pencil on a scrap of paper and sent it wet with her tears to my mother. Unhappy, ill-fated haste ! The paper was despatched to Lord Stanley. Everything was shortly settled, and no blandishments that power and passion could bestow were spared to dazzle the unhappy victim." Before London had ceased to discuss the Devonshire marriage, or the festivities at Wimbledon, the newspapers contained columns of descriptions of a gigantic *fête champêtre* at The Oaks, Lord Derby's country house near Epsom. " It will cost £5,000," wrote Horace Walpole. " Lord Stanley has bought all the orange trees round London."

Was the entertainment in rivalry to the *fête* at Wimbledon ? Possibly, for the age was essentially one of absurd pretensions and family pride. The Devonshire marriage had taken place on the 4th ; the Derby feast was held on the following Thursday in the same week. Three hundred members of the fashionable world, including all the foreign ministers, journeyed from London to Epsom, arriving at the Oaks about six o'clock in the evening.[1] The countryside turned out in thousands, and the trees were black with clusters of uninvited sightseers. The visitors were greeted by groups of shepherds and shepherdesses, " variously attired, who skipped about, kicking at the tambourines which were pendent from the trees." Many persons, " habited as peasants," attended swings and formed quadrille parties. It was Rosherville on a large scale and ultra-modish.

The day closed with dancing. Then the guests entered a suite of rooms, illuminated with coloured lights, and draped in crimson and gold. A Druid appeared with a bough of mistletoe ; Fauns and Dryads, in tigerskins and oak leaves over " fine rose coloured silk " (or, in other words, pink tights) bounded in and danced a ballet under the direction of Signor Lefoy of the Italian Opera. " A pantomime story was reproduced by the dance in which Cupid and Hymen were introduced as principal characters. The little blind god was robbed of his wings by Hymen by way of expressing his wish that a like fate should ever attend his victims." As for the extensive supper-rooms,

---

[1] They left for town at four the next morning, so that Mayfair must have been reached in time for breakfast.

" the profusion displayed on the table and sideboards was equal to the elegance of the occasion.' And in the grounds a temple had been built with an inscription imploring the protection of Venus.

There was reason to propitiate the goddess. The parade was a mockery. Amongst the guests was the Duke of Dorset, who had returned from his diplomatic mission in order again to disturb the feelings of Lady Betty. The wretched girl exerted her utmost to escape from an engagement she dreaded. The newspapers announced that the marriage was to take place on Sunday, June 12. Lady Charlotte Campbell tells us that up to the last moment her sister endeavoured to break away. The marriage was postponed, but it was too late. All the orange trees in London had been bought and over £5,000 had already been spent upon joy and festivity. Lady Elizabeth Hamilton was married under her mother's roof in Argyll Street, Oxford Street, on June 23. " Lady Betty Hamilton was married to-day to Lord Stanley, quite privately, very few people at the wedding," wrote Lady Mary Coke, entering the deed like a Sibyl in her book of fate.

The Duchess of Devonshire was presented at Court, a happy and smiling bride. When Lady Stanley made her curtesy a few weeks later the verdict was different. " 'Tis said she did not look so satisfied a bride as the Duchess of Devonshire," wrote Lady Mary Coke. " Her dress was approved of, and her diamonds are very fine. She returns no visits, excuses herself upon the account of her going so soon into Lancashire, where she will find a scene very new to her. She goes to ' plain work and to purling brooks, old fashion'd halls, dull aunts, and croaking rooks, etc.' " The last lines were a reminiscence of Pope's epistle to Mrs. Teresa Blount :

> She went to plain-work, and to purling brooks,
> Old fashion'd halls, dull aunts, and croaking rooks :
> She went from opera, park, assembly, play,
> To morning walks, and prayers three hours a day.

Poor Lady Stanley was evidently doing her best to gain

the goodwill of the " dull aunts." Lady Mary Coke did not approve of the manners of both the brides. " Lady Elizabeth Stanley has in my opinion behaved with greater politeness than the Duchess of Devonshire : her card of thanks was the civilest I ever saw. As she did not stay in Town it was impossible for her to return her visits, and I think anybody who was not content with that card must be very unreasonable. The Duchess of Devonshire was backwards and forwards in Town, and for the last fortnight never out of it, said she should return all her visits, and indeed in that time had little excuse not to do so, yet she never came, or sent me a card of excuse, which, considering my intimacy in both families, appears very extraordinary, but, having shown the civility that I thought was due, I have done and shall certainly go no more."

This was in July. When Lady Mary met Lord Frederick Cavendish she complained that his niece had not treated her with the politeness due to her position. The handsome bachelor was too wise to disagree with the indignant Lady Mary. " He seem'd to be of the same opinion," she entered in the journal. Then she left town for Wentworth Castle. In August, Mayfair was abandoned to its caretakers. The fashionable world of London had scattered to every county in England, and most of the countries of Europe.

CHAPTER VI

"SHE was so *peculiarly* happy as to think his Grace *very agreeable*. The Duke's intimate friends say that he has sense and does not want merit—to be sure the jewel has not been well-polished: had he fallen under the tuition of the late Lord Chesterfield he might have possessed *les Graces*, but, at present, only that of his Dukedom belongs to him."

Old Mrs. Delany had no high opinion of the young Duke, but she was seldom tired of praising the Duchess. For her there was a chorus of praise. Those who knew Georgiana Cavendish loved her, and she never lost their affection to the day of her death. There can be little question as to the secret of the power she exercised over her contemporaries. Samuel Rogers described the Duchess as being more fascinating than beautiful. Her beauty, he added, was not that of features but of expression. This is the unanimous verdict of her contemporaries.

It is interesting to compare the opinions of Horace Walpole and Fanny Burney. Both were keen observers of the social drama and met all the most famous men and women of their time. One was a sarcastic, somewhat ill-grained man about town, with no illusions and very few ideals, the

73

other a brilliantly gifted woman always ready to see the bright side of life and to judge humanity at its best. Neither had much prejudice in favour of or against the noble houses of Cavendish and Spencer. Walpole knew Chatsworth, but he spared his friends almost less than his enemies. Fanny Burney belonged to the Court, and had lived with people who looked upon Devonshire House as a hotbed of sedition. After her first conversation with Georgiana Cavendish she expressed surprise that she should ever meet on friendly terms " the head of the opposition public, the Duchess of Devonshire! " Yet their descriptions tally to a phrase, and support the recollections of Samuel Rogers and Nathaniel Wraxall.

In 1775, some months after the ducal marriage, Horace Walpole attended a ball at " the Lady's Club," and returned with a sheaf of comment. The company pleased his refined taste. " It was all goddesses, instead of being a resurrection of dancing matrons as usual. The Duchess of Devonshire effaces all, without being a beauty ; but her youth, figure, flowing good-nature, sense, and lively modesty and modest familiarity make her a phenomenon."

Presumably the other goddesses were not distinguished for such a combination of the virtues. Horace Walpole never altered his opinion. Eight years later he expressed it anew to Sir Horace Mann in identical words. " The Duchess of Devonshire, the empress of fashion, is no beauty at all. She was a very fine woman, with all the freshness of youth and health, but verges fast to a coarseness." This was written in 1783, when the Duchess was twenty-six.

Miss Burney's description is so valuable that it must be repeated in her own words. She met the Duchess at Bath. " I did not find so much beauty in her as I expected, notwithstanding the variation of accounts; but I found her more of manner, politeness, and gentle quiet. She seems by nature to possess the highest animal spirits, but she appeared to me not happy. I thought she looked oppressed within, though there is a native cheerfulness about her which I fancy scarce ever deserts her.

"There is in her face, especially when she speaks, a sweetness of good humour and obligingness, that seems to be the natural and instinctive qualities of her disposition; joined to an openness of countenance that announces her endowed, by nature, with a character intended wholly for honesty, fairness, and good purposes."

Two or three days later, after several conversations with the Duchess, she added to the portrait. "I now saw the Duchess far more easy and lively in her spirits, and cousequently, far more lovely in her person. Vivacity is so much her characteristic, that her style of beauty requires it indispensably; the beauty, indeed, dies away without it. I now saw how her fame for personal charms had been obtained; the expression of her smiles is so very sweet, and has an ingenuousness and openness so singular that, taken in those moments, not the most rigid critic could deny the justice of her personal celebrity. She was quite gay, easy, and charming: indeed, that last epithet might have been coined for her."

This piece of word-painting has a grace peculiar to Fanny Burney. She was indeed, as her friends called her, a "character monger," and her pen had the light and feathery skill of Gainsborough's brush. She was ready to smile with all who would smile with her. The vivacity of the Duchess was sympathetic to her own high spirits and gentle wit.

But these lines, written at Bath as late as 1791, are doubly interesting, because they prove that the Duchess never altered in the essentials of her character. Mrs. Delany met the girl six months after her marriage, in January 1775. The old lady was seventy-five, her visitor seventeen. Most of us have passed through the ordeal of such examinations when age wisely blinks at us over its glasses, and we feebly wonder what devastating judgment is being secretly formulated behind the wrinkled brow. Posterity has got Mrs. Delany's verdict. It was wholly favourable. The Duchess was "so handsome, so agreeable, so obliging in her manner, that *I am quite* in love with her."

With generous appreciation she summed up her manner as
" kindness embellished by politeness."

Lastly must be added the well-considered phrase of
Sir Nathaniel Wraxall. He was a diplomatist who mixed
gall in his ink. But he agrees with Rogers, Walpole, Miss
Burney, and Mrs. Delany. " Her personal charms constituted her smallest pretension to universal admiration ;
nor did her beauty consist, like that of the Gunnings, in
regularity of features and faultless formation of limbs and
shape ; it lay in the amenity and graces of her deportment,
in her irresistible manners and the seduction of her society.
Her hair was not without a tinge of red, and her face, though
pleasing, yet had it not been illuminated by her mind,
might have been considered as an ordinary countenance.
. . . In addition to the external advantages which she
had received from nature and fortune, she possessed an
ardent temper, susceptible of deep as well as strong impressions ; a cultivated understanding, illuminated by a taste
for poetry and the fine arts ; much sensibility, not exempt,
perhaps, from vanity and coquetry."

The Duchess was loved for her " kindness." The word
is simple and unassuming. It means as much, or as little,
as we wish to read into it. In the case of Georgiana Cavendish it was intended to mean much. She did not pass
unsullied through an age which was often coarse, and
generally scurrilous. Much evil was spoken of her by
political opponents, and charges made which to-day we find
impossible either to prove or to deny. But there was always
an undercurrent of public sentiment running strongly in her
favour. Even in such a publication as " The Jockey Club,"
where the author not only repeated all the scandals of the
moment but undoubtedly invented a few additional ones to
give a stronger spice to his work, the Duchess of Devonshire
is treated tenderly. Her " liberal, noble spirit " is praised.
Her charities are said to be universal. " The cold unfeeling
mind may condemn her warmth of temper, as hurrying
on many occasions to extremes, not properly belonging to
feminine reserve ; but sensibility, like hers, disdains the

fastidious delicacy of etiquette or punctilio, when the interest and happiness of a friend are at stake ; nor suffers any consideration to restrain her from pursuing all possible means of promoting both one and the other. Let us therefore consider such trifling peccadillos as serving only to heighten the general beauty of her character. All her foibles and levities originate in a purity of heart, and a consciousness of her own innocence, which makes her overlook those forms of ceremony and restraint which prudence may require, but of which, even the strictest observance is not always sure to stop the breath of calumny."

This extraordinary charm which enabled the Duchess to dominate such opposite personalities as the Prince of Wales and Dr. Johnson, was probably inherited in an almost equal degree from her mother, the Countess Spencer, and her grandmother, Mrs. Poyntz. " The Fair Circassian " certainly had a host of friends, in Paris as well as London. Edward Gibbon met her in France and liked her. She was a gossip, ready to give her whole family history to every newcomer, very proud of her daughter, still prouder of her granddaughter. She undertook to cure one of the daughters of Louis XV. of a painful disease, and Madame Victoire improved so rapidly that when Mrs. Poyntz left Paris for Spa the royal family kissed her and took leave of her as one of their dearest friends. That Mrs. Poyntz could stand upon her dignity is evident from the journals of Mrs. Calderwood, but she was generally welcomed in her own circle as a kindhearted old lady with a wealth of amusing *bavardage*.

Lady Spencer was probably less sympathetic to those who were not to be classed amongst her intimate friends. Although she held a regular salon, and attended most of the fashionable assemblies, the few references to her in the multitude of eighteenth-century correspondence and diaries suggests that her character was notable for little more than a pleasing amiability. In 1791 Fanny Burney met her at Bath, and the peeress takes her place in the gallery of portraits collected by that sparkling author. Lady Spencer is described as " a sensible and sagacious

character, intelligent, polite and agreeable. . . . She
would be one of the most exemplary women of rank of the
age, had she less of show in her exertions, and more of
forbearance in publishing them." And Miss Burney makes
a reference to " vain glory " which was evidently the keynote
of an otherwise charming character. Horace Walpole
gave her the nick-name of " the goddess of Wisdom,"
which was pretentious and far from true in fact. Possibly
it is another example of Strawberry Hill sarcasm, for she
was certainly not a wise mother.

Yet one of the most pleasant pages in the history of
Georgiana, Duchess of Devonshire, is the mutual affection
of Lady Spencer and her two daughters. Of Georgiana's
love for her sister we must speak later. The bond between
Lady Spencer and her eldest child was even stronger.
The eighteenth century was an age of letter writers. There
was much to be said, and many of the writers, nurtured
on the *Spectator* or the *Rambler*, had caught an engaging
manner of saying it. Georgiana, like her companions,
did not spare paper and ink. And as her mother held the
chief place in her thoughts, after her marriage she wrote
what was practically a daily journal of her doings to be sent
to Lady Spencer.

A few of these letters have been published. They record
her interests and amusements, her most private thoughts.[1]
They allow us to obtain some slight idea of her sensibility
and intelligence, and of the delight with which she
approached life. The earliest deal with the days she spent
at Chatsworth and Hardwick after her marriage.

Whatever may have been the extent of her husband's
neglect (and it evidently commenced early in their married
life), the summer of 1774 must have proved months of
glorious delight. She was mistress of Chatsworth and its
dependencies, and, as queen of such a wonderful domain,

[1] The present Duchess of Devonshire edited and published a
selection in the *Anglo-Saxon Review*, June and September, 1899,
with the explanation that " much of what she wrote remains too
trivial, and not a little too intimate for publication."

her high spirits could not have been entirely subdued.
Chatsworth has always remained the most beautiful of the
country homes of the British aristocracy. Indeed, in many
respects, there are few palaces in Europe which can surpass
it. Horace Walpole, who knew everybody and went
everywhere, must be cited again. Hardwick did not appeal
to him, but Chatsworth excited his pen to a rare enthusiasm.
" It is a glorious situation ; the vale rich in corn and verdure,
vast woods hang down the hills which are green to the tòp,
and the immense rocks only serve to dignify the prospect."
As an amateur architect, landscape gardener, and man
of taste, he naturally suggested many improvements,
and pointed out faults of construction. His remark that
internally the great mansion is rather gloomy is not far
from the truth. " The inside is most sumptuous. . . .
The heathen gods, goddesses, Christian virtues, and allegoric
gentlefolks, are crowded into every room, as if Mrs. Holman
had been into every room and invited everybody she saw.
The great apartment is *trist ;* painted ceilings, inlaid
floors, and unpainted wainscot make every room sombre. '

The young Duchess filled the rooms with music. Felice
de Giardini, the director of the London Opera, and the first
violinist in Europe, spent part of his holiday at Chatsworth.
" As for Giardini," grumbled the critical Walpole, " I would
not go across the room to hear him play to eternity."
The same connoisseur refused to find either force or simplicity in his music. However, the Duchess considered
Giardini's minuets " vastly pretty," and said that he played
on the harpsichord " amazingly well." She told Lady
Spencer that he was composing a new trio for her, " extremely pretty, but requires practising," for technical
accomplishment is demanded even from a princess. Giardini
was a lively companion, with a fund of anecdote. He was
prodigiously tall and stout, somewhat awkward—when
he wore a sword he always tripped over it—but able to
charm angels' music from the strings. Miss Burney,
who knew him well, as he was a constant visitor to her
father's house, said that " he loved mischief better than

any man alive." He helped to dissipate some of the gloom of Chatsworth that summer.

Another resource was reading. The girl's taste was a tribute to the excellence of Lady Spencer's scheme of female education. Thirty years earlier, John, Duke of Argyll, forbade his daughters to learn French because " one language was enough for a woman to talk in." Lady Mary Coke quarrelled with her husband over a book, which was cited in Westminster Hall as one of the causes of their separation.[1] During the early Hanoverian age girls were taught to read and write, whilst their father's steward instructed them in a knowledge of accounts. Lady Mary Wortley Montagu had " a professed carving master " three times a week. in order that she might preside at her father's table with skill as well as dignity. It was practical enough, but the lessons did not go very far. Lady Mary preached in and out of season the necessity of a higher standard of female education. " We are educated in the grossest ignorance, and no art omitted to stifle our natural reason ; if some few get above their nurses' instructions, our knowledge must rest concealed, and be as useless to the world as gold in the mine. I am now speaking according to our English notions, which may wear out, some ages hence, along with others equally absurd . . . Learning is necessary to the happiness of women, and ignorance the common foundation of their errors both in morals and conduct. . . . The first lady had so little experience that she hearkened to the persuasion of an impertinent dangler ; and if you mind, he succeeded in persuading her she was not so wise as she should be." Lady Spencer belonged to the new school of thought as to female education.

In November, 1774, the Duchess was reading Goldsmith's *History of Greece* and Voltaire's *Siècle de Louis XIV*, for,

[1] " Lord Coke finding her employed in reading Locke on the Human Understanding told her she could not understand a word of the book, and was an affected —— for her pains." (Lady Louisa Stuart's recollections).

as she told her mother, " these two periods are so distant there will be no danger of their interfering so as to puzzle me.''

Despite the volumes at her call in the ducal libraries, she took under her protection " a poor bookseller " (the phrase is her own—but then booksellers are traditionally poor as publishers are naturally rich) who had a shop in Chesterfield. She commenced to buy books, always a sign of grace and a visible mark of intelligence. She mapped a course of serious study, picking out the *Histoire des Révolutions arrivées dans le gouvernement de la République Romaine*, by the Abbé Aubert de Vertot, and William Robertson's *History of Scotland*. In addition she had a permanent music master and was taking lessons in drawing and painting.

She was also being initiated into a far more serious art—the art of politics. In November both Duke and Duchess were visiting Lord Rockingham at Wentworth Castle, that mansion which is reputed to cover over two acres of ground. Horace Walpole, who knew Wentworth as he knew Chatsworth and every other palace in Britain, sums up its pretentiousness in a few words. " There are temples in cornfields ; and in the little wood a window frame mounted on a bunch of laurel and intended for a hermitage.'' The enormous building overcame him. " The chimney pieces are like tombs.'' [1]

[1] Sir Algernon West in his *Recollections* says that Wentworth is a quarter of a mile long. Two of his stories give some idea of its immense size. The property passed from the Rockinghams to the Fitzwilliams, as the first Earl Fitzwilliam had married the eldest sister of the Marquess of Rockingham. One of the earls was told by his wife that he ought not to be so entirely in his servants' hands, and should sometimes visit the offices. Next day he started on a voyage of discovery, and, wandering through the deserted lower regions, found a solitary boy. He asked the boy who he was. " Why, I'm the boy who does all the work in this 'ere 'ouse, and who the devil are you ? " was the reply. The same Lord Fitzwilliam before going to bed one night rang the bell two or three times, without any answer. At last a servant came, and was asked for a glass of water. The water was not brought, and so, in a resigned way, the head of the house said : " I suppose I must go without the glass of water.''

The Duchess sent her mother a long account of her entertainment at Wentworth. Lord Rockingham had taken her through his house and park. She had been to see the new stables he was building. Giardini's music had been " vastly pretty " ; Rockingham's stables were " vastly well designed." " Vastly " in 1774 was the " awfully " of a later generation. They strolled through the park —probably to admire the temples. As they crossed the lawns they talked of other affairs than the planning of stables and blacksmith's shops, or the correct proportions of a Palladian temple. The Marquess of Rockingham was one of the many territorial princes of the century who naturally fell into the scheme of party government. He was " a man of plain and sound understanding, unquestionable probity, great benevolence, the most liberal munificence, and patriotic intentions." He was also by inclination and inheritance a bigoted Whig, who, as a boy, had sneaked away from Wentworth in order to enlist under Cumberland's banner at Carlisle and fight against the Jacobites. Georgiana's father, Lord Spencer, had taken no very active part in the political animosities of his time. But his daughter had been brought up in the true faith, and there was little that Rockingham could teach. However, now she was making

---

But a glass of cold water, the traditional right of every beggar, was always a difficulty in these great houses. In 1823 Mr. Creevey was the guest of Mr. Lambton, afterwards the Earl of Durham. " The night before last, between 12 and 1, I being in the library where the same cold fowl always is with wine and water, Lambton came in out of the hazard room, and finding no water, began belabouring the bell in a way that I thought must inevitably have brought the whole concern down. No effect was produced, so he sallied forth, evidently boiling, and when he returned he said :—' I don't think I shall have to ring so long another time.' This is all I know of my own knowledge : but, says Lady Augusta Milbank to me yesterday—' Do you know what happened last night ? ' ' Du tout,' says I. ' Why,' says she, ' Mr. Lambton rung the bell for water so long that he went and rung the house bell, when his own man came ; and upon saying something in his own justification which displeased the Monarch, he laid hold of a stick and struck him twice ; upon which his man told him that he could not stand that, and that if he did it again he should be obliged to knock him down. So the master held his hand and the man gave him notice he had done with him.' "

the acquaintance of the leaders in the battle, for the Marquess was a Cabinet minister together with one of her uncles by marriage, Lord John Cavendish. And Rockingham's private secretary, a certain Edmund Burke, who had been found a safe seat in the little borough of Wendover, was going to become one of the stars of her future circle at Devonshire House. That morning's walk across the Yorkshire fields was Duchess Georgiana's initiation into the political world. We know what Rockingham was troubled about. His attitude towards the American struggle was that of all his fellow Whigs. They deprecated the continuance of the war against the rebellious colonies, and some of them— like Rockingham—stood apart from politics while the struggle was in progress. These were the problems which the statesman unfolded to the girl by his side.

But the hours were not wholly serious. For the first time in her life the Duchess shot " two or three guns " at a mark in company with the Duke and Lord Rockingham. The great unfinished house was full of interest, and her letters display delight and astonishment.[1] Some of the host's improvements were " glorious," and she became so engrossed that she was late for dinner. All the company had assembled. She chronicles their names, Sir George Armytage [2] with his fine voice, and several whist players. After dinner, music and cards, and the light-hearted letter ends with " Adieu, mon adorable Maman, croyez que je vous aime de tout mon cœur."

October had been spent at Hardwick, and a lengthy

[1] In September, 1827, Mr. Creevey was at Wentworth. He writes : —" At dinner I heard Princess Lieven say to Lord Fitzwilliam :— ' Your house, my lord, or your palace, I should rather say, is the finest I have seen in England. It is both beautiful and magnificent.' —To which old Billy (as nickname for the fourth Earl of Fitzwilliam) replied—' It is indeed.' She then proceeded :—' When foreigners have applied to me heretofore for information as to the houses best worth seeing in England, I have sent them to Stowe and Blenheim ; but in future I shall tell them to go down to Wentworth.' The last compliment was received by Old Billy *in solemn silence !* Not an atom of reply ! "

[2] Sir George Armytage, of Kirkleis Park, near Brighouse, Yorks. He succeeded to the baronetage in 1768, and died in 1783.

chronicle was despatched to her " dearest Mama." She
went to a county ball. With glee she describes her dress,
" a demi-saison silk, pink trimmed with gauze and green
ribbon." The colours are scarcely in harmony, but her
fresh young face was always pleasant and charming. The
dance, evidently a political function, was held at some
assembly rooms in Derby. " Nobody was refused at the
door ; the Ball Room was quite full of the Daughters and
Wives of all the voters in check'd aprons.' There was
plenty of drink about. Upon their entry, as they went up
the stairs, they met *F.* " extremely drunk." *F.* was probably
Lord Frederick Cavendish, the Duke's uncle, a valiant
soldier and M.P. for Derby.[1] There was difficulty with the
music, for the band had gone to sleep, and when it was
aroused the musicians mixed their parts. What a discord
to ears trained by Giardini !

She danced with Mr. Coke. " The handsome Englishman," who was only twenty-two, had recently returned
from abroad, and was already the hero of romance. He
was credited with being hopelessly in love with the Pre-

[1] Lord Frederick Cavendish, third son of the third Duke of Devonshire, was then in his forty-fifth year. He was elected M.P. for
Derbyshire in 1751 when his elder brother, the Marquess of Hartington, was summoned to the House of Lords as Lord Cavendish of
Hardwick, and he sat as M.P. for Derby from 1754 until 1780. His
career in the army was not without distinction, and he was one of
the four young officers (Wolfe, Monckton, and Keppel were the others)
who, on the outbreak of the Seven Years' War, made a compact not
to marry until France had been conquered. He never did marry.
Being a Cavendish and a Whig he refused to accept a command
during the American War of Independence. He died a Field-
Marshal in 1803, and left a large fortune to his nephew, Lord George
Cavendish, afterwards first Earl of Burlington.
There has been no greater change in social manners than in the
attitude towards drunkenness. In the eighteenth century it was
not only a venial sin, but the subject of merriment. The third Earl
of Lichfield, Chancellor of Oxford University, was always drunk.
In 1765 Gilly Williams wrote to George Selwyn concerning a private
political meeting : " At the rehearsal on Wednesday night of the
Speech at Lord Halifax's, Lord Lichfield came extremely drunk
and proposed amendments and alterations to the no small amusement of the company." Drunken men sometimes rose and spoke
in the House of Commons.

tender's queen, the Countess of Albany, who permitted him to carry her portrait. Lady Mary Coke's squabbles with her husband had made this youth the first commoner in England, for he succeeded to the estates destined for her child. He became famous as "Coke of Holkham," and was created Earl of Leicester—sixty years after this dance with the young Duchess in the ball-room at Derby.[1]

One other activity employed her leisure. She wrote verse. The "Summer and the Rose" belongs either to 1774 or 1775:

> As Summer, with declining ray
> To autumn's sober shades gave way
>   A Rose that ow'd its blooming pride
> Its budding charms and perfumes sweet
>   The blushing leaves that deck'd its side
> All to her gentle friendly heat
>   Now finding that its bloom must go
> And droop to every gazer's eye
>   Its leaves dispers'd must to the zephyrs flow
> Adrest Her thus with many a scented sigh.

> "Sweet Season lov'd by ev'ry flower
> Blest parent, of the Vernal Hour
>   Why was I ever doom'd to taste
> The pleasure of thy blooming reign
>   Since thou to other climes must haste
> And leave thy votary in pain—

The "laughing Season" promised the Rose that—

> . . . . Soon again thy rosy hue
> Thy leaves that with the Zephyrs play
>   Thy gentle tints shall brighten at my view
> And dazzle in the vermil dawn of Day.

The last lines end with considerable feeling:

> No Rose could ever droop its head
> As Summers much lov'd moments fled
>   Could ne'er its grief sincere impart
> In sign of Melancholy woe
>   With half the grief that feels my heart

---

[1] In December, 1837, Creevey was at Holkham. There was the usual Christmas ball for the servants in the audit room. "The Earl of Leicester, aged 85, opened the ball. He is a marvellous man, but I think he is *going out*, tho' he burns as bright to the last." He outlived Creevey, however, by four years.

When what it loves is forc'd to go.
Nor when the blooming days appear
No Rose could half that pleasure prove
As that with which my beating heart must burn
At the Dear presence of the friend I love.

These are the verses of a romantic school girl   They are not great poetry, but they reveal much depth of tenderness. " Her heart," wrote Wraxall, " might be considered as the seat of those emotions which sweeten human life, adorn our nature, and diffuse a nameless charm over existence." The praise is not excessive, and the words came from the pen of an old diplomatist who might have been pardoned for a display of cynicism.

CHAPTER VII

THE marriages of the Cavendishes and the Spencers soon passed into the limbo of the forgotten. The *fête champêtre* at the Oaks was turned into a comedy and presented at Drury Lane Theatre by its author, General John Burgoyne.[1] Other more exciting events engrossed the drawing-rooms of Mayfair and the coffee-houses of Fleet Street. For example, Grace Elliott, the pretty wife of a fashionable physician, eloped with Lord Valentia. During her three years of marriage, Mrs. Elliott had already given the town much material for gossip. With her elopement, her career of scandal as " Dally the tall " was at its beginning. Then, in June, Lord Holland was dying. Before the month had ended both he and his wife were dead. There was speculation as to the fortunes bequeathed to the new lord and his brother, Charles James

---

[1] John Burgoyne (1722-1792), statesman, gambler, soldier, actor, playwright. At the age of twenty-one he married and eloped with Lady Charlotte Stanley, daughter of the eleventh Earl of Derby. In September, 1774, he was sent to America to reinforce General Gage, arrived at Boston in 1775 and was defeated at the battle of Bunker's Hill. Returning to London he wrote and produced the *Maid of the Oaks* (founded on the Derby marriage *fêtes*) at Drury Lane Theatre, in which Mrs. Abingdon took the part of Lady Bab Lardoon. In 1777 he commanded the troops at the victorious battle of Ticonderoga. In 1786 he wrote another successful play, *The Heiress*. He was a close friend of Sir Joshua Reynolds and a visitor at Devonshire House.

Fox. Yet, with all these subjects for small talk, Horace Walpole, surveying the world from his retreat at Strawberry Hill, was able to tell the Countess of Upper Ossory that " the reigning dullness is so profound that it is not even ridiculous."

The Duchess of Devonshire returned to town in January, 1775. Her success as a leader of fashion was immediate. The mansion, which had not known a mistress since the death of the last Duchess in 1754, at once became the centre of an active and important circle, active because most of its members were young, important because their rank was high and the influence they exerted over the fortunes of the Whig party far-reaching. But the personal attraction was even stronger, and the secret of this girl's power over her contemporaries was due simply to the fascination of her manner and the overflowing kindness of her heart.

A letter from Mrs. Delany to her friend Mrs. Port, dated January 19, 1775, gives more than a clue. Mrs. Delany belonged by birth and temperament to an age which had passed. She was a distant relative of the Spencers, and, although a woman of position, hardly a conspicuous member of the fashionable world. The earliest visit the Duchess paid upon her return to London was to Mrs. Delany in her rooms in St. James's Place, and this mark of respect from the young woman flattered and delighted the elderly dame.

On that Tuesday morning in January, Mrs. Delany was not alone. By her fireside sat an old friend, Mrs. Hester Chapone. Horace Walpole did not care for Mrs. Chapone, and protested that he was unable to read her books. He thought, however, that they might go a long way towards making the Bible fashionable. Mrs. Chapone did not need the approbation of Walpole or suffer from his sarcasm, for she was the famed author of *Letters on the Improvement of the Mind*, a book every parent gave his children in the eighteenth century. Altogether Mrs. Chapone and Mrs. Delany were a formidable couple of elderly ladies for a girl of eighteen to encounter.

Georgiana Cavendish conquered them both. " In came the Duchess of Devonshire," wrote Mrs. Delany enthusiastically, " so handsome, so agreeable, so obliging in her manner that *I am quite* in love with her. She ask'd most kindly after you, made apologies for not having been to see you at Ilam, but hopes when you have thoughts of favouring her with a visit at Chatsworth that you will *not* come in a formal way on her day, and that she came to me in a morning to break thro' all ceremony between us, and to desire I would give her leave to call on me sometimes. I can't tell you all the civil things she said, and really they deserve a better name, which is *kindness* embellished by politeness. I hope she will *illumine* and *reform* her contemporaries ! "

The radiant Georgiana left St. James's Place in the glory of her new sedan, surrounded by eight footmen in the laced livery of the Cavendishes. The two old dames peered above the window-blinds with delight as the beauty was processionally carried round the corner into St. James's Street.

For, in the eighteenth century, a Duchess was a superior being, not ordinary clay, ruled by strange conventions, subject to a distinctive code of social laws, in Heaven as well as on earth a Duchess first, a woman after. " Dry up your tears, my brethren," said a divine, when preaching the funeral sermon of Mary, Duchess of Queensberry, " weep no more, for this most illustrious Princess, who, though she was a great and good Duchess on earth, is now a great and good Duchess in Heaven." [1] The admiration for dukes and duchesses has always been a characteristic

---

[1] " God Almighty would think twice before he damned a person of good family," said a lady of quality. Lord Hervey records the remark of another, who, referring to her *femme de chambre*, observed : " Regardez cet animal, considérez ce néant, voilà une belle âme pour être immortelle." The Duchess of Buckingham told Lady Huntingdon " it is monstrous to be told that you have a heart as sinful as the common wretches that crawl on the earth. This is highly offensive and insulting." Sarah, Duchess of Marlborough, declared that she was " not only sure of going to Heaven but of obtaining one of the best places." In the same connection may be related C. K. Sharpe's story of the country gentleman who took his child to the Bishop of Durham's confirmation. " My Lord, this young lady is *my* daughter. Pray give her a double portion."

of English society, and is not confined to any particular class. The true-born Briton, in the words of one of Disraeli's heroes, " is opposed to all privilege, and indeed to all orders of men except dukes, who are a necessity."

The Duchess had however now been married long enough to learn that even the members of her exalted circle were governed by the ordinary rules of human conduct, not those laws that are supposed to control morals, but the hidden springs of feeling, which from time to time over-whelm all conventions. In her unhappy case she suffered from neglect, from a negation rather than an excess of passion.

General Fitzpatrick, an intimate friend of Fox, and a prominent supporter of the Whigs, told Samuel Rogers that the Duke of Devonshire's love for his wife grew quite cool a month after their marriage. There is no corroboration of this statement in the few letters which have been published written by the Duchess during her early married life. But it was evidently the belief of their friends at the time. Lady Mary Coke hints at it slightly coarsely. Mrs. Boscawen's comment has already been cited.

" Our freeborn weather, which on Monday was as hot as Lord George [Gordon], is now as cold as the Duke of Devon-shire," wrote Horace Walpole. Another portrait, with the shadows etched in, is to be found in the reminiscences of Sir Nathaniel Wraxall. " He was a nobleman whose constitutional apathy formed his distinguishing character-istic. His figure was tall and manly, though not animated or graceful, his manner always calm and unruffled. He seemed to be incapable of any strong emotion, and destitute of all energy or activity of mind. As play became in-dispensable in order to arouse him from his lethargic habit and to awake his torpid faculties, he passed his evenings usually at Brooks either at faro or whist."

This was the husband of the girl who described herself as " animated nature." He belonged to a family constitu-tionally silent and retiring. There is a story that the Duke and his brother, Lord George Cavendish (afterwards Earl of

Burlington, and father of the seventh Duke), were travelling to Yorkshire, and at one inn were shown into a three-bedded room. Two of the four-poster beds were for the brothers, the curtains of the third bed were drawn. Each brother, in turn, walked across the room to the bed, peeped between the curtains, and then went to bed. During the next day's journey one brother said to the other :

" Did you see what was in that bed last night ? "

" Yes, brother," was the laconic reply.

The bed contained a corpse.

At another time, at Chatsworth, he was aroused from his sleep by the news that the house was on fire. He merely turned himself in bed, and said sleepily that he hoped they would put it out.

This attitude towards life was partly natural and partly acquired. " It is *bon ton* to be tranquil," wrote Disraeli in " Coningsby." We can understand how the continental tradition of the phlegmatic Englishman was built up. The Englishman is more reserved than his European neighbours, but he is not quite so calm under the ups and downs of fortune as foreign critics would have us believe. And when Saxon and Celtic blood intermingles it is easy to find temperaments as active and excitable as any Frenchman from the Meridional.

The Duke did not lack intelligence. He was a classical scholar of considerable attainments, whilst " to know Shakespeare as well as the Duke of Devonshire " was a proverb amongst his acquaintance. But there was no incentive urging him to take his true place in society. He had no ambitions. Decorated with the green sash of a noble order, his only remark was that a green coat would be of more use to him.

He was not a man without a certain kind of affection. Wraxall wrote that he was " by no means insensible to the seduction of female charms." He certainly was insensible to the charms of his beautiful wife.

The *Town and Country Magazine*, in an issue dated 1777, told a curious tale of an adventure that happened to the Duke before marriage. The magazine lived on its scandal, and its " *tête-à-tête* portraits " were sufficiently notorious. As far as they can be checked the facts were seldom exaggerated. In dealing with the Duke of Devonshire, the writer said :—

" His rank and family entitled him to admission into the first companies wherever he went. He has often been admitted at the *petits soupers* of the late King of France, when Mademoiselle Du Barré has done the honours of the table. This lady, considering her situation, and that a very short time would perhaps expose her to the resentment of a young king, or a new ministry, cast her thoughts towards the d——. Her possessions were capital, her influence extensive, her interest unbounded ; such a predicament was sufficient to intoxicate any young female, possessed of more prudence and penetration than Mademoiselle Du Barré. Her personal attractions she thought irresistible, as they had captivated one of the greatest monarchs in Europe ; but she forgot to distinguish between royal dotage and d——l juvenility. In a word, she thought her pretensions sufficient to be no less than the wife of our hero. The report got wind, and it came to the ears of the d——'s preceptor. He cautioned his pupil in the strongest terms, to be upon his guard against the artifices of a subtle courtezan. She had already made such advances as required an *éclaircissement ;* he had not yet made it : the field was, therefore, his own. Finding she had built too much upon her charms, influence, and attractions, and, at the same time, that her heart was too far engaged in the conflict, she became the dupe to her own artifice ; and the young English nobleman had his vanity so far gratified as to be the rival of the *grand monarque.*"

This entanglement with the Dubarry was a passing infatuation. The purpose of the particular *tête-à-tête* in the *Town and Country Magazine* was to draw attention to the Duke's interest in Miss Charlotte Spencer, an interest which extended long after his marriage. Miss Charlotte Spencer, the daughter of a country curate, came to London at the death of her father. After some adventures of an ordinary nature, she found herself the possessor of a sum of money. With this she opened a milliner's shop. Here the Duke saw her and raised her to a position less onerous and more lucrative than that of stitching feathers on to bonnets.

Their relationship was known and recognised, and the *Town and Country Magazine* made the following curious comment. " A paradox still remains to be solved ; which is, that after some years intercourse with Miss S——r, who was now rather approaching the decline of beauty, our hero should marry a nobleman's daughter, an universal toast, still in her teens, with every personal accomplishment, who gives the *Ton* wherever she goes, and that he should still be fond of his antiquated (by comparison) Charlotte ? There is a caprice in mankind, it is true, that cannot be accounted for—whim prevails more than reason—but that the blooming, the blythe, and beautiful D—— should be neglected for Charlotte S——r is really astonishing ! "

Between 1775 and 1780 a daughter was born which the Duke recognised. The young Duchess, without children of her own, showed her magnanimous spirit by caring for the child—the fate of Miss Spencer we do not know— and engaging a governess for her early education. The governess was Lady Elizabeth Foster, the child the mysterious " Miss W."

But the Duchess could not remain indifferent to her husband's coldness. From 1775 to 1783, when her eldest child was born, she amused herself with the lightest pleasures. Her name became the synonym for aimless folly. She became the subject of a pamphlet war, a one-sided campaign, for there was no defence. *Heroic Letters, Interesting Letters,* a *First Letter,* and then a *Second Letter,* were quickly issued from the press. Some were coarse lampoons, others dignified remonstrances, written more in sorrow than in anger. It is far from clear how the girl managed to attain such a notorious position in London life within a period of four or five years.

An Interesting Letter to the Duchess of Devonshire,

written and published in 1778, evidently came from a
clerical pen. The author addressed his remarks to the
whole sex, as well as to the Duchess, who, he explained,
" is an undoubted source of female example. . . .
The subject is very interesting to the female sex ; and
without any diminution of the respect I bear to the great
lady to whom it is addressed, I present it as an offering
of great goodwill to the attention of my countrywomen."
He trusted his remarks would open the door for Prudence
and Discretion.   " Even if they fail to impress her they may
yet help to fortify some minds against the prevailing contagion."

The age was charged with pessimism. The loss of the
American colonies had profoundly impressed thoughtful
opinion. Horace Walpole was convinced that Great
Britain was on the down grade, and most of his friends
agreed with him. The navy was not to be relied upon.
When La Galissonnière overcame Byng in the Mediterranean
the old Duke of Newcastle cried to a judge of the Admiralty :
" My dear Sir Thomas, England has seen her best days.
We are all undone. This d—— fellow has done for us,
and all is over." Georgiana Cavendish was cited as an
example of the decadence of society. The author of the
Interesting Letter announced with an air of conviction :
" We certainly live in times of universal depravity. . . .
A shameless, daring effrontery, a carelessness of reputation,
an inattention to the good opinion of the World, with
an open and avowed prostitution of real honour, are the
notorious and very reproachful characterictics of the present
age—and, as a great addition to the calamity, the Female
part of Society is greatly involved in this description."

The author, very diplomatically, paid an elaborate
compliment to the sex he was trying to convert. " A fair
and unprejudiced History of the Female Character yet
remains to be produced to the world," he writes on one of
his earliest pages. " Indeed, where is the Man who is
qualified to write with due impartiality on a subject of such
an interesting nature ? For where is the man to be found

Maria Cosway pinxt. V. Green sculpt.

GEORGIANA, DUCHESS OF DEVONSHIRE

As when fair Cynthia in darksome night   Breaks forth her silver beams, and her bright
  Is in a noyous cloud envelcped,   head
Where she may find the substance thin and   Discovers to the world discomfited.
  light   *Spencer: "Fairy Queen."*

who has lived in the World, that does not in a great degree, if not. entirely, owe his comforts and his sorrows to the Female part of the creation ?·''

There is no bitterness in his gentle soul, though he admits that '' strict partiality cannot be expected where prejudice will inevitably arise from Gratitude or Resentment.'' But, aghast at the prevailing lack of moral tone, he makes the unfortunate Duchess his target. '' I am fully persuaded that your Grace might give Vice and Folly a very consider-able check by becoming yourself an example of Christian Virtue.''

In the course of one hundred pages he tackles the poor lady with severity, telling her that she has acquaintance with many '' who cannot be fit companions for any Woman who fears the loss of reputation, and retains the love of Virtue.

'' Instead of unfolding your charms to catch the gaze of a curious multitude, or as traps for the flattering and admiration of the idle and dissipated Men of Fashion which surround you, instead of resting your consequence on that Beauty whose duration will be so short, use the winning graces which are yours to give Virtue its most lovely appearance. . Extend your example to the applause and imitation of distant Times, when your fine form shall be mouldered into dust '—hardly a pleasant reflection for a young and beautiful woman.

Putting generalities aside, he becomes personal. '' You have hitherto been approached either as a Duchess, a Beauty, or a young person of rank and levity, who thought .she had a right to exhibit herself in any manner she might think proper, and to promote any fashionable amusements that might suit her fancy.

'' In the latter capacity, you certainly possess an allowed supremacy :—however, it is but a sorry pre-eminence ; for little is gained by it, but being the adopted parent of every absurdity which Fashion, fertile in absurdities, administers to your Sex.

'' Your Grace, by the singular manner in which you

adorned your person, not only placed an exorbitant plume upon the heads of all who frequent the polite places of public resort, but gave the same decoration to every unhappy Female who patrols the purlieus of Prostitution. If the influence of your Grace's virtues and future prudence should be as extensive as your late display of fashionable levities, the formation of a *coterie* would be an Herculean labour,—and the *Magdalen* will become a useless establishment." Then grandiloquently he writes:

" Sorrow has perched upon your Toilette : that Altar of Vanity has received the tribute of your tears. '

Poor Duchess ! She was barely twenty-one when she read these lines. Not one bird of misfortune but vast flocks had already settled upon the toilette-table of Devonshire House.

The closing pages of the pamphlet foreshadow this volume—" The conclusion which I would derive from these observations is this :—that from the rage after anecdotes and private history, which at present prevail, and the uncommon pains which is taken to gratify it, Posterity will possess a degree of biographical information, which neither this nor any former Age has ever known. A person, therefore, of your high rank and personal qualifications will be, without doubt, the subject of some future Domestic Historian, who, if your present love of pleasure should continue, and he should take his description from thence, will probably form something like the following character of your Grace :

" This lady was married at a very early age to the Duke of ————, who signalised his affection for her by every mark of the most unbounded generosity. At this time she was considered as one of the most beautiful Women in the Kingdom, and, from the virtues of her noble parents, the uncommon attention which was paid to her education, and the precautions which had been taken to preserve her from the contagion of the Age, great expectations were formed of her future conduct, and it was not doubted that she would prove an unrivalled example of female excellence. But youth cannot be trusted amid the seductions of Pleasure, when it possesses the utmost means of enjoying them. Inspired with an uncommon vivacity of temper, and having experienced no medium between parental control and the boundless indulgence of a husband, her Grace yielded to the delusions which played around her, and suffered herself to be tempted into a rage after pleasure which at once blasted all the fond expectations concerning her. Fashion submitted its capricious fancies to her control, and she was delighted to direct them. Flattery was continually at her ear, and she encouraged its adulations. Vanity prepared her Temple, and she became the Priestess of it. Pleasure solicited a place in her heart, and she gave up the whole of it to that deluding Syren ;—while Discretion and Good Sense, finding themselves deserted and unnoticed, resigned their care ; and of all the Virtues which once possessed an interest in her, Chastity alone refused to abandon her. The consequences of such a conduct did not belie the source of them. Her health was lost, her constitution impaired, and she proved a barren Wife, to the great disappointment of her noble family. With her beauty, her flatterers fled away ;—with her health, the means of enjoying pleasure were at an end ;—and having rested her dignity upon caprice and fashion, it sunk with them. In short, she languished an unrespected and hypochondriac character to her death, which was scarce lamented, and happened at a period when the wise only begin to know the real pleasure of life."

This was plain speaking, and the writer touched upon several incontrovertible facts. " Be known as the Christian Duchess ! " cried the preacher, and he drew a picture of such a saint. " Her piety was warm but rational, and took the middle course between indifference and enthusiasm." The phrase could not better convey the milk-and-water latitudinarianism of the eighteenth century.

Another shorter pamphlet, issued by the same publisher, bore on its title-page a line from Pope :

" Pleas'd with a feather, Tickled with a straw,"

evidently intended to sum up the character of the Duchess.

H

The opening sentence explained the author's intention.
" Every character whose follies may be the source of mischief to Society, deserves reproof and chastisement."
He administered both to the Duchess. " When you began
to breathe from the hurry which must have accompanied
your marriage with the Duke of Devonshire, and to turn
your thoughts to the character you ought to support in the
world ; it was rather singular that among the many parts
of importance and dignity which solicited your choice,
you should fix upon one so trifling in its nature and so
unworthy your rank and understanding as the Dispenser
of Fashions and the Genius of Pleasure."

In the same year William Combe published anonymously,
The First of April, or the Triumphs of Folly, which he
dedicated to " a celebrated Duchess."   The author describes the universal worship before the altar of folly :

> " When Devonshire, uprising from her seat,
>   With careless gesture to the altar moves.
> Then *Virtue* shriek'd, and all the *laughing loves*
>   That play'd around, droop'd instant with dismay,
>   And spread their wings, and weeping, fled away !
>   The noble dame her offering now prepares,—
>   A father's counsels, and a mother's cares,
>   Upon the altar's gilded surface lie,
>   With winning grace and sweet simplicity ;
>   The gay, yet decent look ; the modest air,
>   Which loves the brow of youth and triumphs there ;
>   The power to give delight, devoid of art,
>   Which stole unconscious o'er the lover's heart ;
>   The wish to bless, with all those virgin charms
>   Which heighten'd rapture in a husband's arms ;
>   Each infant friendship, each domestic care,
>   Each elevated thought was offer'd there.
>   Nor did the lavish votary deny
>   One solid charm—but chilling chastity."

The last words of " Peter Pindar's " easy flowing rhyme
touch upon an aspect that must not be forgotten. In all
except the very coarsest and most scurrilous lampoons,
no reflection was ever made upon the honour of the Duchess.
She was a giddy, mad-headed girl who had not sufficiently
realized the dignity and responsibility of her position.
She was fascinated and engrossed by balls, *fêtes-champêtres*,

and similar dissipations, she gave too much time to dress and the delights of fashion. Combe suggests in *The First of April* that :

> " her rosy lips dispense
> *Double entendres* and impertinence."[1]

The impertinence was probably true, but there is no suggestion that her conversation was open to objection. Miss Berry distinctly says that " her suppers were blamed only by those who were not admitted to them—by those who knew not that her good taste was well as her principles, permitted no unbecoming levity on any subject, for the improper discussion of which neither wit nor rank were deemed an excuse ; and that the tone of her society was as perfectly proper, as if it had consisted of the dullest individuals who took upon them to censure her."

Her greatest faults were youth and high-spirits. The first she grew out of ; sorrow cured her of the second. Her love of dress was another subject of criticism. But the women who is not interested in clothes forfeits half her charm and loses most of her power.

CHAPTER VIII

Scandal busy—the Duchess as a leader of fashion—headdresses
and feathers—exacting dissipation—days in the country—
visits to the House of Commons and Drury Lane—" The Maid
of the Oaks "—the Duke of Dorset—Georgiana Cavendish and
Elizabeth Stanley—the fate of the Countess of Derby—
fears for the Duchess of Devonshire—naval and military
adventures—the camps at Coxheath—Dr. Johnson—gaieties
at Tunbridge Wells—Mrs. Thrale and Mrs. Montagu—a pen
portrait by Fanny Burney—Mrs. Montagu on the adders of
scandal.

GOSSIP was busy with the name of the Duchess
before she had been three months in London. In
January Mrs. Delany was delighted at her behaviour. March brought a different tale. An
ominous letter was sent from St. James's Place to Mrs.
Port, of Ilam, on March 10, 1775.

" The longer I live in the world the more I am convinced
that the happiest people are those who make the *best of
their lot*, and keep their minds untainted with ambitious
views. Ambition's ladder is very treacherous ; when you
have taken one step you are deluded to another, not considering your airy situation, and that if a step fails your fall
is so much the more dangerous for having left the ground
you stood on before. I do not mean that this lesson is
wanting at Ilam, where innocence and peace, with every
virtuous inclination, possess one of the most beautiful spots
in England. O, my Mary ! I really can say with Cato, *I am
sick of this bad world*, when I suffer my imagination to
wander among the multitude ; it would be more supportable
could one select a number of any considerable magnitude
not affected by the great whirlpool of dissipation, and (indeed

I *fear*, I may add) *vice*. This bitter reflection arises from what I hear *every* body say of a *great* and *handsome* relation of ours just *beginning* her part ; but I do hope she will be like the young actors and actress' who begin with *over* acting when they first come upon the stage, and abate of her superabundant spirits (that now mislead her) and settle into a character worthy of applause and of the station she possesses ; but I *tremble* for her ! which has led one into this tedious animadversion.'

Mrs. Delany's trembling fears were hardly justified, although the Duchess did wake up the town with her vivacity and youthful energy. Her early triumphs were in the field of fashion. She did not invent plumes. Eve was probably the first woman to pluck a feather from the tail of a peacock in order to decorate her hair. But the Duchess of Devonshire wore feathers which were larger than the feathers ever worn by any other woman. This surprising feat not only made her immediately famous, it made her notorious, it excited the bitter pens of the Grub Street pamphleteers, and the far bitterer tongues of the other ladies of quality who sought to set the *ton*.

Her success was thus complete. " Nothing is talked of now so much as the ladies' *enormous* dresses, more suited to the *stage* or a *masquerade* than for either *civil* or sober societies," wrote Mrs. Delany. " The three *most* elevated plumes of feathers are the Duchess of Devonshire, Lady Mary Somerset, and Lady Harriet Stanhope, but some say Mrs. Hobart's exceeds them all. It would be some consolation if their manners did *not* too much correspond with the lightness of their dress ! But the Lady H. Stanhope is much commended for the propriety of her behaviour." [1]

---

[1] Lady Harriet Stanhope, thus commended, was a daughter of the Earl of Harrington. She married in 1776 the Hon. Thomas Foley, afterwards second Baron Foley, and died in 1781. They were very extravagant, and there came a time when it was reported that the family had not enough to eat. Lady Harriet's son sold the estate at Witley to Lord Ward (afterwards Earl of Dudley) for £890,000, and was able to pay the debts accumulated by his father and mother. The balance brought him in an income of £19,000 a year without debt, instead of being " the wretched impoverished man he was."

Every gossiping letter, every memoir, every tale sent abroad by strangers in the land, contain references and comments on this fashion. In the spring of 1775 a Mrs. Harris wrote to her son : " the Duchess of Devonshire had two plumes sixteen inches long, besides three small ones ; this has so far outdone all other plumes, that Mrs. Damer, Lady Harriet Stanhope, etc., looked nothing." No mention here of the presumptuous Mrs. Hobart. Mrs. Mary Moser, the female Royal Academician, invited a friend to " come to London and admire our plumes ; we sweep the sky ! A Duchess wears six feathers, a lady four, and every milkmaid one at each corner of her hat." Some of the husbands feebly objected. " He could not bear flowers, nor feathers, nor stays, so to please him we have almost left off feathers— *c'est bien complaisant*—but we can go no further." Wonderful that they could go so far. The same lady, one of the Eliots of Minto, writes : " The heads are higher than ever, with feathers *en rayons de soleil* and *le jardin Anglais*— fruit, turnips and potatoes ; the gowns trimmed the same way. To give you some idea, my gown for the birthday was trimmed with grapes, acorns and roses, so that I looked like a walking hothouse, but on the whole it was pretty."

The most astounding feather worn by the Duchess was that of an ostrich. Lord Stormont gave it to her. Tradition says it was an ell long, but as an ell is nearly four feet tradition probably romances.

It was long enough, however, to arouse a spirit of frantic emulation. But where could feathers of such size be found ? Rivals searched London in vain until an undertaker was induced to sell the huge waving plumes from the top of his hearse. From six feathers the number rose to eleven in one coiffure, and by degrees the hair was raised on cushions from ten inches to a yard above the forehead. Truly had *The Spectator* once remarked that " there is not so variable

---

Lady Mary Somerset, the youngest daughter of the Duke of Beaufort, married the Duke of Rutland. " I saw Lady Mary Somerset," wrote Horace Walpole in 1774. " She had moulted her feathers, and wore a hat over her nose, so I only fell in love with her chin."

a thing in nature as a lady's head-dress : within my own
memory I have known it rise and fall within thirty degrees."
That was in the reign of Queen Anne. Now, under Queen
Charlotte it was growing as rapidly as the Tower of
Babel.

So important a matter could not fail to have a political
significance. "The Queen and her ladies never wear
feathers," wrote Miss Mary Moser. "They say here that
the minority ladies are distinguished from the courtiers by
their plumes." A foreign correspondent in the *Cologne
Gazette* repeated the same tale. "It is become a general
fashion with the women to wear large feathers on their
heads, which often hinder their entrance into their apartment, and which fashion now so increases that we may
truly call them not the feminine but the feathered sex. The
Queen, the example of her sex in every virtue, has forbidden
any of the plume-headed ladies to appear at Court."

Samuel Foote, the comedian, stepped on to the stage of his
little theatre in the Haymarket in the character of Lady
Pentiveazle, and wearing a headdress which satirised the
mode, for it was stuck full of feathers and was about a yard
wide. King George and Queen Charlotte were present, and
gave the actor their heartiest applause. Foote waddled up
and down the boards until the whole fabric of feathers,
hair and wool dropped to pieces. The audience roared with
pleasure. But the fashion, despite the Queen and the mob,
did not alter.

"Extravagance of fashion is vulgar, and shows levity
of mind," said Mrs. Delany, but she was forced to admit
that the headdresses were still growing and meant to reach
the skies. In 1776 she went to a rout. "The company
assembled for the entertainment consisted of a good many of
the *bon ton* ; waving plumes, preposterous Babelonian heads
towering to the sky, exciting both my wonder and indignation at their immense folly." Lady Mary Coke "could not
reconcile herself to the headdress of the young ladies ; it is so
like the dancers on the stage that it seems very improper
for ladies of distinction."

When plumes diminished the coiffures were built up with a medley of ornaments.   Chanted a poet :

> " Sing her daub'd with white and red,
> Sing her large terrific head,
> Nor the many things disguise
> That produce its mighty size ;
> And let nothing be forgot,
> Carrots, turnips, and what not,
> Curls and cushions for *imprimis*,
> Wool and powder for the *finis* ;
> Lace and lappets, many a flag,
> Many a party-coloured rag,
> Pendent from the head behind,
> Floats and wantons in the wind."

It is easy to conceive how such aberrations of taste annoyed the older critics.   At a state ball, held January, 1776, a London newspaper recorded that " Lady Gideon sported an extraordinary head upon the occasion which forced a smile from Her Majesty.   The lower part of her hair was like a man's wig, and the upper part terminated in a lofty peak like a grenadier's cap with a bouquet on top of it.'

In a letter to the Countess Spencer, written in the winter of 1776, the Duchess sketches on the margin of the page the lines of the current mode.   " The heads are quite as high, and in this shape my father says I look like the head of a Base," evidently meaning the capital of a column.

Lord Carlisle (in after years Byron's guardian) was so overcome when he saw the Duchess in full dress that he was excited to verse :

> " When on your head I see those fluttering things,
> I think that Love is there, and claps his wings.
> Feathers helped Jove to fan his amorous flame,
> Cupid has feathers, angels wear the same.
> Since then from Heaven their origin we trace,
> Preserve the fashion—it becomes your Grace."

And this was the opinion of Her Grace, who refused to change the mode at the dictation of Queen Charlotte.

To recreate the gaieties of those early years is now almost impossible.   The life of the Duchess was an endless round of receptions, balls, parties of pleasure, visits to the theatre and the opera. " Twenty-four idle hours, without a leisure one among them," was Mrs. Montagu's description of a fashionable day. Her Grace's letters reveal glimpses of her interests. She is never dull, and if her occupations are generally aimless she nevertheless concentrates her mind upon them as if they were of the utmost importance. A Frenchman called Texier or Tessier was one of the lions of the winter of 1775. The Duchess enjoyed his mimicry more than once. " The best actor that ever was seen," she writes with her usual enthusiasm. " Mr. Walpole and all the audience agreed it equal'd a performance at Paris, he sung and play'd on the harp like an Angel." She implored her " dear Mamma " to accept an invitation to a supper where this phenomenon was to perform. " The thing is unique, and will charm papa and you." This Coquelin of his day is mentioned in much of the contemporary correspondence, and his monologues were the sensation of the season. Mrs. Boscawen told Mrs. Delany that he acted a French tragedy so perfectly that all his audience wept, and he himself, " se blessa de son propre épée," wept in sympathy. Horace Walpole studied him at Monsieur de Guinés, when the ambassador gave " a vast supper " in honour of the Prince of Pless and " the goddesses most in fashion," those goddesses naturally including Georgiana Cavendish. Twenty-eight sat down to supper (the " vastness " must have been in the supper rather than the company) and Tessier acted a play of ten characters, varying his voice for each so perfectly that he did not name the persons that spoke, nor was it necessary. " I cannot decide to which part he did most justice, but I would go to the play every night if I could see it so acted," wrote Walpole in conclusion. Tessier acted several times in the drawing-room of Devonshire House, and Lady Cowper came up to town specially to see him at the request of the Duchess.

Tessier was undoubtedly clever. Mrs. Montagu saw him act the part of Pygmalion. " Modern nymphs are so warm and yielding that less art than that of Monsieur Tessier might have animated the nymph," was the gibing remark of the middle-aged bluestocking.

The letters to the Countess Spencer spoke of many things beside Tessier. They present a picture of innocent and happy hours. In July, 1776, she was staying at a country house with the Beauclerks and Lord Westmorland, who, although described as "a very good humour'd awkward boy," was but two years her junior. The party attended a regatta on Whittlesea mere which she found dull. "The thing most worth seeing was Lord Orford's fleet, who passes six weeks every summer on the water without either dining or sleeping on shore, it is compos'd of four wooden cabins fix'd on small boats, the first his bedchamber, the second his dining-room, the third his attendant's apartment, and the fourth his kitchen. . . . We had the pleasure of seeing his cook and his mistress, who is the strangest animal I ever saw, but we did not see him."

Then followed the history of a runaway horse at Chatsworth. Lord Carlisle, Anthony Morris Storer, and Brooke Boothby were of the party. Luckily she escaped a serious accident, but, she tells her mother with undisguised glee, "I never saw such dismal figures as the Duke's, Lord Carlisle's, Mr. Storer's, and Mr. Boothby's. They sent for a chaise to come home in." Then there was horse racing in which young Everard Fawkener joined, and, one Sunday morning, the weather being extremely bad, Lord Edward Bentinck and the Duchess of Portland, his mother, taught her the steps of the *menuet de la cour*. "It is quite luxury dancing to Giardini's playing, as every tone encourages me to dance gracefully and to make one's steps imitate the softness of his music."

A visit to Welbeck and the Portlands—Whig invariably visited Whig—brought a long description of the family and particularly the younger children. "C'est la santé, l'innocence, et la gayté personnifiés," wrote the Duchess warmly, and the words applied exactly to her own character, despite all slanderers. Her portrait was painted by Reynolds and Gainsborough, and later by Romney. On the immense panels James Barry executed for the Society of Arts she is to be found amongst the most distinguished men and women of her generation.[1] James Sherwin painted and engraved an absurd composition, entitled, " The finding of Moses," in which the Duchess appears in sixteen different positions—one as Pharaoh's daughter, and then as fifteen of the Egyptian handmaidens.

In November of the same year (1776) she accompanied Lady Jersey to the House of Commons, where, to her mind, the Whigs had the best of the speaking. " Charles Fox outdid himself." A few days later she went after dinner to the theatre and saw " The Maid of the Oaks." " The play was stupid and ill-acted, and the orchestre played so badly that one of the French dancers came before the curtain in a great passion and cried, ' Je demande bien pardon au public, mais Messieurs (to the orchestre) il est impossible d'avoir moins de tête que vous n'avez.' "

As she sat in her box whilst Burgoyne's comedy was being acted she thought of her own marriage and the famous nuptials of Lady Elizabeth Stanley. The story of Lady Betty and the Duke of Dorset was well known to her, but it was a tale that had not yet ended. In 1777 the Duke of Dorset was visiting at Chatsworth. He had just left York, and was on his way to the Earl of Derby. " I always have look'd upon him as the most dangerous of men," she wrote to her mother. " For with that beauty of his he is so unaffected, and has a simplicity and a persuasion in his manner that makes one account very easily for the number of women he has had in love with him.'

The child of twenty had already taken her bearings in the fashionable world. She was not blind to its dangers

---

[1] The subject is the distribution of premiums. Barry wrote : " Towards the centre of the picture is a distinguished example of female excellence, Mrs. Montagu. . . . Near Mrs. Montagu stand the two beautiful Duchesses of Rutland and Devonshire ; and if I have been able to preserve one half of those winning graces in my picture that I have so often admired in the amiable originals, the world will have no reason to be dissatisfied with what has been done."

and hidden shoals, and when her old friends, such as Mrs. Delany, feared for her future they were thinking of the fate of the unfortunate Lady Elizabeth Stanley.

The married life of Georgiana Cavendish was an overcast tragedy. That of Elizabeth Stanley was an open scandal almost from the commencement. Charles Pigott, the author of the *Whig Club*, distributes the blame somewhat impartially between husband and wife, with an inclination towards the latter. " The noble lord,' he wrote in his scurrilous volume, " led to the altar a reluctant beauty of nineteen, who was sacrificed to his arms by the vanity of her mother." This was hardly correct, for Lady Elizabeth Hamilton was more than nineteen at the date of her marriage, and the Duchess of Argyll and Hamilton was an over-indulgent mother to both her children by her first marriage. " Such an union promised but little happiness ; and the sighs of the fair were heard frequently amidst the shades of the Oaks. She found however resources in town . . . ." Lord Derby had other interests as well. " Their mutual infidelities were soon the general theme of the town, and those of the lady were made public in a Court of Justice. But as she had full proof of recrimination against her husband, a separation was all he could obtain, and he has been forced to leave her in the possession of the title of D——y. She has since languished under the accumulated misery of a wounded fame and broken constitution ; friendship has alone remained to dart a ray of comfort through the gloom. Pure in herself Lady C—rl—le has disdained the censure of the world, and regarding the errors of her friend as arising rather from the ambition of a parent, than from her native disposition, with a magnanimity which disgraces that of most men, she has not forsaken her in the hour of her distress. Whenever Lady D——y is in town, she is invariably invited to the entertainments given by Lady C—rl—le ; though with a propriety peculiar to herself, in her cards of invitation to her other acquaintance she mentions that it is to meet Lady D——y."

These paragraphs are tolerable specimens of the materials

supplied by Charles Pigott in such books as *The Jockey Club,* *The Female Jockey*, and *The Whig Club.* Vivaciously written they had a considerable circulation in the seventies and eighties of the eighteenth century. As sources for contemporary history they cannot be wholly disregarded, though the facts they state must often be amply discounted. Unfortunately in the pages devoted to Lady Derby there is little exaggeration.

In many respects her London establishment was conducted in active rivalry to that of Devonshire House. Both she and her husband became notorious as the most extravagant people in the town. Her portrait was painted by Reynolds and Romney. In the canvas by the president we see her clothed in elaborate silk flounces and garlands of flowers, and wearing the towering head-dress which had been ordained fashionable by the Duchess. She leans against a stone pedestal upon which is perched a cockatoo. In the distance are the wooded groves of the park at Knowsley. Reynolds never painted a finer portrait, and to-day, in the saleroom, the mezzotint is one of the most valuable that comes under the hammer, whilst the canvas would be worth a king's ransom.

But her face is not wholly sympathetic. Perhaps her troubles were beginning to weigh on her mind when she sat to the artist. The anxiety for the morals of the Duchess of Devonshire can be understood when we realise that both these great ladies of fashion were moving on parallel lines, both were light-headed, and one was probably doomed to fall into the pits and traps that had engulphed the other. In February, 1779, in the midst of the acrimonious pamphlet war over the Duchess, Lady Sarah Lennox wrote about the Countess of Derby. " It is no scandal to tell you it is imagined the Duke of Dorset will marry Lady Derby, who is now in the country keeping quiet and out of the way. There is a sort of party in town of who is to visit her and who is not, which makes great squabbles, as if the curse and blessing of the poor woman depended upon a few tickets more or less. . . . I am told she has been and is still most thoroughly attached to the Duke of Dorset, and if so I should suppose she will be very happy, if the lessening of her visiting list is the only misfortune ; and what with giving up her children, sorrow for a fault, dread of not preserving his affection, I think she is much to be pitied." [1]

Forgiving her errors of conduct, that was the general opinion. For the Duchess of Devonshire, who, despite her flightiness, had been most careful not to cross the rubicon, there was public and private criticism of the bitterest description. The Countess of Derby received much sympathy. She needed it. Her husband, far from guiltless, refused to take her back. For years she travelled on the Continent an outcast. Queen Charlotte refused to allow her to be presented at Court until she had returned to Lord Derby, well knowing that the earl had contemptuously disregarded her applications for his forgiveness. Another enemy was a travelling Englishwoman of uncertain age and temper. " Poll Coke," who had not been sparing of her comments upon the Duchess of Devonshire, loved to vent her accumulated spite upon the younger women of her circle. Lady Derby wrote to her mother, the Duchess of Argyll and Hamilton, from Spa, in 1778 : " Poll Coke is here —and I know has said everything you can imagine disrespectful and shocking of me. To Lady Morton, upon her asking her why she did not visit me, she even said she was

[1] " Since I wrote the enclosed I have heard that Lord Derby announced to his lady on Friday last that their divorce was begun in the Commons, which news threw her into fits. She went as soon as she was able to her brother, then the Duke of Dorset waited on Lady Derby and Duke Hamilton, and declared to both his intentions to marry her as soon as possible. Next day she had a *levée*, when she received with a smiling countenance Lady Essex, Lady Betty Delmé, Lady Julia Howard, Lady Melbourne, Mrs. Meynell . . . ' Let wealth, let honours, wait the wedded dame : August her deed and sacred be her fame.' "—Mrs. Boscawen to Mrs. Delany, December 7, 1778. The Duchess of Devonshire told her mother that she had always considered the Duke of Dorset one of the most dangerous of men, for, added to his great beauty, he was unaffected, simple and persuasive. The Duchess added that for these reasons she could account very easily for the number of women who had fallen in love with him.

sure nobody of character and reputation would visit me, an evil speech to Lady Morton, by the bye. Lady Morton assured her on the contrary every (one) did, and that my behaviour was not to be found fault with, and that all ranks and all nations paid me the attention and respect due to me "—a statement only partly true. The rehabilitation of Lady Derby became a matter of party feeling. Women attached to the Court naturally took their lead from the Queen. Augusta, Duchess of Brunswick, sister to George III., a broad-minded member of a narrow and bigoted family clique, did her utmost for the poor Countess, going so far as to write to her brother the King to receive the lady. Queen Charlotte merely answered, " Not till Lord Derby takes her back." But this, as Lady Derby found, after a correspond-ence with her husband, was " a determined impossibility."

The reason was patent. " His Lordship," to quote the author of *The Jockey Club*, "impatiently waits the moment of her decease, that he may at last reap the harvest he has long promised himself from a marriage with a well-known fashionable actress." In his rage he had the portrait by Reynolds burnt. " This attachment does not prevent my Lord from indulging in the other amusements of the fashionable world ; his racers, his hunters, and his hounds, are all in a superior style ; and in the sports of the field, and the hospitality of his table, he has deserved and acquired the character of an obliging, good-tempered, generous man." Possibly Charles Pigott wrote this flowing sentence whilst still under the influence of the superior style and the hospitable table. Lady Derby, deserted by the fickle Duke of Dorset and spurned by the good-tempered, generous Earl of Derby, lingered on, a solitary ghost, until 1797. And not till then did Elizabeth Farren marry the little man who was supposed to be the ugliest as well as the richest peer of the realm. Lady Betty had been long forgotten. The actress-countess was described by Lady Granville, " digni-fied, like a heroine in a genteel comedy, and seems a sensible, excellent, superior woman." Lord Derby remained in his age what Lady Mary Coke had said of him in his youth.

"Somebody was saying the other day that they thought Lord Stanley made ducks and drakes of his money. Lady Abercorn, who was present, said if he had made ducks and drakes of his money, his money had been even with him, for it had made a goose of his Lordship."

The social wreck of Lady Stanley had a slightly sobering influence upon the Duchess. Countess Cowper, in a letter to Mrs. Port, noted it as early as February, 1778. "The Duchess of Devonshire is *much quieter* than she was, and is always at home *before* the Duke ; and whatever people may say, and tho' *so much admired*, she has no cicisbeo,[1] which is now much the *ton*." The elder lady announced this information without surprise. The age was a gallant one, and the Duchess had already been assured by a correspondent that he had "no right to flatter himself on being excluded from the general combination against husbands."

Surrounded by "bucks, beaux, fribbles, macaronis,[2] and dandies," she continued to rule a little world which arrogated to itself a position sustained by money rather than merit. She travelled abroad with her mother, Lady Spencer, and her younger sister. Returning from Spa one September, they embarked at Ostend on the *Fly*, sloop for Calais. During the voyage the sloop was attacked by two French cutters. After a long engagement the French were beaten off. Gibbon refers to the incident in his letters. "Lady Spencer, Lady Harriet, and D[uchess] of Devonshire behaved like heroines in the Engagement, which they saw very distinctly ; the latter exposed herself to save them." Accounts, given by Mrs. Delany, state that Lord Spencer was also of the

[1] A term applied in Italy, according to the dictionary, to a professed admirer of a married woman. But the Duchess had many professed admirers, and Lady Cowper meant more than the dictionary suggests.

[2] "Macaroni" were originally young men, who, said Horace Walpole, wear long curls and use spying glasses. A later definition is more explicit. "There is indeed a kind of animal, neither male nor female, a thing of the neuter gender lately started up amongst us. It is called a Macaroni. It talks without meaning, it smiles without pleasantry, it eats without appetite, it rides without exercise, it wenches without passion."

party, and that the sloop was chased for two days by French privateers.

England and France were at war, but Spa was neutral ground where public enemies met comfortably as private friends. In a long letter from Henry Ellis to William Knox we obtain a view of Spa two months before the privateer adventure. "Spa is very thin of company, and likely to continue so by the war, and the shutting up the passage from Calais to Dover, or rather from Dover to Calais. This was certainly a right measure ; I greatly approve of it, although it is to be highly inconvenient to me. Had it not taken place, I should have been in England ere now. . . . Of the French nation who are at this place, the most distinguished are the Duchess of Bourbon and her suite, the Duke de Coigny, Count Polignac, le Marquis Vaudreuil, their ladies, etc. These latter are of the Queen's party, and consequently not well with Madame de Bourbon, but both sides court the English with as much zeal and assiduity as if they liked them. The Spencers, the Duchess of Devonshire, Lady Clermont, and the Archbishop of Tuam and his family are the whole of our country of any note. . . . There are, besides, a considerable number of persons of condition from other parts, but principally Russians, who are neither the most opulent or the most animated people, and consequently the diversions are more languid than usual. A general intercourse, however, is maintained, and were it not for the newspapers and some puffing letters now and then from Paris, such is the tranquillity that reigns at private and public resorts, that one might well imagine there were no wars in the world."

In England the attitude towards the enemy was very different, and ladies who had been chased for two days by hostile fleets were convinced of the necessity of guarding their native land. The nation rallied to the army. Large camps were formed in the south and east of England, at Salisbury, Bury St. Edmunds, Coxheath in Kent, Warley Common in Essex, and Winchester. Wives followed their husbands, and if they could not live under canvas, took lodgings at the nearest country town. The clothes they wore were passable imitations of their husband's uniforms. The whole affair became a delightful picnic, officered by a multitude of charming amazons. And although there was laughter in the air the menace was a real one.

The Duchess of Devonshire threw herself into the movement with her usual vivacity and enthusiasm. " The only news I have heard I cannot believe," wrote Mrs. Boscawen to Mrs. Delany. " It is that the Duchess of Devonshire marched through Islington at the head of the Derby militia, dressed in the uniform of that regiment." The fact was not so impossible, for the Duchess was keenly interested in the regiment of which her husband was an officer. In a letter written to her mother about the same time she describes a military ball. " I went to the ball at eight. I danced a minuet and four country dances . . . I got vastly acquainted with all the ladies, and the ball made a brilliant figure. The Duke and all his officers were there, they looked vastly smart and though there are two or three ill-looking *dogs* amongst the captains there are some very handsome ones—and a great number of young ones who will turn out very well." Then followed some comments upon the officers. " The Duke saluted to-day in public with great success, for Colonel Gladwin told me he did it better than any of the officers, though he has but just learnt." After which graceful tribute it is not surprising to read that " Colonel Gladwin is a charming man, he is brave as his sword and has the true soldier's spirit which you like so much, for at this instant he is persuaded he could conquer America with the Derbyshire Militia." The Colonel was a veteran of the American war, where he had seen hot service. " He is very passionate and a great disciplinarian."

Two days later came a letter describing the Duke's martial exercises. A major whose gout prevented him from marching sat on horseback to be saluted as general. " The Duke of Devonshire," wrote his wife to her mother, " took his post at the head of his company, and after marching about they came by Major Revel and saluted him, the Duke really does it vastly well, and so indeed do most of the officers except an old Captain Jebb who has been four years trying to learn it."

The next year, in 1778, the ducal party was at Coxheath. A poet wrote an *Ode to the Warlike Genius of Britain*, and poet and ode were presented by Boswell to Dr. Johnson.

" Here is an error, sir," growled the sage. " You have made Genius feminine.

" Palpable, sir," replied the poet. " I know it. But it was to pay a compliment to the Duchess of Devonshire, with which her Grace was pleased. She is walking across Coxheath in military uniform, and I suppose her to be the Genius of Britain."

The poet was undoubtedly forgiven, for Dr. Johnson had already been entrapped into the charmed circle of Devonshire House and received an invitation to Chatsworth. " I have seen the Duchess of Devonshire," wrote Wraxall, " in the first bloom of her youth hanging on the sentences which fell from Johnson's lips and contending for the nearest place to his chair. All the cynic moroseness of the philosopher and the moralist seemed to dissolve under so flattering an approval, to the gratification and distinction resulting from which he was far from being insensible." Dr. Johnson, indeed, was always fond of female society and that " purring " adulation which simmers over the afternoon tea when a great man condescends to relax. And Johnson, an ugly, disagreeable, clumsy man, with a tendency towards rudeness, could talk impersonally about love to coquettes of various ages without losing his presence of mind or his ready wit. His conversation was thus brilliantly attractive.[1]

[1] An apt example of this will be found in Mrs. Piozzi's writings. " As we had been saying one day that no subject failed of receiving dignity from the manner in which Mr. Johnson treated it, a lady at my house said she would make him talk about love ; and took her measures accordingly, deriding the novels of the day because they treated about love. " It is not," replied our philosopher, " because they treat, as you call it, about love, but because they treat of nothing, that they are despicable. We must not ridicule a passion which he who never felt never was happy, and he who laughs at never deserves to feel—a passion which has caused the change of empires, and the loss of worlds—a passion which has inspired

At the manœuvres of the Derbyshire militia the Duchess was present in the field. " The soldiers fir'd very well, and I stood by the Duke and Colonel Gladwin, who were near enough to have their faces smart with the powder, but I was not fortunate enough to have this honour." Whilst the Duke was at Coxheath the Duchess stayed with a large party of friends at Tunbridge Wells. The day commenced with a glass of water at the Pantiles. Then a journey was made to the camp, which bustled with the excitement of a royal visit and a sham fight. Dinner was shared with the warriors, but the *régime* was not Spartan. " We had a turtle . . . the D. has a fire in his tent, and it is very comfortable." At the royal review the Duke surpassed himself. " The D. of Devonshire is at present in great fame, for his saluting, he is reckon'd to have saluted the best of anybody." The Duchess had a less congenial duty. " Duchess of Grafton, Lady Cranborne, Duchess of Gordon, Lady Aston and I, were sent to, to come to the queen in her tent and stayed there, I believe, two hours—it was a great bore as we had been standing all day and as we could only sit down there for a minute."

Upon one of these great days Lady Cranborne opened her tents to whist and cribbage, and supper was served to a large company. The Duchess met a lady she did not like, and the letter to her mother is too curious not to be quoted. " I believe I am growing very deceitful, for I take great pains to get into Lady F. Marsham's good graces, and yet I detest her vastly, but my reason is that I hear her

---

heroism and subdued avarice." He thought he had already said too much. " A passion, in short," added he, with an altered tone, " that consumes me away for my pretty Fanny here, and she is very cruel." The Fanny was Miss Burney.

When Miss Monckton (afterwards Lady Cork) said that Sterne's writings were very pathetic, Johnson bluntly contradicted her. " I am sure," she replied, " they have affected me." " Why," said Johnson, smiling and rolling himself about, " that is because, dearest, you are a dunce." Afterwards she mentioned his remark to him. " Madam, if I had thought so, I certainly should not have said it."

Such a man's conversation was irresistible.

abuse everybody so much the instant they have turn'd
their backs, that my vanity is peak'd to *concilié* myself of
her suffrage. She is an odious mixture of notable ill-nature,
and she puts me into ten thousand passions because she
always talks to me as if she thought I had not my five
senses like other people, you cannot conceive the astonishment she expressed on my saying I walked very often in the
garden at D[evonshire] House. I am sure you know the
kind of person I mean, who, because I was dissipated and
what they call the *ton*, imagine that I scarcely breathe like
other people." The confession in the final lines is naïve.

At Tunbridge Wells the dissipation was of a healthy
nature. Countess Spencer told her daughter how to behave
in the plainest terms. " You should especially at such a
place as Tunbridge keep up a civility and dignity in your
behaviour to the Men of your own Set—and a courteous,
good-humour'd affability to the Company in general whom
you are little acquainted with, whereas I suspect if you will
examine your own Conduct, you put on that killing Cold look
you sometimes have to those you should be *prévenante* to,
and a great deal more familiarity and ease than is either
necessary or proper to the Men about you."

To which grave exordium the daughter replied in a
few days that " our amusements in this place, and I suppose
our minds have degenerated into infancy. In the beginning
of the summer our evenings were past in conversation and
singing of fine songs, we then got by degrees to Macao, cribbage, whist and catches, and now we are come to the point
of diverting ourselves with ' Laugh and lay down,' and ' I'm
come a lusty wooer, my dildin, my doldin, I'm come a lusty
wooer, lilly bright and shinee,' and ditties of that sort."

In playing a trick with a red-hot poker the Duchess nearly
set Mrs. Greville on fire, " upon these occasions I always
think it right to go into something like an hysteric." Then
the Duchess and Mrs. Crewe get a trick of " whenever anybody tells a story to act it," which sadly disconcerted Mr.
Greville, who had a long and evidently dull story about a
duel. " He saw that we were acting it but would not be

disturb'd, and kept his countenance, till upon his saying one of the gentlemen went to town Mrs. Crewe pretended to whip some horse and said, St, st, st—quelle bêtise, et quelle folie à moi de vous la conter," cries the light-hearted Duchess.

There was a more serious circle at the Wells which looked towards higher things than " lilly bright and shinee." Mrs. Thrale and Mrs. Montagu were present. " I have a great curiosity to know her," wrote the Duchess of the first. " Her singularity will amuse me, and like our books one may draw something out of it." Mrs. Montagu was an old friend, who described her morning at the Wells as " going to chapel, philosophical lecture, viol d'amore, controversy with a Jew or a Quaker." The Duchess found her rather heavy, for when she paid an afternoon visit she informed her mother : " I staied there three hours and a half . . . but I must confess that one reason of my long stay was a difficulty I found in getting up from my chair and out of the room."

These learned ladies were a trial. " Mrs. Thrale was ridiculous, she play'd at Whist and was affecting inattention to her game and talking Latin and quoting verses "—which must have been disastrous to the hand and trying to her partner. The Duchess summed up the evening in Verse :

> "When Madam Thrale was prest to play at whist
> Her love of learning warn'd her to desist—
> At last the Dame gave way, the table came
> She own'd she was a novice in the game,
> No sooner seated, than the Lady saw
> That Madam Montagu began to jaw
> She could not bear to lose the palm of wit
> And turning on her chair uneasy sit—
> ' That line is Gray's—pray was it I that won
> Te duce Caesar, who that trick begun.'
> The game and learning trying to pursue
> She lost her money and her reason too."

" A poetical licence,' added the author, " for she won the rubber."

Mrs. Montagu admired the youthful Duchess, and mentions her spirits and good-humour. But she doubted the advisability of encouraging a military spirit amongst the ladies of England. Describing a ball at the Wells, at which both Lady Spencer and the Duchess of Devonshire were present, Mrs. Montagu remarked : " minuet dancing is just now out of fashion ; and by the military air and dress of many of the ladies, I should not be surprised if backsword and cudgell playing should take the place of it. I think our encampment excellent for making men less effeminate, but if they make our women more masculine, the male and the female character, which should ever be kept distinct, will now be more so than they have been."

The Duchess, to employ her own phrase, had all her five senses. She was never a masculine woman. The greatest fault she committed in those early years was an inordinate love of pleasure. " The Duchess of Devonshire cannot be very ill," wrote Mrs. Delany, " as she danced at the Knights of the Bath's ball till four o'clock in the morning. The young ladies by their manner of living will be soon old ones, and no wash will ever make them appear well.'

It must have been after one of these late nights, or early mornings, that Fanny Burney met the Duke and Duchess walking together in the Green Park. " The dear discerning little creature ' vividly sketched the ducal couple.

" Mr. Burney, Hetty and I took a walk in the Park on Sunday morning, where among others, we saw the young and handsome Duchess of Devonshire, walking in such an un-dressed and slatternly manner, as, in former times, Mrs. Rishton might have done in Chesington Garden. Two of her curls came quite unpinned, and fell lank on one of her shoulders ; one shoe was down at heel, the trimming of her jacket and coat was in some places unsown ; her cap was awry ; and her cloak, which was rusty and powdered, was flung half on and half off. Had she not had a servant in superb livery behind her she would certainly have been affronted. Every creature turned back to stare at her. Indeed, I think her very handsome, and she has a look of innocence and artlessness that made me quite sorry she should be so foolishly negligent of her person. She had hold of the Duke's arm, who is the very reverse of herself, for he is ugly, tidy, and grave.   He looks like a very mean shop-keeper's journeyman."

This portrait, the unpinned curl, the shoe down at heel, the rusty cloak, and the unstitched trimming, could only have been written by a woman.   There is an animus of tone which Miss Burney could not disguise, despite her feeling of sorrow.   She was judging the Duchess upon her public reputation, the notoriety of the pamphlets and the scurrilous magazines.   When, in later years she met the Duchess at Bath her own journals prove how quickly she changed her mind and acknowledged the influence of a singularly beautiful character.

Mrs. Montagu was an older woman than Fanny Burney. Despite her pedantry she was wiser than the author of *Evelina*.   She moved in circles Miss Burney had not yet reached, and she knew Georgiana Cavendish intimately.   In July, 1777, she wrote to a friend : " Of all the vices of the human disposition a love of scandal and detraction is the most contemptible.   It is now got from the gossip's tea-table to the press.   The scribblers weekly let fly their pop-guns at the Duchess of Devonshire's feathers.   Her grace is innocent, good-humoured, and beautiful ; but these adders are blind and deaf, and cannot be charmed."

CHAPTER IX

The men of the circle—Dr. Johnson and the Duchess—his manners in society—the Strawberry Hill group—the Fox group—Charles James Fox—the Duchess on his "amazing quickness"—his character—Richard Brinsley Sheridan—his "gallantry"—the Duchess helps his political career—Colonel Richard Fitzpatrick—Lord John Townshend—"Fish" Crawford—Lord Robert Spencer—a visit to Woolbeding.

THE men who bowed to the charm of the mistress of Devonshire House were strangely varied in temperament and disposition. Some, despite their genius, were often wearisome in society. Burke's presence was more coveted than enjoyed. Dr. Johnson was a less frequent visitor, and, happier in the more homely atmosphere of the Thrales at Streatham, could not have appeared to the best advantage in the Piccadilly *salons*. He was by no means insensible to the tangible advantages of the entry into so select a circle as Wraxall would like us to believe. When Mrs. Thrale praised Garrick's song in *Florizel and Perdita*, dwelling with peculiar pleasure upon the line :

" I'd smile with the simple and feed with the poor,"

Johnson's comment revealed his own position very clearly :
" Nay, my dear lady, this will never do. Poor David ! Smile with the simple !—what folly is that ? And who would feed with the poor that can help it ? No, no, let me smile with the wise and feed with the rich." [1]

[1] And " the great " appreciated his wisdom more than his table manners, for, when he went to Chatsworth, the Duchess reported to her mother, " He din'd here and does not shine quite so much in eating as in conversing, for he eat much and nastily."

He was invited to Chatsworth, but Boswell chronicles little in relation to his friendship with the Duchess, for the sufficient reason that Boswell himself was never admitted amongst the intimates of Devonshire House.   Johnson belonged to the higher ranks of Grub Street, and was accepted as one of the "characters" of the time every hostess could occasionally open her doors to.   He was not an easy guest to entertain.   His social manners were irregular, his conversation often more rude than just.   " He loved late hours, or, more properly, hated early ones," said Mrs. Thrale. Even Mrs. Boswell objected to his uncouth habits, such as turning the candles with their ends downwards when they did not burn brightly enough, and thus allowing the wax to drop on the carpet.   He had fantastic notions about crossing the squares of a carpet with right or left foot foremost, and dinner and host could wait indefinitely whilst he was vainly endeavouring to pass a particular spot in the anteroom.   Such eccentricities might amuse a great lady once, or perhaps twice.   A performing lion cannot fail to attract attention, but there is always a sigh of relief when he is back in his cage.   As a rule, however, when a hostess makes out a list of her house-party she pins more faith upon the success of her gathering if her guests are socially agreeable rather than abnormally gifted with genius or intelligence.

The visitors to Devonshire House and Chatsworth belonged to several distinct groups.   The Strawberry Hill *coterie* was formed of men who had passed the first flush of youth.   Most of them were striving to live up to their reputations.   It is as easy to gain a reputation for wit as for wickedness, but the first is far more difficult to sustain than the second.   Horace Walpole, the leader of this small but important companionship, was a cynic who had seen much of the world.   Like all brilliant conversationalists he was ever ready to sacrifice a friendship to an epigram.   His allegiance to the Duchess was not wholehearted, and the "empress of fashion " (as he delighted to call her) was always at the mercy of his destructive and acrid criticism. But the Cavendishes were too important a family to neglect, and his best friends could often be found in the drawing-rooms of Devonshire House. George Selwyn was welcome, although it was never definitely settled if he was to be classed amongst the wits or the humorists. He, too, had a bitter tongue. Probably the Duchess was the first to enjoy his description of her kinsman, Lord John Cavendish, as a " learned canary bird." For Lord John was a fair-haired little prig who, quoting Walpole, " under an appearance of virgin modesty, had a confidence in himself that nothing could equal, and a thirst of dominion still more extraordinary."

The Strawberry Hill group, which included " Gilly " Williams, Edgcumbe and Lord March (better known as " Old Q "), were less assiduous in their attendance at the shrine than those men of the town who followed the lead of Charles James Fox. Amongst these were Colonel Fitzpatrick, a soldier, a politician and a poet ; Anthony Morris Storer, a man of fashion with a sincere love for scholarship, and praised by his associates for his " sense and good nature " ; James Hare, the " Hare of many friends," according to the Duchess of Gordon, whose bow at the opera was a more valued distinction than an invitation from the Prince of Wales ; and the Earl of Carlisle, the most finished " macaroni " of his time. His activities were various.

" What heterogeneous honours deck the Peer !
Lord, Rhymester, Petit-Maitre and Pamphleteer ! "

But he was not such a fool as Byron, in his anger, would have us believe. Storer, Hare and Carlisle had been contemporaries at Eton, and were turned to a similar pattern. They were highly cultivated gentlemen, clever and fascinating men of the world, but they could not hope to rival the two most brilliant stars in the constellation. Charles James Fox and Richard Brinsley Sheridan stood alone. The friendship of Georgiana Cavendish for these great souls was deep and sincere. And because their characters mingled in almost equal proportions—strength and weakness, genius and a childlike *naïveté*—they were irresistibly attractive to an impulsive woman whose conduct and friendships were so largely governed by feeling and sentiment.

" I think how much better a good dull man is than a Charles Fox, and many others, whose talents and vices have grown together in a superlative degree," wrote Mrs. Montagu in a letter to an acquaintance. But Mrs. Montagu was over sixty. " There was nothing feminine about her," said Wraxall truthfully. Her masculine intellect did not reflect the opinion of her sex, and even she did not encourage dull men to attend her assemblies in Hill Street or Portman Square. " I never invite idiots to my house," she told Garrick, in an unpublished letter.

For Fox dullness was one of the few impossibilities. On his mother's side he could boast of a descent from the royal house of Stuart, and his qualities and defects were those of that unfortunate family. " Charles," wrote Boothby,[1] his most intimate friend, " is unquestionably a man of first-rate talents, but so deficient in judgment as never to have succeeded in any object during his whole life. He loved only three things—women, play and politics. Yet at no period did he ever form a creditable connection with a woman. He lost his whole fortune at the gaming-table ; and, with the exception of about eleven months of his life, he has remained always in opposition." His life, judged upon its results, was a failure. Yet a man who can secure the love of his friends has not failed in the struggle. Had Fox been given the opportunity of a second existence upon earth he would again have devoted it to women, play and politics. " Let nothing be done to break his spirit," wrote Lord Holland, his father, when speaking of his child's education. " The world will effect that business soon enough."

---

[1] Sir Brooke Boothby (he succeeded to the baronetcy in 1789) belonged to a Derbyshire family, and was often seen at Piccadilly and Chatsworth. He was a friend of the Darwins, the Sewards, and the Edgeworths, attached to the literary circle at Lichfield ; a strong upholder of the principles of the French Revolution, and a minor poet. " A pretty gentleman *du premier ordre* " rather captiously describes his undoubted ability. He died in 1824, at the age of eighty.

CHARLES JAMES FOX

Charles Fox's spirit remained unbroken to the day when he died, under the roof of the Cavendishes at Burlington Villa in Chiswick.

The Duchess of Devonshire was eight years younger than Fox. She was immediately fascinated by the charm of his personality, but at first a trifle nervous as to his opinion of her own character. In 1777 he was a guest at Chatsworth, and, in a letter to her mother, she described his conversation in a vivid phrase : " I have always thought that the great merit of C. Fox is his amazing quickness in seizing any subject—he seems to have the particular talent of knowing more about what he is saying and with less pains than anybody else—his conversation is like a brilliant player at billiards, the strokes follow one another, piff-paff." She admitted that the conversation was too rapid for her. In company with Fox was the Duke and Mr. John Townshend. " Their chief topic is politicks and Shakespeare. As for the latter, they all seem to have the most astonishing memorys for it—and I suppose I shall be able in time to go through a play as they do."

Fox had been carefully taught the arts of rhetoric and the tricks of declamation. Dr. Barnard, his headmaster at Eton, prided himself upon his gifts of elocution, and was famous for the "absolute perfection" of his reading of the Church Service. When a debate in the House of Commons promised to be interesting the boy had no difficulty in obtaining leave to spend a few hours at Westminster. At school Fox committed to memory long passages from the dramatists, and won his earliest successes in the speech-room.

His " quickness in seizing any subject," which so amazed the young Duchess, although partially an inherited gift, was raised upon the securer foundation of a very real scholarship. His knowledge of the classics was sound. Passages from Virgil, Horace, Tacitus, Juvenal, and Cicero presented themselves to his memory without effort. During a single winter, according to his biographer Trevelyan, in addition to his private studies he read aloud to Mrs. Fox, Tasso,

Ariosto, Milton, Spencer, Apollonius Rhodius, Lucretius, Virgil, and Homer. At Oxford he had worked hard at mathematics, which he liked " vastly "—a word much used in the fashionable vocabulary of that age. His tours on the Continent combined instruction and pleasure. He was one of the many youths who

" Sauntered Europe round,
And gathered every vice on Christian ground."

But these journeys were not devoted entirely to dissipation, although he is said to have returned from one tour the poorer by £16,000. He could speak in French as fluently and as correctly as in his mother-tongue. The only men who criticised his diction were Napoleon and Talleyrand. His knowledge of Italian was almost as perfect. He could rise from the fluctuating delights of the faro table to spend a quiet hour with Dante, Ariosto, and Tasso. *Orlando Furioso* was his favourite Italian poem. " For God's sake,' he wrote to his friend Fitzpatrick, " learn Italian as fast as you can, to read Ariosto. There is more good poetry in Italian than in all other languages I understand put together. Make haste and read all these things, that you may be fit to talk to Christians."

It is not, however, in this direction that we can find the secret of his undeniable personal attraction. He was a good companion. A letter from the Duchess describes him playing billiards in the early hours of the morning with the Duke and Mr. John Townshend, the second son of the fourth Viscount Townshend. In another letter she tells her mother how she played a rubber of whist " in fear and trembling." Fox was her partner, and their antagonists were Lord Robert Spencer, the eccentric son of the third Duke of Marlborough, and Mr. Parker, a Devonshire member of Parliament. The Duchess and Fox won, and then Fox " betted Mr. Parker 25 guineas against a horse." There was sufficient reason for her " fear and trembling." Fox was famous for his genius at cards. Sir Nathaniel Wraxall praises his skill at whist and picquet. At Brooks' Club it was said that he might have made £4,000 a year at these games if he would have confined himself to them. Unfortunately, he did not restrict his energies to games of skill. His brother, Stephen Fox, sat down one evening with thirteen thousand pounds to his credit and rose without a penny. Charles Fox was equally unfortunate. At hazard his bad luck was notorious.

> "At Almack's of pigeons I am told there are flocks,
> But it's thought the completest is one Mr. Fox.
> If he touches a card ; if he rattles the box,
> Away fly the guineas of this Mr. Fox. . . .
> In gaming, 'tis said, he's the stoutest of cocks. ;
> No man can play deeper than this Mr. Fox ;
> And he always must lose, for the strongest of locks
> Cannot keep any for this Mr. Fox."

In the betting book, still preserved at Brooks' Club, are innumerable wagers against the name of Charles Fox. He bets against the Duke of Devonshire receiving the Garter within seven years ; against Turkey becoming a European power ; against Dr. North being raised to the See of Durham ; against Lord Northington swimming a mile in the Thames or any other river. And " Fish " Crawfurd made a safe wager which is entered as follows :—" Lord Clermont has given Mr. Crawfurd 10 guineas upon the condition of receiving £500 from him whenever Mr. Fox shall be worth £100,000 clear of debts." It was not the nature of Charles Fox or his friends ever to be clear of debts. And their bad example was largely responsible for the financial anxieties of the Duchess when she, in her turn, worshipped the fickle god of Chance.

Lord George Germain asserted in the House of Commons that " Ministers had some property to lose as well as the gentlemen on the other side of the House." Fox was able to reply with perfect truth, " It is well known that I have no stake to lose." Within a few years his father's wealth had vanished over the faro tables of Mayfair and St. James's.

At the time of the Devonshire marriage Fox was a prominent " macaroni." Wraxall says that he dressed *en petit maître*, wearing a hat and feathers even in the House of

Commons, whilst his shoes had the red heels which were the distinguishing mark of the aristocracy at the Court of France. Within six years his dress had changed. He usually wore a shabby and threadbare blue frock coat with a buff waistcoat. In 1781 he was reduced to the utmost distress owing to his gambling losses. He borrowed money from the club waiters. He lacked sufficient small change to pay the chairmen who carried him from house to house. Excess impaired his health, and he suffered from acute pains which could only be alleviated by doses of laudanum. Yet he never lost those good spirits which formed so essential a part of his character. The heavy lines of his saturnine face—almost Jewish in type—were always ready to break into a smile. Beneath black and shaggy eyebrows glowed orbs of fire whose brightness was never dimmed by the most fantastic midnight extravagances. His figure grew fatter and more unwieldy. Rapidly he lost all desire to cultivate the exterior graces. Gone were the days when an exigent taste rendered it necessary to drive post from Paris to Lyons to select the patterns for an embroidered waistcoat. His manners were not always those of a gentleman, if we accept Wraxall's story of his rudeness to the devoted Mrs. Hobart. Morals he had discarded since his visit to France as a school-boy,[1] although in later years he remained faithful to one woman without, characteristically enough, invoking the sanction of law or Church. When, in 1768, Fox visited Voltaire at Geneva, the philosopher wrote to Lord Holland : " Your son is an English lad, and j an old frenchman. He is healthy, and j sick. Yet j love him with all my heart, not only for his father, but for himself." Charles Fox was loved for himself, despite his errors and weaknesses, as few men of his age were loved.

" Do you not hate that fellow ? " he was once asked.

" I am a bad hater," replied Fox.

[1] For this his father was chiefly responsible. "Lord Holland (wrote Lord Shelburne) educated his children without the least regard to morality, and with such extravagant vulgar indulgence that the great change, which has taken place among our youth, has been dated from the time of his son's going to Eton."

His character was a mass of contradictions. He was a rake with a chivalrous respect for women ; a spendthrift who asked for little more than a crust ; a terrific worker, with extraordinary powers of dissipation ; an idler, equally at home in the vitiated club-rooms of St. James's or the open air of his beloved gardens on St. Anne's Hill. In the House of Commons his power as an orator carried an audience which has never been famous for its enthusiasm. As a politician he was as uncertain as a weathercock. The Duchess herself wrote of him as " a man whose idol was popularity," which she curiously interpreted as " perhaps the greatest proof of the real greatness of his mind—and must give security of the sentiments he professes." Those sentiments were often hard to follow. In 1792, when the allied armies were defeated at Valmy, he declared : " No public event, not excepting Saratoga and Yorktown, ever happened which gave me so much delight."

Fox, like most of the men and women of the Devonshire House circle, was governed by his feelings. The Duchess recognised his weaknesses, and lamented his faults and negligences. But, quoting her own words, " The virtues and foibles of Mr. Fox, the comprehensive mind, undaunted genius, and unabating kindness, which, added to the most unaffected simplicity, constitute his character," these qualities formed good and sufficient reasons for a personal love which far surpassed the admiration of his party for his powers as a statesman. He was a man without hatred in his heart.

The character of Richard Brinsley Sheridan was less complex. Fox was able to enter Devonshire House by right of birth ; Sheridan had to conquer his position. In the earliest days of her marriage the Duchess was not sure if she could admit the son of a player to her *salons*. The genius of Sheridan soon set at rest all questions of social rank and precedence, and the songs of Miss Linley distinguished the drawing-room of any hostess she was pleased to honour. Fox was worshipped by the Duchess ; Sheridan worshipped the Duchess. The distinction was very real, for Fox had

K

nothing to gain from a friendship with the " goddess of fashion," whilst Sheridan was a penniless genius with his way to make in the world.

There is a picture in the water-colour gallery at South Kensington Museum in which Francis Wheatley sketches a crowd of connoisseurs at the Boydell Gallery in Pall Mall. Amongst the fashionable gathering are the Prince of Wales and his brothers, and, by the side of the Duchess, stands R. B. Sheridan. Their acquaintance dated from the early days of her marriage. Mr. Walter Sichel, in his engrossing biography of the author of the *School for Scandal*, believes that she first met Sheridan at the Cootes'. Despite the difference in their upbringing there was a similarity in their temperament. They were both impetuous, uncertain, and not wholly to be relied upon, ready to seek distraction in practical jokes and horseplay, inclined towards sentimentalism, and very restless and ever seeking for incessant distraction from the dull round of everyday life. Sheridan told the Duchess that there was something " mysterious and unaccountable " about him. In reality, there was nothing of the kind, and Sheridan was adopting a melodramatic pose, later to be termed Byronic. Sheridan had a lingering tenderness for the Duchess. His own domestic circle was not blind to the perils of her fascination. In 1786, when he was staying at Chatsworth, Mrs. Tickell, in a letter to her sister, Mrs. Sheridan (who was also one of the party), wrote : " How I laughed at S. not being in time for my lady Duchess. Oh, dear ! what a fine name would hers have been at the head of his list of captives." Only two years later, to quote Mr. Walter Sichel, when Sheridan's fame was at its height, Elizabeth Sheridan describes the lover-like attentions of the same enchantress and her sister at a masquerade, though she intimates that the hero of the hour disregarded them.

Sheridan was the son of an actor, and assumed the rôle of a gallant as lightly as an actor struts through a new character. " He employs a great deal of art with a great deal of pains to gratify not the proper passion in such affairs, but vanity ; and he deals in the most intricate plotting and underplotting, like a Spanish play." This was the verdict of Sir Gilbert Elliot, better known as Lord Minto. He did not stand alone. The Duchess herself loved to play a mysterious part, and to impress the groundlings. Her letters are full of romantic affectations.

Within a few years Sheridan became one of the most prominent members of the society which gathered at Devonshire House. His high spirits and good humour, his gifts of entertainment, made him the petted favourite not only of the Duchess, but also of most of the ladies of the moment, such as the Duchess of Rutland, Mrs. Crewe, Lady Craven, and the Countess of Jersey. His wife's wild jealousy is easy to understand, though there was little reason to justify it. But when a poet of Sheridan's grace and facility begins to praise "majestic Stella," and the beauty of " Myra's eyes," he courts trouble, especially when Stella was a Duchess of Rutland and Myra a Duchess of Devonshire.

Sheridan studied the fashionable types immortalised in the *School for Scandal*, in the drawing-rooms of Devonshire House. When that play was produced in 1777 the Duchess sat in one of the boxes of DruryLane with Mrs. Crewe, to whom the comedy was dedicated. In a few years Sheridan entered political life and, according to Creevey, he was able to make good use of the influence of his powerful friends. In 1780, the year of the general election, it was his intention to make a trial for a seat at Wootton-Bassett. The night before he set out to open his campaign he visited Devonshire House. Every one was talking about the forthcoming election. " Lady Cork [1] asked Sheridan about *his* plans, which led to her saying that she had often heard her brother Monckton say he thought an opposition man might come in for Stafford, and that if in the event of Sheridan failing at Wootton he liked to try his chance at Stafford she would give him a letter of introduction to her brother. This was immediately done. Sheridan went to Wootton-

[1] Second wife of the seventh Earl, and youngest daughter of the first Viscount Galway.

Bassett, where he had not a chance. Then he went to Stafford, produced Lady Cork's letter, offered himself as a candidate, and was elected. For Stafford he was a member till 1806—six and twenty years."

The Duchess of Devonshire had a more important share in the transaction than Lady Cork, for Stafford belonged to the Spencer interest. Sheridan took with him a letter of recommendation from Lady Spencer, and the electors of Stafford followed the advice of Lord Spencer's agent. When the poll was declared Sheridan found himself a member of the House of Commons. He admitted long after to Creevey that it was the happiest moment in his life, and upon his return to London he thanked his benefactor. " It is no Flattery to say that the Duchess of Devonshire's name commands an implicit admiration whenever it is mentioned, and I found some that had opportunities of often seeing and of hearing more of your Grace, who were so proud of the distinction as to require no other motive to support anyone who appear'd honor'd with your Grace's commendation." He finishes his letter with the sentence : " I have avoided asking Mr. Fox to thank Your Grace on my account, because I am perhaps even unfairly ambitious to owe all the Gratitude myself."

This was a formal letter between friends who could speak to each other with greater intimacy. Then the Duchess became " dear T. L." " Sheridan goes to-morrow," wrote the lady to her mother in 1787. " We kept him to-day by main force, absolutely. He is amazingly entertaining. He is going to Weirstay to shoot for a silver arrow ; he is such a boy."

In his powers of amusing a drawing-room Sheridan was probably more successful than Fox. His wit was finer, and, unlike many of the men of his circle, it was a kindly wit. Most of his stories miss their point in the recapitulation. He is warned that alcohol will destroy the coat of his stomach. " Well then my stomach must just digest in its waistcoat ! " A footman drops a pile of plates without a breakage. " You silly fool, all that d——d noise for

RICHARD BRINSLEY SHERIDAN

nothing," is his quick cry across the table. This is not an intellectual wit, but it is the simple humour that convulses a party and sets each man on good terms with his neighbour. With women who do not ask for a deep or cutting wit its effect must have been irresistible. There are few English women who aspire to wit at all, which on their gentle tongues becomes perilously akin to shrewishness.

Fox and Sheridan were giants. The lesser men who formed their *entourage* had many fine gifts. Colonel Richard Fitzpatrick, a younger son of the first Earl of Upper Ossory, was twelve years older than the Duchess. Like his friends, his talents were distributed amongst the arts of peace and war. In 1782 he was acting as secretary to the Duke of Portland, then Lord Lieutenant of Ireland, and in the following year he was Secretary of State for War. General in the army and Colonel of the 47th Regiment of Foot, he was also a skilful maker of *vers de société*. Wraxall, speaking of Fox's poetic talent, is careful to add that for " ease, delicacy, and playful satire he could not stand a competition in that branch of accomplishment with his friend and companion Colonel Fitzpatrick."

At Devonshire House he was familiarly known as " Fitz." Sheridan, who did not lack the double vanity of a poet and an Irishman, argued with him over the merit of their respective verses. The quarrel was very friendly, for Fitzpatrick wrote the prologue to *The Critic*, and proposed his rival as a member of Brooks' Club—a doubtful benefit. Fitzpatrick wrote several of the verses in *The Rolliad*, which has long since lost the relish of contemporary interest. Another visitor to Devonshire House could do better. John Townshend's portrait of George III. is a document of historical value :

> " Hail, inexhausted, boundless Spring
>   Of sacred Truth and holy Majesty !
> Grand is thy form—'bout five feet ten,
> Thou well-built, worthiest, best of men ;
> Thy chest is stout ; thy back is broad ;

The pages view thee and are awed !
Lo ! how thy white eyes roll !
Thy whiter eyebrows stare !
  Honest soul !
Thou'rt witty as thou'rt fair."[1]

John Townshend, of almost the same age as the Duchess, the younger son of Viscount Townshend, recited Shakespeare with the Duke of Devonshire. " Jack Townshend is really a very amiable young man. He has great parts, though not such brilliant ones as Charles Fox's, and I dare say he will make a very good figure hereafter—he is just twenty now, though he has the appearance of being older," was her criticism in 1777.

Townshend, who became a bosom friend of Sheridan, was soon involved in a scandal which threatened the position of the Duchess. Miss Poyntz, her first cousin, had been married against her will to William Fawkner. " The lady," wrote Lord Glenbervie a quarter of a century later, " had been in a manner educated in Devonshire House, and continued to live principally in that society of easy manners after her marriage." Townshend eloped with Mrs. Fawkner, and the Duchess was accused of giving cover to the intrigue. After a duel the injured husband was divorced by act of Parliament, the Duke of Devonshire being called as a witness by the defendant. Mrs. Fawkner became Lady John Townshend and lived happily in retirement with her second husband. She was one of the last members of the circle, for her death did not take place until 1851. Lord John Townshend was described by Lord John Russell as " a young man of very lively parts, who by his talents and devotion seems to have gained at one time an influence with Mr. Fox, the results of which were of great importance." Socially he was famed for his power of mimicry. According to Lady Holland, no mean judge, he was "one of the wittiest men there is ; his verses are excellent."

---

[1] George III. was the butt of every Opposition wit. Because his articulation was indistinct, the Duchess of Chandos used to speak of her visits to " the drawling-room " at St. James's Palace.

James Crawford of Auchinames, usually called "The Fish," or "Fish" Crawford, wandered from circle to circle in the West End, but was most at home in Devonshire House. He, too, was an amateur of life, obtaining a certain fame without distinction as a politician, and a wit. He complained of his gout, and, when Cagliostro came to London, consulted that charlatan for advice. He drew attention to the selfishness of his friends, forgetting, as Glenbervie reminds us, that his nickname of "Fish," which had been given to him at Eton, was an abbreviation of the word "selfish."

Lastly must be mentioned that Prince Charming, the eldest son of George III., a constant visitor to Devonshire House. "Perdita," describes the "graces of his person, the irresistible sweetness of his smile, the tenderness of his melodious yet manly voice, the polish and fascinating ingenuousness of his manners."

The least important member of this circle was the person usually referred to as "Bob Spencer." A son of the third Duke of Marlborough, the gates of Devonshire House and Chatsworth were always open to him. He had been an old school friend of Sheridan at Harrow, and seems to have been one of those simple-hearted, good-natured, dissolute younger sons who are welcomed in every gathering.[1] As he grew older his manners did not improve. In 1808 he was described by Lady Sarah Spencer (afterwards Lady Lyttelton) as "our not respectable cousin," and his house "a curious one for Papa to have been in." "Papa" was the second Earl Spencer. "The honours of the house" (wrote the Earl's indignant daughter) "were done by Mrs. B——, a lady

---

[1] Lord Robert Spencer had to sell the greater number of his pictures, as well as his town house, in 1799, "all from poverty," according to Lady Di. Beauclerk. He bought the house known as Woolbeding, in Sussex. This house and collection of works of art was left by him to Mrs. Bouverie's youngest daughter, Diana, and who was generally supposed to be his own child. Lady Louisa Stuart called her "the tell-tale Bouverie . . . for there never was such a perfect indisputable Spencer, Lord Robert's walking picture, and the very prettiest creature that ever was seen." Lord Robert married Mr. Bouverie's widow in 1811.

still very beautiful though past fifty, and who is in more than one sense the mistress of that abode. Her ill-fated husband, a poor old twaddler, was there too, and three of her children grown up. Besides these there were a German baron and an American sportsman, very fit company for the host and his fair friend. Papa saw several children playing about, but thought it most prudent not to inquire minutely into their birth and parentage, for fear of getting into some scrape in the style of poor Lady Ducksworth at your Torquay dinner. I forgot to mention two of the guests; Mrs. Fox (Charles Fox's widow) [1]—you must have heard of her character, not the clearest—and a Miss W——, an humble companion and *protégée* of hers, and natural daughter to Charles Fox by someone else. There's a set of people for you ! Pleasant enough and respectable is Lord Robert's old age, spent in so infamous a collection of people."

The date of the letter—September—suggests that Lord Spencer was enjoying Lord Robert's hospitality at Woolbeding, with a gun as well as an easy conscience. And as Mrs. Bouverie became Lady Robert Spencer in 1811, there was not much left for Lady Sarah to complain of.

[1] Elizabeth Bridget, the widow of Mr. Armistead, married Fox in 1794. " By the way," wrote Lady Sarah Napier to Lady Susan O'Brien, " Charles Fox's marriage was just then *sur le tapis*, and Lord Fitzwilliam said to my sister that all things considered he was glad of it, for that it would be much *less* disadvantage to Charles to be seen with his *wife* than his mistress." Although their domestic arrangements were regularised rather late their life was ideally happy, and Mrs. Fox was a most devoted companion.

CHAPTER X

BURKE said of the eighteenth century that it was an age " distinguished by producing extraordinary women." His flattering verdict was undoubtedly the result of observations taken in the drawing-rooms of Devonshire House. To describe adequately the charms and eccentricities of all the *grandes dames* who crossed that magic threshold is an almost impossible task, only to be attempted by a brave heart and a patient pen in a library of many volumes. In a single chapter the attempt would be absurd. Some delightful personalities and a few odd characters may however be roughly sketched.

The ladies who formed part of the inner and most intimate circle of Devonshire House were ardent Whigs. The female Tories were rigidly excluded, and the rival princesses met only on neutral ground. Men who owed allegiance to the opposite party were often admitted. Dr. Johnson's strictures upon Whiggism were never suppressed, but his heretical views were freely forgiven, and Duchess Georgiana welcomed him both in Piccadilly and at Chatsworth. Edward Gibbon, a far closer friend of the house, remained throughout his life a most unsatisfactory party man. He viewed the world of affairs from a standpoint of philosophical detachment. He admitted to his friend Deyverdun that he was not

uninfluenced by personal interest. " You have not forgotten that I went into parliament without patriotism and
without ambition, and that all my views tended to the
convenient and respectable place of a lord of trade." When
he lost his office—a comfortable sinecure with a salary of
£800 a year—he relinquished politics without a regret. In
his memoirs he even denied that he ever was a Whig.
He possessed a " cross-bench " mind. At the house in
Piccadilly his political shortcomings were overlooked for
the pleasure of his company. He was a " character " as
well as an author of genius. Any hostess in London could
feel proud when the fat little man with the falsetto voice
strutted across her carpet and posed in front of the fireplace.

As politicians the ladies who intrigued and caballed at
Devonshire House left much to be desired. They worshipped Fox and Sheridan and were eager to follow their
leaders in any mad adventure. If their principles were
open to criticism they were in a position to advance other
arguments which have never lacked weight. We know
that they were witty and high-spirited, although many
of the records of their conversational sprightliness have long
passed from memory. Happily their good looks were
immortalised by the greatest of our portrait-painters.
Nearly every habituée sat at one time or another in Reynolds's studio. And from his gallery of portraits we can
make sure of one fact which helps to reveal the true character
of the Duchess. Her soul was without envy or jealousy.
She was singularly free from any littleness of mind or spirit.
She admired beauty in other women, and did not seek to be
the most beautiful of the nymphs who surrounded her throne.

Although generally known as " the beautiful Duchess "
she was far from being the unchallenged paragon amongst
the great ladies who accepted her hospitality. Indeed, in
turning over engravings of her portraits by Reynolds, Cosway, and Lady Diana Beauclerk, we are compelled to doubt
if she was ever really beautiful judged from a classical
standard. " Her beauty was not that of features but of

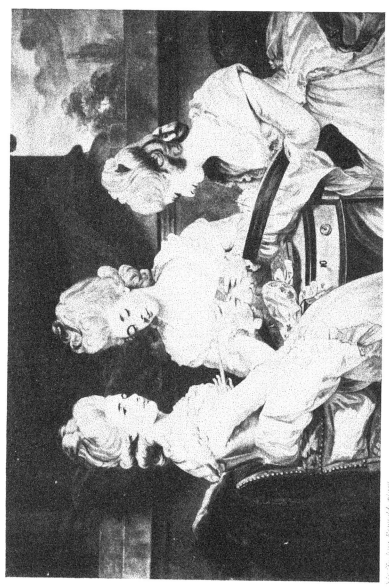

Sir Joshua Reynolds, pinxt.   Valentine Green, sculpt.

LADIES ELIZABETH LAURA, CHARLOTTE MARIA AND ANNE HORATIA WALDEGRAVE

expression," wrote Samuel Rogers. " Her personal charms constituted her smallest pretension to universal service," said Wraxall. These judgments have already been quoted, but it is necessary to repeat them. Portraits of the Duchess corroborate the comments of her critics. Her features were by no means regular, and easily surpassed by those of her sister, the excitable Lady Bessborough. Another duchess, Isabella of Rutland, was much handsomer. A poet endeavoured to explain the secret of her influence and power :

> Whatever here seems beauteous, seem'd to be
>   But a faint metaphor of thee :
> But then, methought, there something shin'd within,
>   Which cast a lustre o'er thy skin.

Her unquestioned supremacy in the society of her age owed much to that " something " shining within. She had a certain spirituality of temperament, a happiness of nature, which made a direct appeal to the goodwill of her friends. " The fascination of her manners appears to have been absolutely irresistible. She was warmly affectionate, and enthusiastically attached to her mother, sister, and children, and this enthusiasm of affection appears to have been reciprocated not only by them, but by all who knew her. Her heart might be considered as the seat of those emotions which sweeten human life, adorn our nature, and diffuse a nameless charm over existence." Wraxall supplies us with the key to the problem when he speaks of the enthusiasm of her affection. The apt phrase sums up the whole character of the Duchess.

We understand her broad-minded and tolerant attitude when we become acquainted with her friends. They added lustre to her own glory and fame. Her closest companion outside Devonshire House was Frances Anne Crewe. Mrs Crewe was certainly the most beautiful member of the coterie, and probably the most beautiful woman of her time. In the seventies of the eighteenth century Mrs. Crewe's only rival was Sheridan's young wife, the ethereal Eliza Ann Linley. " The elegance of Mrs. Sheridan's beauty is unequalled by any I ever saw except Mrs. Crewe," wrote

Fanny Burney.   Sheridan himself at one period was frankly in love with Mrs. Crewe.   How far she encouraged him is one of the many secrets of an amorous age into which we need not enquire too closely.   " When ugly circumstances come out against our acquaintance I own I always love to think the best," said Mrs. Candour.   Assuredly Mrs. Crewe's behaviour was not discreet.   Sheridan, with an exaggerated exuberance of flattery, attributable to his Irish blood, laid the *School for Scandal* at her feet with a dedication which would have been disconcerting to any other woman. Amongst her friends she was familiarly known as " Amoret," and, as Amoret, the playwright addresses her with the poetic fervour of a man who has lost both his heart and his head.   She is " inshrined Modesty."   Whilst celestial blushes check her conscious smile, he bids her stand " the perfect model."   Reynolds's art is subdued by her incomparable grace.   Even " Granby's cheek " and " Devon's eyes " must give place to her surpassing charms.

> But, praising Amoret we cannot err,
> No tongue o'ervalues Heaven, or flatters her. . . .
> Adorning fashion, unadorn'd by dress,
> Simple from taste, and not from carelessness ;
> Discreet in gesture, in deportment mild,
> Not stiff with prudence, nor uncouthly wild :
> No state has Amoret ; no studied mien ;
> She frowns no goddess, and she moves no queen,
> The softer charm that in her manner lies
> Is framed to captivate, yet not surprise ;
> It justly suits the expression of her face,—
> 'Tis less than dignity, and more than grace.

Sheridan's pen is as masterly as Reynolds's brush.   His raptures explain the worship of Mrs. Crewe by the men of her society.   She was the good-hearted friend rather than the great lady.   And in her character there was a spice of devilry, a bohemian charm of unconventionality, which, added to a quick wit and unparalleled beauty, rendered her presence a joy to all beholders.

The *School for Scandal* was played for the first time May 8, 1777.   The audience included Mrs. Crewe, the Duchess of Devonshire, and the most prominent members of the circle. They gazed across the footlights at a mimic reproduction of the world in which they moved, and recognised their portraits. " I can assure you that the Farce is charming, and the Duchess of Devonshire, Lady Worseley, and I cut very good figures in it," wrote Mrs. Crewe to Lady Clermont. The dramatist found the models for his puppets in the drawing rooms of his acquaintance. When Snake told of Mrs. Clackitt's industry, and the *tête-à-têtes* in the *Town and Country Magazine* there must have been an uneasy movement throughout the boxes. For many of the audience had already been pilloried in the pages of that scandalous and highly popular chronicle, and others were qualifying for inclusion. Lady Sneerwell and Sir Benjamin Backbite were no creatures of fancy.[1]

Within the next few years Sheridan's interests widened. His life as a dramatist ended ; his career as a politician opened. His passion for Amoret melted away. But, towards the end of his days, when reviewing the doings of a hot youth, the dying Sheridan reflectively exclaimed of Mrs. Crewe that "in truth she was the handsomest of the set."

That was the unanimous opinion of her associates from her earliest girlhood. Her beauty was inherited from both father and mother. Fulke Greville, the friend and patron of Dr. Burney, had eloped with Miss Frances Macartney. There was no good reason for the elopement, which was a mere *secret de polichinelle*. " Mr. Greville had taken a wife out of the window whom he might just as well have taken out of the door," wrote a contemporary. Greville became

---

[1] Mrs. Montagu, writing, July 9, 1777, spoke of the new play and the Duchess in the same paragraph :— . . . " The warmth of the weather prevented my seeing the *School for Scandal*, but every one agrees with you to commend it. Of all the vices of the human disposition, a love of scandal and detraction is the most contemptible. It is now got from the gossips' tea-table to the press. The scribblers weekly let fly their pop-guns at the Duchess of Devonshire's feathers. Her grace is innocent, good-humoured, and beautiful ; but these adders are blind and deaf, and cannot be charmed. However, the scribblers are all of them hungry ; but the circulators of scandal, who have neither hunger for their excuse, nor wit to give it a seasoning, are sad vermin, and I am glad Mr. Sheridan has so well exposed them."

Envoy Extraordinary to the Elector of Bavaria, and gained a reputation for erratic temper. Mrs. Greville acted as godmother to Fanny Burney, who saw much of Frances Anne, the beautiful daughter. She, the only child, was married at an early age to John Crewe, of Crewe Hall, in Cheshire. " I am sure you will be very glad,' wrote Lady Sarah Lennox to Lady Susan O'Brien, in sending the news. " You liked her I know, and he is a very amiable man, and there is no harm in his having £10,000 a year, you know. She is much prettier this winter than when you saw her, as she was then than other people." [1]

Had John Crewe not been so amiable a man he might well have objected to the undisguised admiration his wife aroused. Sheridan was not the only moth attracted by so vivid a flame. Fox openly asserted that he preferred Mrs. Crewe to any woman living. Praise of this nature from Fox could not have been gratifying to any husband, for the reputation of Fox was notorious. His feelings were not merely expressed by word of mouth. Like Sir Benjamin Backbite he was a pretty poet as well as a pretty wit, and verse alone could adequately convey his enthusiasm. Horace Walpole set up the rhymes at his private press, and

---

[1] Lady Sarah Lennox, born in 1745, was sister to the third Duke of Richmond. Her parents dying while she was quite young, she was educated by her grandmother, Lady Cadogan, and lived for some time with her sister, Lady Caroline Fox. At the age of sixteen George III., then Prince of Wales, fell in love with her and proposed marriage. Had not Lord Bute intrigued against her Lady Sarah would have sat on the throne of England, and the modern history of England might have evolved upon different lines. At the king's marriage to Princess Charlotte of Mecklenburg she acted as one of the bridesmaids. Shortly after she married Thomas Charles Bunbury, a Suffolk baronet. In 1769 she left her husband, and lived for some months with her cousin, Lord William Gordon. This was the single mistake of her life. Divorced in 1776, she married the Hon. George Napier in 1781, dying at the age of eighty-one in 1826. Her eldest son by her second marriage, General Sir Charles Napier, was the conqueror of Scinde. Her constant correspondent was Lady Susan Fox Strangways, daughter of the Earl of Ilchester. In 1764 she eloped with a handsome young Irish actor, William O'Brien, and, despite the indignation of the family, lived happily ever after.

a limited edition of this superfine broadsheet was issued from Strawberry Hill.

Was Fox really in love with Mrs. Crewe? Were his ecstasies the outward sign of an *à la mode* flirtation? The answer is difficult to give, for Fox's lines are not less exaggerated than those of Sheridan:

> Where the loveliest Expression to Feature is join'd,
> By Nature's most delicate pencil design'd,
> Where Blushes unbidden and Smiles without Art
> Speak the sweetness and feeling that dwell in the heart;
> Where in Manners enchanting no Blemish we trace,
> But the Soul keeps the promise we had from the Face,
> Sure Philosophy, Reason and Coldness must prove
> Defences unequal to shield us from Love.

In a single sentence Fox sums up the charming good-nature which radiated from Mrs. Crewe.

> Though Brightness may dazzle, 'tis Kindness that warms."[1]

---

[1] Sir George Trevelyan writes in his *Early History of Charles James Fox* :—

" Fox, from twenty to twenty-five, had doubtless not the air of a rigid moralist. The world could not believe that the king of the maccaronis wore the most audacious costumes, and carried the largest nosegay in London, for nothing; and the suspicions of the world were freely expressed by the verse-writers of society.

> " Here Charles his native eloquence refined,
> Pleased at the Toilet, in the Senate shined;
> And North approved, and Amoret looked kind.

" But he was involved in no overt scandal. He broke up no man's home. He did not add a paragraph to the chronicle of sin and misery in which companions and relatives of his own conspicuously figured. A Lovelace never would have won, or valued, the enthusiastic friendship with which Fox was honoured by so many high-minded women, whose loyalty to his interests, at a great crisis, has furnished some of the most agreeable among the stock anecdotes of English history. The secret of the certainty with which he pleased those of the other sex who were best worth pleasing is clearly revealed in the letters addressed by the Duchess of Devonshire to her mother, and still more clearly in the letters which Fox addressed to the Duchess herself. His notion of true gallantry was to treat women as beings who stood on the same intellectual table-land as himself; to give them the very best of his thought and his knowledge, as well as of his humour and his eloquence; to invite, and weigh, their advice in seasons of difficulty; and, if ever they urged him to steps which his judgment or his conscience disapproved,

From the moment of her marriage Mrs. Frances Crewe commenced to shine as one of the most interesting and brilliant hostesses of London society.   Her salon was never a rival to that of Devonshire House, although her friends. were equally the friends of the Duchess.   She, herself, was. to be found as freely in Piccadilly as in Grosvenor Street, where she entertained lavishly.   Her villa at Hampstead was a crowded resort for "week ends," and during the summer and autumn she reigned mistress of the great mansion at Crewe.   Her position was as unchallenged as her beauty.   In every memoir, in every collection of letters, runs a constant undercurrent of Mrs. Crewe.   The theme is always one of admiration.   The criticism is invariably in a friendly spirit.   Like her companion the Duchess, she had few, if any, enemies.   Both ladies had warmed the hearts of their acquaintances to a degree of unhesitating appreciation.

As late as 1792 Fanny Burney and her father went on a three days' visit to Hampstead.   " The villa at Hampstead is small, but commodious.   We were received by Mrs. Crewe with much kindness.   The room was rather dark, and she had a veil to her bonnet, half down, and with this aid she looked still in a full blaze of beauty.   I was wholly astonished . . .   The form of her face is so exquisitely perfect that my eye never met it without fresh admiration.   She is certainly in my eyes the most completely a beauty of any woman I ever saw.   I know not, even now, any female in her first youth who could bear the comparison.   She uglifies every-thing near her."   And when the fair object of this enthusiasm died, in 1818, Miss Burney declared that she was still beauti-ful in her coffin.

Sheridan contended that Mrs. Crewe was not only beauti-ful but also exceedingly intellectual.   In the eighteenth century every woman of quality wrote verse.   " Making

not to elude them with half-contemptuous banter, but to convince. them by plain-spoken and serious remonstrance."   This is a most delicate piece of whitewashing, and would have delighted some of Fox's friends.

verses is become almost as common as taking snuff," acidly commented Lady Mary Wortley Montagu. " God can tell what miserable stuff people carry about in their pockets and offer to all their acquaintances, and you know one cannot refuse reading and taking a pinch." Mrs. Crewe was no exception to the rule which governed her circle of friends. Literature was in her blood. Her mother had written an " Ode to Indifference,' as well as an unfinished novel. Mrs. Crewe wrote verse and journals, but her activities were not on so large a scale as those of the Duchess. She took her place amongst the " blue-stockings," although " blue-stocking " in the ordinary acceptation of the term she never was. When satirical verses were published about the literary ladies of her time Mrs. Crewe was named in company with Mrs. Carter, Mrs. Chapone, Mrs. Cowley, Hannah More, Mrs. Boscawen, Mrs. Thrale, Mrs. Montagu, Sophy Streatfield, and her mother, Mrs. Greville.

Possibly her association with these learned ladies tinged her conversation with a slight trace of pedantry. She enjoyed the company of Edmund Burke, and may have caught some of his ponderous mannerisms. At Crewe Hall is preserved a lengthy manuscript which gathers together a number of notes she made from time to time of Burke's conversation. The manuscript proves her to have been a good and clear-headed listener, for Burke's profundities were not always easy to report. It also explains a suggestion that now and again there was a forced brilliancy and feeling of strain in her own small talk. This is evident in a long letter written from London by Sir Gilbert Elliot of Minto to his wife in the north.

" I rode to Beaconsfield on Sunday, and found Mrs. Crewe, Windham, young Burke, and a Mr. Adie. I have got into a certain degree of intimacy now with Mrs. Crewe, and find her like ninety-nine in a hundred—a mixture of good and bad. I mean only in respect to agreeableness and sense, for I know *no* bad in her in any other acceptation of the word. She likes good conversation—takes an interest, and even a share, in all subjects which men would naturally talk of when not in women's company—as politics and literature ; and she likes arguments and discussions of all sorts. She seems to have a clear understanding, and a good deal of refinement and ingenuity in her own ideas. All this is good. On the other hand, she is certainly not without a degree of pedantry and *over*-refinement. She betrays as much vanity and desire of admiration in her pursuit of *male* conversation, as real taste and genuine pleasure in it ; in short, she seems to be struggling to maintain the same place and consequence by wit and conversation which she once held as a beauty ; and for a wife, or one to live constantly with—begging your pardon—you know I always protested against a professed beauty, and so I do against a *professed* wit, but more especially a professed wit grown out of a professed beauty."

Maybe the environment was at fault. With Burke and his heavy batteries in reserve there could never have been an easy flow of conversation. Windham, too, must have charged the atmosphere with weighty politics. Conversation with women upon philosophical or economic subjects is never easy. There is bound to be a striving of sex against sex for mastery in debate. Man is generally handicapped. If he says all he thinks he lays himself open to a charge of brutality. The conversation of men and women is only at its best when it becomes personal or sails round the coast-lines of gossip.

Mrs. Crewe was very beautiful, exceedingly witty, certainly intelligent. She was also warm-hearted, impulsive, and indiscreet. Yet scandal never seriously sullied her good name, despite the Sheridan incident. The real nobility of the characters of Georgiana Cavendish and Frances Anne Crewe preserved them from the abundant evil of their age. And Mrs. Crewe never changed. Nearly twenty years after her marriage Lady Sarah Napier described her as " the same honourable, generous minded creature, fair to all parties, to all sets, firm to old friends tho' out of fashion, laughing at the follies of the world, but still giving them a *value* from habit which her sense disowns ; she is a *dear* creature still."

But if we want criticism we may always find it amongst our closest friends. Some years later Lady Sarah met the " *dear creature* " for a week and found her a trifle tiresome. Mrs. Crewe did not lack sense. She had " the purest principles of everything that is good, but it is all so *jumbled* in her little pate." She chats, gossips, laughs, has an odd way of expressing herself, talks incessantly, never waits for an answer, " all bustle and joy, and grievance, and anxiety, and indifference too about politics." Perhaps she was tired of politics, as well she might have been in 1794. Yet Lady Sarah came back to her earlier and softer judgment. In 1799 she wrote : " I love her very much and like her company but her politics worry me like those of many other people."

Women take politics too seriously to be good politicians. Their politics—in the eighteenth century at least—were based upon personalities, and the personalities were men. No wonder they worried each other when they gossiped about affairs of State.

Fox and Sheridan loved Mrs. Crewe for a variety of reasons. The Hon. Charles Arbuthnot, a name which has not come down in history, met her in 1790, and his description agrees with those of the statesmen. " She, I think, is a charming person, and I find her particularly pleasant. . . . Instead of a fine lady, she is a comfortable kind of a creature, that has read a great deal and is amazingly well-informed." Finally must be quoted Mrs. Piozzi's frank note. " She never lost an atom of character, I mean female honour. She loved high play and dissipation, but was no sensualist."

Sir Joshua's art was not unequal to the task of depicting Mrs. Crewe's beauty, although Sheridan's verse suggested the contrary. The President has given us several canvases to prove that her friends did not exaggerate her charms. The most lovely portrait is that best known by means of Watson's mezzotint. The group of Mrs. Crewe and Mrs. Bouverie—the canvas belongs to Lord Rosebery—is more famous. Mrs. Piozzi has a story in her memoirs about the picture and the sitters. " Mrs. Crewe and Mrs. Bouverie, the two fashionable belles about the Court and Town, had been painted by Reynolds in a character of two shepherdesses, with a pensive air, as if appealing to each other, about the year 1770 or perhaps earlier, and there was written under the picture *Et in Arcadia ego*.   When the Exhibition was arranging, the members and their friends went and looked the works over : " What can this mean ? " said Dr. Johnson.   " It seems very nonsensical.   ' I am in Arcadia ! ' "

" Well ! What of that !   The King could have told you," replied the painter.   " *He* saw it yesterday, and said at once, ' Oh, there is a tombstone in the background.   Ay, ay, death is even in Arcadia ! ' "

The beautiful Mrs. Bouverie was as enthusiastic a Foxite as Mrs. Crewe.   She married Edward Bouverie, M.P. for Northampton, and second son to the first Viscount Folkestone. Like Mrs. Crewe, she lived in an atmosphere of " high play and dissipation."   She wrote much verse, and owed her introduction into Devonshire House through the claims of kinship.   She was born a Fawkener, and therefore cousin to the Duchess.[1]

To re-create some suggestion of the personal fascination of the women of that circle by words, and by words alone, is not easy. The material, although extensive, is yet insufficient. Lady Bessborough, sister to the Duchess of Devonshire, was in many respects an interesting study.   She was as attractive as her sister, to whom at one time she was held up as an example.   Upon her marriage to Lord Duncannon (afterwards Earl of Bessborough) Mrs. Delany declared her to be

[1] In 1793 Lord Glenbervie met Mrs. Bouverie, who looked " very handsome and is still armed with a great deal of matron-like seduction.   She looks very like a lady to be such a democrat. ' Last summer Lord Orford (Horace Walpole) said a good though a very severe thing about her.   Somebody reported to him that Mrs. Bouverie had been talking a great deal of democratical language, and had declared that she hoped to see the time when there would be no overgrown fortunes, and when the poor would be in easy circumstances and the fine ladies lay down their coaches and walk the streets.   Lord Orford said he had no doubt a great regard for his relation, Mrs. Bouverie, but that he owned he always thought she had a turn for street walking."   The turn of fancy is not very refined, but it allows us to judge the form of conversation when Walpole was in the room.

" a very valuable young woman, and I hope will have the good sense not to fall into those giddy errors which have hurt her sister, who I also hope is now sensible of those errors. I believe she never meant to do wrong, but pleasure and flattery and violent youthful spirits plunged her into danger before she was aware of the bad consequences."

Lady Bessborough's ill-health removed her from society at the height of the Duchess's reign. But she has left the impression of a creature of impulse—a tradition which was intensified by the behaviour of her daughter, Lady Caroline Lamb. Her interests were wide. She played with art, literature, and politics. She was very sensible and very frivolous. To a certain extent the same description applies to all the great ladies who crossed the threshold of Devonshire House, such as the Duchess of Rutland, Lady Craven, the Countess of Jersey, Mrs. Hobart (afterwards Lady Buckinghamshire), Lady Lucan, Lady Cork, and their like. Some were more dissipated than others. They were not all angels, or all fiends. But whatever they did, good or bad, right or wrong, they did with enthusiasm. Their energy was extraordinary.

They were wondrously good-looking. Sir Joshua leaves us no room to doubt on that score. He flattered his sitters, but he never absolutely falsified the truth. But beauty alone does not explain the whole degree of their attraction. Their manners and conversation must have been charming. Diaries, letters, memoirs, fragments of forgotten history, reveal their hidden character. Scraps of light-hearted badinage float through half-opened doors. Laughter peals along empty corridors—and dies away. The doors have been softly closed. We cannot reopen them.

The late eighteenth century was an admirable mixture of body and soul. Manners during the reigns of the earlier Georges were gross. The age of the Regency had many black aspects, and not many redeeming features. But the society over which the Duchess of Devonshire reigned was highly educated as well as highly dissipated. The " blue stockings " formed an integral part of the best society.

In December, 1775, Mrs. Boscawen wrote to Mrs. Delany :
" I went to Mrs. Vesey, where there were fine ladies indeed !
Duchess of Devonshire, Lady Jersey, Lady Claremont, Mrs.
Crewe, Mrs. Walsingham, Lord Edgcumb, Mrs. Dashwood."

For good breeding and elegance of learning Mrs. Vesey's
drawing-room rivalled that of Mrs. Montagu.   In 1775
its mistress was a lady of some sixty years, the wife of a
member of Parliament who was also accountant-general
of Ireland, " a man of very gentle manner," recently elected
to full membership of the Club.   Mrs. Elizabeth Vesey
was a lion-hunter.   She " sought to see everything and
everybody."   All the notorieties and celebrities of the season
were brought together in the tiny rooms of her little house
in Bolton Street, Piccadilly.   She was described as collect-
ing " all the graduates and candidates for fame, till they
are as unintelligible as the good folks at Babel."   Dr.
Johnson sat in her salon surrounded by a circle five deep.
Her social duties were so heavy that Mrs. Handcock, a
sister-in-law, relieved her of the dull but necessary cares of
household management.   We begin to picture Mr. Vesey
and his " gentle manners."   Mr. Jellaby was also a man of
gentle manners.   Probably Mr. Vesey used to sit in a corner
of the Vesey drawing-room with his head against the wall,
in the intervals of accounting for Ireland and supporting
his party in the House.   For, though we hear much of Mrs.
Vesey, the chronicles are silent about Mr. Vesey.

Mrs. Vesey received the nickname of " mind " because
of her " spirit, wit, and vivacity."   She was also sometimes
called " the Sylph."   Mrs. Handcock was known as " body."
Under such direction the salon became very popular and
crowded, for Mrs. Vesey was " vastly agreeable."   Yet
there were critics of such perfection.   Boswell and Lady
Diana Beauclerk discussed their hostess.   Lady Di. said
that Mrs. V. was an idiot.   Boswell replied that she
was so much less of an idiot than he had expected that he
did not think her an idiot at all.   " I think," said Lady Di.,
" she is bad enough, if that is all a lawyer can find to say for
her, that she is only less an idiot than he imagined."   Bos-

well then considered the different species of idiots loose upon this world, the land idiots and the water idiots, and so on. " I think," said Lady Di., " that is worth writing down." And so they drifted away from the subject of Mrs. Vesey.

She was too active to be an ideal hostess. " Her fear of ceremony is really troublesome,' Lord Harcourt told Fanny Burney. " Her eagerness to break a circle is such that she insists upon everybody's sitting with their backs one to another, that is the chairs are drawn into little parties of three together in a confused manner all over the room."

This was trying. No man wished to sit with his back to the Duchess of Devonshire or Mrs. Crewe.

Mrs. Vesey often received the Duchess. Another constant hostess was Mrs. Montagu, who had much affection for the beautiful daughter of the Spencers. A clever woman who has left her mark upon that age cannot be included in the circle. Although Mrs. Thrale met the Duchess in society, she never appears to have been included in any of the gatherings at Devonshire House. The Duchess thought her " vulgar," one of the most blighting accusations that can be made by one woman upon another. The criticism had little justification. Vulgar in family origin Mrs. Thrale most certainly was not. The Salusburys were of distinctly more ancient stock than the Spencers.[1] She had the same intense interest and gusto in life which characterises all the Georgian women. Probably she expressed her feelings too openly to be loved by all who knew her. Her second marriage was never forgiven. Johnson's wrath is historic. Her contemporaries judged her severely, but she was a woman more than ordinarily gifted with intelligence and fine feelings.

Leaving the ladies who were pretty, or witty, or intellectual, and those who were accorded all the graces as well as most of the virtues, we come to the artists. If art be a

[1] Mrs. Thrale was distantly related to Topham Beauclerk. The brewer's wife was born a Miss Salusbury. Beauclerk's mother was a Miss Mary Norreys, of Speke Hall, Lancashire, a house mentioned in Domesday Book. The Norreys were descended in the female line from the still older family of Salusbury.

sign of high civilization, and it is hard to deny such a contention, the Devonshire House circle reached a very advanced standard of refinement. Lady Diana Beauclerk and Mrs. Damer were prominent members of the set. Both had passed through the unhappiest domestic complications, and both found in the practice of the fine arts a relief from their personal troubles. Lady Di. painted and designed. Mrs. Damer was a sculptor of more than amateur ability.

Lady Diana Beauclerk was sister to Lady Betty Spencer, Countess of Pembroke, and wife to Johnson's aristocratic companion, Topham Beauclerk. She was an artist of finer attainments than Mrs. Damer ; with whom she does not appear to have been on intimate terms, although they lived close to each other, had similar tastes and employments, and moved in the same circles.

Mrs. Damer affected a severely classical manner. She was a daughter of the age of Winckelmann, who taught his followers that " the sole means for us to become—ay, if possible, inimitably great—is the imitation of the ancients." So at No. 9, Upper Brook Street, she raised a shrine of classicism which was admired without stint by her friends.

Lady Di. displayed the difference in her temperament in her choice of exemplars. In her decorative panels she reflected somewhat obliquely the spirit of Fragonard. She was inspired by Wedgwood. She sat at the feet of Cosway and Bartolozzi, and, to a limited degree, was a forerunner of Morland, Stothard, and their lesser followers. She met Sir Joshua, and her tiny amorini and baby fauns have the faces of Sir Joshua's children. She was a woman of gifts, but her work was always strongly derivative.

Elder daughter of Charles, fifth Earl of Sunderland and third Duke of Marlborough, great-granddaughter of the great Duke and Duchess Sarah, Lady Diana entered Devonshire House by right of birth, for she was cousin to Duchess Georgiana. There was a strong artistic vein in her branch of the family. One brother, Lord Charles Spencer, brought the Ansidei Raphael to England. The youngest and favourite brother, Lord Robert Spencer, formed a fine collection of works of art as well as a good library. Educated amidst the art treasures of Blenheim, she copied the pictures of Rubens as a child, and met the celebrated artists who visited the palace in Oxfordshire. During those early years she doubled the parts of connoisseur and fine lady, for, at the coronation of George III, she walked in the procession to the Abbey as a Lady of the Bedchamber to Queen Charlotte.

Her marriage in 1757 to the second Viscount Bolingbroke was a disaster. " Bully " was no ideal husband. He had already fallen in love with the beautiful Gunning who became Lady Coventry. His morals were those of a Moslem, without, however, the restraints of the Koran. His manners were those of the stable. In judging Lady Diana we must remember these facts. Eight years after the marriage Lady Bolingbroke met Topham Beauclerk, great-grandson of Charles II. and Nell Gwynn, whose striking resemblance to his royal forefather had already fascinated that sturdy Jacobite Samuel Johnson. Lady Bolingbroke had already left her husband when she became infatuated with Beauclerk. There were soon rumours of a divorce. In January, 1766, Lady Sarah Lennox wrote to Lady Susan O'Brien suggesting that both lord and lady were mad.

" Seriously speaking, I believe Lord B. is much the same as mad when he is drunk, and that is generally. . . . Everybody that don't love her pities him, but, as I had heard he had got a woman in the house already I can't say I do, for if he was unhappy at the thoughts of having used her so cruelly as he has done, surely a man that had any feeling would not recover his spirits so easily."

" Bully " attempted to reform, and friends worked hard to effect a reconciliation. But there were awkward facts to ride over, and the lady had no wish to go back. " It is a great pity," wrote Gibbon to Madame Boufflers. " She is handsome and agreeable, and ingenious far beyond the ordinary rate." The moral atmosphere was not clear. [1] An

[1] Lady Di.'s sister married Lord Pembroke, who had a notorious escapade with Miss Kitty Hunter, a Maid of Honour. Lord Pem-

Act of Parliament was passed dissolving the marriage, and, two days after it received the royal assent, Lady Diana Spencer and Topham Beauclerk were married at St. George's, Hanover Square. The only witnesses were Lord and Lady Spencer, the parents of the future Duchess of Devonshire.

Topham Beauclerk and his beautiful wife were frequent visitors to Devonshire House. In 1778 Lady Di. drew a portrait of her cousin the Duchess which was engraved by Bartolozzi. " A Castilian nymph conceived by Sappho and executed by Myron, would not have more grace and simplicity ; it is the divinity of Venus piercing the veil of immortality," wrote Walpole, who was never stingy of his praise when it concerned a member of the *ton*. " The nymph-like simplicity of the figure is equal to what a Grecian statuary would have formed of a dryad or goddess of a river."

Walpole had been telling the poet Mason that he did not intend to go to the Academy banquet. " I shall not leave my little hill for the dinner at the Royal Academy on Thursday, only to figure the next day in the newspapers in the list of the Mæcenas of the age." Then he reflects upon Lady Diana's drawing. " The likeness is perfectly preserved, except that the paintress has lent her own expression to the Duchess, which you will allow is very agreeable flattery ; what should I go to the Academy for ? I shall see no such *chef d'œuvre* there." [1] Mason wanted one of these prints, which became exceedingly scarce. The Duke of Marl-

broke went off to the Continent with Miss Hunter, and a little later asked his wife to join the party, bringing with her a guitar, two servants who could play the French horn, and his dog Rover. Had it not been for the advice and influence of her brother, Lady Pembroke would have gone. Afterwards, according to Gilly Williams, Lord and Lady Pembroke lived in " extreme conjugal felicity," whilst Miss Kitty Hunter made a very good marriage.

[1] And yet, as Mrs. Steuart Erskine reminds us in her exhaustive biography of Lady Diana Beauclerk, that Academy exhibition of 1778 included Gainsborough's great portrait of the Duchess. What a pity that Walpole, " the most artificial, the most fastidious, the most capricious of men " could not have exercised a little of his gift of appreciation upon Chatterton when that " marvellous boy " asked for help and friendship.

borough bought the plate, and ordered two hundred impressions. Soon there was not one left. The world of fashion " tore them away."

Meanwhile Walpole continued to chant hymns in praise of Lady Diana's art, which he declared combined the peculiar qualities of Guido, Albano, Poussin, Salvator, and Sacchi. " Just at present," he wrote in 1775, " I am the vainest creature in the universe. Lady Di. has drawn the scenes for my tragedy, which if the subject were a quarter as good as the drawings would make me a greater genius than Shakespeare, as she is superior to Guido and S. Rosa. Such figures! such dignity! such simplicity! Then there is a cedar hanging over the castle that is more romantic than when it grew on Lebanon." He realised that his remarks were extravagant. " How an author's sanity can bestow bombastic panegyric on his flatterers! " Lady Di. knew how to exert all her charms upon this king of the diletantti, and, in these nervous phrases, we can obtain some impression of his small talk at Devonshire House.

The artist did not make many portraits. She caricatured her friend Gibbon, and there exists a clever sketch of another member of the circle, C. J. Fox. If she did not accept Dr. Johnson's dictum about portrait painting as a profession for women, she certainly followed his advice. " Public practice of any art," observed the sage, " and staring in men's faces, is very indelicate in a female."

Johnson loved Topham Beauclerk more than any of his friends. " Thy body is all vice, and thy mind is all virtue," he summed up. " There is in Beauclerk a predominacy over his company that one does not like. But he is a man who has lived so much in the world that he has a short story on every occasion ; he is always ready to talk, and is never exhausted." He told Mrs. Thrale that " Beauclerk's talents were those which he had felt himself more disposed to envy than those of any he had known." But Beauclerk was a difficult man to live with despite " his wit and his folly, his acuteness and his maliciousness, his merriment and his reasoning." In 1780, the year of his death, Lady

Diana retired to Devonshire Cottage, Richmond, over-looking Petersham meadows and the river. It had belonged at one time to Duchess Georgiana, and many of the men and women of her circle had houses in the neighbourhood. Lady Buckinghamshire (Mrs. Hobart) lived at Marble Hill, Horace Walpole at Strawberry Hill, the Sheridans at Douro House on Richmond Hill, " Old Q." at Queensberry House, the Duke of Clarence at Ivy Hall, whilst other frequent visitors and residents were the Prince of Wales, Mrs. Fitz-herbert, the Bouveries, the Bunburys, Edmund Burke, and Sir Joshua Reynolds.

In 1780 Miss Burney was one of the guests at a dinner party given by Reynolds in his house on Richmond Hill.

" From the window of the dining-parlour, Sir Joshua directed us to look at a pretty white house which belonged to Lady Di. Beauclerk. ' I am extremely glad,' said Mr. Burke, ' to see her at last so well housed ; poor woman ! the bowl has long rolled in misery ; I rejoice that it has now found its balance. I never, myself, so much enjoyed the sight of happiness in another, as in that woman when I first saw her after the death of her husband. It was really enlivening to behold her placed in that sweet house released from all her cares, a thousand pounds a year at her own dis-posal, and her husband was dead ! Oh, it was pleasant, it was delightful, to see her enjoyment of the situation ! '

" ' But without considering the circumstances,' said Mr. Gibbon, ' this may appear very strange, though when they are fairly stated, it is perfectly rational and unavoidable ! '

" ' Very true,' said Mr. Burke ; ' if the circumstances are not considered, Lady Di. may appear highly reprehen-sible.' He then, addressing himself to me (Miss Burney) as the person least likely to be acquainted with the character of Mr. Beauclerk, drew it himself in strong, marked expres-sions, describing the misery he gave his wife, his singular ill-treatment of her, and the necessary relief the death of such a man must give. He then reminded Sir Joshua of a day in which they had dined at Mr. Beauclerk's soon after his marriage with Lord Bolingbroke's divorced wife, in company with Goldsmith, and told a new story of poor Goldsmith's eternal blundering."

Miss Burney gently closed the door, and we have lost for ever the new story of poor Goldsmith's eternal blundering. But we listen to Burke's ponderous gossip, the bowl of misery rolling in its balance, and the poor lady whose circumstances were rational and whose character, unless carefully considered, highly reprehensible.

There was not a spot upon the stainless reputation of Anne Seymour Damer, the daughter of Walpole's closest friend, Henry Seymour Conway. Her connections were of the highest. Her mother, Lady Ailesbury, was the daughter of the fourth Duke of Argyll and the beautiful Mary Bellenden. Her uncle, the fifth Duke of Argyll, had married the Duchess of Hamilton, who had been born one of the famous Gunnings.

Anne Conway's life should have been a dream of happiness. Her father was a man " whom nature always designed for a hero of romance, and who is *déplacé* in ordinary life." Her mother, according to Walpole, the same authority, was " handsomer than fame." Amongst the guests of the household, were Hume, Rousseau, Gray, Thomson, Shenstone, Reynolds, Angelica Kauffmann, the Garricks, the Farrens, and Mrs. Siddons. There was plenty of money, and loads of debts. The Duke of Devonshire, father to the Duke who married Duchess Georgiana, bequeathed £5,000 to Henry Conway. " You might despise the acquisition of £5,000 simply," wrote Walpole. " But when that sum is a public testimonial of your virtue, and bequeathed by a man so virtuous, it is worth a million."

General Conway probably wished it had been worth a million. He was extravagant, his wife gambled, and his daughter had little idea of the value of money. In such a household the only child soon gets married. Miss Conway, " very pretty and agreeable," to quote Lady Sarah Lennox, married John Damer, eldest son of Lord Milton. The bride was nineteen, the bridegroom twenty-three. The result was far from satisfactory.

"I think one has no right to blame her more than him,"
wrote Lady Sarah Lennox. "He had no business to marry
a girl he did not like than she to accept a man she was totally
indifferent to, and he was as much to blame in giving her
the example of never living at home, as she was to make all
her life opposite to his. In short I cannot think it fair to
blame one more than other, but as it is evident love was out
of the question, I must give her credit for her present
conduct."

John Damer was a brainless fop. After his death his
wardrobe was sold for £15,000. He was of the same type
as "Bully" Bolingbroke. The young wife engaged in
endless excitement and fashionable dissipation. Soon they
were both in the hands of the Jews. Early in 1775, a few
months after the marriage of her friend the Duchess of
Devonshire, husband and wife separated. Their joint
debts amounted to £70,000.

Her father had helped her to the best of his ability. But
General Conway was no economist, and his own affairs were
heavily involved. Her father-in-law, Lord Milton, although
one of the richest of noblemen, declined to reduce his son's
liabilities, and refused even to see his heir. Horace Walpole
tells the story of the tragedy of John Damer in a letter to
Mann. On August 15, 1776, at the Bedford Arms in Covent
Garden, "having had supper with four common women, a
blind fiddler, and no other man, he dismissed his seraglio,
Orpheus being ordered to come up again in half-an-hour.
When the fiddler returned he found a dead silence and smelt
gunpowder. He called, the master of the house came up,
and found Mr. Damer sitting in a chair dead, with a pistol
by his side, and another in his pocket ; the ball had not
gone through his head or made any report ; on the table lay
a scrap of paper with these words : ' The people of the house
are not to blame for what has happened, which was my
own act. . . .' What a catastrophe for a man of thirty-
two, heir to two-and-twenty thousand a year."

Charles James Fox broke the news to Anne Damer. Lord
Milton seized her " diamonds, furniture, carriages, and

everything to pay the debts with." She left her house in a hackney coach, taking only her inkstand, a few books, her dog, and her maid." She had three guineas in her pocket. Her half-sister, the Duchess of Richmond, took pity on her, and gave her a roof for shelter.

Walpole told Mann that he loved Anne Damer " as his own child." From his letters we learn much of the young widow. " Mrs. Damer is going abroad to confirm a very delicate constitution ; she has one of the most solid understandings I ever knew ; astonishingly improved, but with so much reserve and modesty, that I have often told Mr. Conway he does not know the extent of her capacity and the solidity of her reason. We have by accident discovered that she writes Latin like Pliny, and is learning Greek. In Italy she will be a prodigy ; she models like Bernini ; has excelled the moderns in the similitude of her busts, and has lately begun on marble. '

In her childhood Hume had encouraged her to model and carve. She had taken lessons from John Bacon and the unfortunate Giuseppe Ceracchi, whilst William Cruikshank was her professor in anatomy. Upon her return from a long European tour she devoted herself to sculpture seriously. Erasmus Darwin celebrated her skill in verse :

> Long with soft touch shall Damer's chisel charm,
> With grace delight us and with beauty warm ;
> Foster's [1] fine form shall hearts unborn engage
> And Melbourne's [2] smile enchant another age.

Walpole boldly called her " a female genius," but there were less indulgent critics. Fanny Burney reported that " her performances in sculpture were of no great merit, but were prodigiously admired by Horace Walpole, who had a notorious weakness for the works of persons of quality."

Both verdicts err, and the truth is to be found between the two. Allan Cunningham spoke of Mrs. Damer as a vain, enterprising woman, who was constantly failing in all

[1] Lady Elizabeth Foster, afterwards the second wife of the fifth Duke of Devonshire.
[2] Viscountess Melbourne.

attempts, and was constantly imagining she had succeeded.
Scandal said that her best works could only be attributed
to the efforts of more skilful but less celebrated craftsmen
known as " ghosts." There is a grace in many of her bas-
reliefs, but her larger compositions are not always happy.
She was at her best when she was at her simplest, as in the
keystones of the centre arch of the bridge at Henley. One
of the fairest judgments is to be found in *The Georgian
Era.* " That her performances were not of the highest
order has never been insisted upon, but a woman of fortune
and fashion who could devote herself voluntarily and enthusiastically to so laborious and difficult an art, and achieve
so much success in it, as Mrs. Damer has done, must surely
be no common genius among her own sex, she at least was
almost a prodigy."

Lady Sarah Lennox, writing from Goodwood in 1778,
outlines a more personal picture. " She likes travelling,
books, and a comfortable home, both in town and (for a
little while, in the) country, and these she prefers to fine
clothes, fine equipages, and finery of all kinds. . . . She is
vain and likes to be at the head of the great world, and is
easily led into that style of life. Upon the whole, I think
she is a sensible woman without sensibility, a pretty one
without pleasing, a prudent one without conduct, and I
believe nobody will have the *right* to tax her with any fault,
and yet she will be abused, which I take to be owing to a
want of sweetness in her disposition ; she is too *strictly
right* ever to be beloved."

Only by such slight character sketches of the more famous
women in society during the late eighteenth century can we
gain any complete picture of the circle which found its
centre at Devonshire House. The Duchess and her friends
were women of considerable intellect, and in many cases
quite able to meet the most celebrated men of their age
upon an equal footing.

Their interests were innumerable, including every de-
partment of human activity. They were able to discuss
in the same breath the wild theories of Rousseau and the

latest vagaries of the *mode*. They were too clever and too sensible to cast aside all the restraints of social law. But their standard of conduct was not governed by ordinary rules. Because they were self-indulgent their judgments were lenient. They were charitable to each other because they needed charity for themselves. Essentially good women, such as Lady Sarah Lennox, left their husbands for their lovers, and suffered all the ignominy of divorce, without losing the respect and affection of their friends.

Body and soul, they enjoyed the wonderful gifts of life and youth with a fervent intensity no other generation of womanhood has attempted to emulate.

M

CHAPTER XI

IN the midst of the distracting whirl of fashion the " beautiful Duchess " found time for the drudgery of literature.
Prose or verse came with equal facility to her. Whilst
dining at St. Albans, on a visit to her mother, the
Countess Spencer, she composed a couple of verses for Mr.
Garrick. Two years earlier Garrick, summoned to read a
play to George III., had composed a fable in which he
described himself as an old and feeble blackbird who had
given up his singing until the eagle had recalled him to
melody. Dr. Johnson, always a critic of " little Davy,"
ponderously remarked, " there is not much of the spirit of
fabulosity in this fable, for the call of an eagle never yet had
much tendency to restore the warbling of a blackbird."
This gossip was in the mind of the Duchess when she wrote :

" The *blackbird* whose melodious throat excel'd each other bird,
Breath'd so sweet its tuneful note that all with rapture heard
Was skimming thro' the air along—'twas on a winter's day—
Sure I, said he, who fly in song
  Must quickly speed my way ;
But vainly did he take a pride in this conceited notion,
For tho' his strains would swiftly glide, he still was slow in motion.

" Meanwhile, a sparrow quick as light, outstripp'd the blackbird's
 wing ;
But tho' she could excel in flight,
  Alas ! she could not sing.
The blackbird with indignant eye thus spoke his angry mind,
Shall birds like you with swiftness fly
  Whilst I am left behind—
Forgive, the timid bird replied, for I, with pleasure too,
Would give my *plumes* and airy pride
  To sing and charm like you."

The conceit is pleasing, but when the Duchess sent a copy to her mother she added, " Don't shew these." Garrick's comment is lost, but the sharp-tongued little actor, who was a poet himself, could not fail to realise the weakness of the amateur.

A poet can never gain more than a limited audience. The novelist appeals to the whole world. In the eighteenth century the young ladies who were not writing verses in each other's albums were composing novels. Sometimes in the neglected library of an old country house we find a shelf of the fashionable romances which fascinated Lydia Languish. They are usually handy little duodecimos published in London or Dublin. They were cheap, about two shillings a volume, and the titles were attractive : *The False Step, The Unguarded Moment, The Fatal Compliance, The Innocent Adultery*. They usually dealt with fashionable life and unlawful love. With very few exceptions, they reached a pitch of dullness that the mind of man can hardly conceive.

Amongst the exceptions was Fanny Burney's *Evelina, or a Young Lady's Entrance into the World*, the success of which set a thousand ardent pens at work. *Evelina* is readable to this day. One of its chief rivals in 1778 was *The Sylph*, which was credited to a far more important person than the music-master's daughter in Leicester Square.

In January, 1779, Fanny Burney was invited to spend an evening with Mrs. Cholmondeley[1] in Hertford Street, " perhaps the most important evening of my life," she entered in her journal. Mrs. Cholmondeley, a lady of fashion, had been educated in France, and was " gay, flighty, entertaining, and frisky." Miss Burney had recently published *Evelina*, and was on view as a literary phenomenon. Into the drawing-room at Hertford Street marched many of the most interesting men and women of the day. Mrs. Sheridan, whose beauty, according to Miss Burney, was only equalled

[1] Mrs. Cholmondeley was a member of the Devonshire House circle. Sir Gilbert Elliot (afterwards first Earl of Minto) met her in 1787. " On Saturday I dined at the Palmerstons'. . . . Mrs. Cholmondeley came in just after supper, and called for a bottle of champagne, and was in one of her high-spirited humours."

by that of Mrs. Crewe ; the sweet singer's sister, Miss
Linley, " heavy and inanimate " ; Sheridan himself, a very
fine figure but not handsome, tall, upright, manly, and
fashionable without being foppish ; and, entering together,
Sir Joshua Reynolds and Dr. Joseph Wharton.   Reynolds
was an old friend of the Burneys.   During the conversation
he went up to her.   Their talk must be reproduced in her
own sprightly words.

" Pray, do you know anything of *The Sylph* ? "

The Sylph had been recently published by bookseller
Lowndes.

" No," replied Miss Burney shortly.   On every side the
question was being asked of her.

" Don't you, upon your honour ? " persisted the artist.

" Upon my honour ?—did you suspect me ? "

" Why, a friend of mine sent for it upon suspicion."

" So did we," interrupted Miss Linley.   " But I did not
suspect after I had read it."

" What is the reason," persisted Sir Joshua, " that
Lowndes always advertises it with *Evelina* ? "

" Indeed I know nothing about it," protested the author
of *Evelina*.

" Ma'am," cried Sheridan, turning to Fanny abruptly.
" You should send and order him not—it is a take-in, and
ought to be forbid."   Then he added with great vehemence :
" It is a most impudent thing in that fellow ! "

The Sylph created much discussion.   Mrs. Thrale wrote
to St. Martin's Street asking if Fanny was the author.   This
moved Dr. Burney to intervene, and he wrote to the
offending publisher.

" Dr. Burney sends his compts. to Mr. Lowndes and
acquaints him that by the manner in which *Evelina* has for
some time been advertised in company with *The Sylph*, it
has generally been imagined that both these Novels have
been written by one and the same Author.   Now, as Mr.
Lowndes must be *certain* that they are the works of different
authors, and as accident has now made the Author of
Evelina pretty generally known, who by no means wishes to

rob the writer of *The Sylph* of whatever praise may be his due, Dr. B. wishes Mr. L. will not only cease to advertise these books in an equivocal way, but inform the Public in *some clear and decisive manner* that they are the work of two different writers. St. Martin's Street, January 27 [1779]."

Lowndes, being a business man and a publisher, was not unwilling to catch the advantage of sales by reason of the novel being credited to the most popular author of the moment. Probably he did not know the name of the real writer, for the novel was published anonymously. A critic hints that the story came from another quarter.

" Sylvanus Urban, Gent.," reviewed it at some length in the *Gentleman's Magazine* for June, 1779. Briefly he describes the plot. " A young lady of exemplary manners, bred in the country, is here unequally yoked with a modern fine gentleman, bred in town, who, after a career of vice and dissipation, concludes it with a suicide. Her ladyship, in the meantime, has her virtue strengthened and conformed by an invisible agent, a kind of second conscience, who proves at last to be a former lover, one as unfashionably virtuous as herself, and in whom, at last, she meets with a more suitable mate. The whole is well intended ; but displays too great a knowledge of the *ton*, and the worst, though perhaps the highest, part of the world, to be the work of *a young lady*, as has been said and supposed."

Fanny Burney was not the " young lady," and Miss Linley had more literary intelligence than Sylvanus Urban or Sir Joshua Reynolds. How could any trained reader after enjoying the wit of *Evelina* give a second thought to the idea that *The Sylph* came from the same hand ? There was another girl, five years the junior of Miss Burney, who possessed a far more intimate knowledge of the *ton*. That girl was Georgiana, Duchess of Devonshire. To her the authorship of *The Sylph* was generally attributed. She never denied the book, and, from internal evidence, it is hardly possible to doubt the ascription.

The Sylph is written in the form of interminable letters.

The eighteenth century was a sententious age ; Dr. Johnson made all his little fishes talk like whales. The men and women in *The Sylph* talk like prigs, and the cynicism is that of a girl of twenty-one. " The gay seductive Sir William Stanley " tells his friend Lord Biddulph that at last he has been " shackled." Love has ever been with him a laughing god. Now he has married " such a woman ! . . . such a rustic ! one of your sylvan deities. But I was made for her." He reminds Lord Biddulph how they said good-bye to each other on the steps of the Thatched House Club in St. James's Street. He went to Wales. At a village near Abergavenny, rambling on the ridge of a precipice—Abergavenny is not very Alpine, although it does glory in the Sugar Loaf—he met " a brace of females." Their beauty so fired his soul and disturbed his equilibrium as he gazed through his glass that he missed his footing on the edge of the precipice and rolled to the foot of the ravine. Naturally the beauties rushed to pick him up, and he was carried to their father's house. Seeing his Julia day by day completed the mischief. Her features were perfect. All she wanted was " a *je ne scai quoi*, a *tout ensemble*, which nothing but mixing with people of fashion can give ; but, as she is extremely docile, I have hopes that she will not disgrace the name of Stanley."

Julia was barely seventeen, the exact age at which Georgiana Spencer became a Cavendish. The third letter is from the bride to her sister Louisa, and describes with considerable brightness the impression made upon a raw country girl by London. " We came into town at a place called Piccadilly, where there was such a crowd of carriages of all sorts that I was perfectly astonished and absolutely frightened." Sir William took her education in hand. She was presented at Court. A dancing master was engaged, and she was given lessons upon the harpsichord and in singing. Taste, she told her sister, is to be acquired, but is variable. " So though I may dance and sing in taste now, a few months hence I may have another method to learn which will be the taste then."

Lady Julia Stanley begins to take her place in town when Lord Biddulph appears. He finds " Stanley's wife . . . the loveliest woman in the town." It is part of the convention that each character should minutely describe the others. Lord Biddulph recapitulates the charms of Lady Julia and the description is that of the Duchess of Devonshire. The amateur author always assumes the part of hero or heroine in a first novel. Julia Stanley " is not a perfect beauty, which, if you are of my taste, you will think rather an advantage than not, as there is generally a formality in great regularity of features, and most times an insipidity. In her there are neither. She is in one word *animated nature.*" No better phrase could be found to sum up the youth and energy of the Duchess.

Lord Biddulph soon thought out his wicked scheme, but he quite decently told his friend that it was not proper to trust to paper. Then, without warning, Henry Woodley walks on. Henry Woodley was a melancholy young man who was visiting the ruined paternal estate. He had however another object in view. " Alas ! how blasted is that view," he moans to his friend James Spencer. " Oh, my Spencer, she's lost, lost to me for ever ! " His Julia had married another, and he poured out an endless recital of his woes. He had watched her from a distance. His emotions were violent, but he subdued them and was careful not to stand on the edge of a precipice. She was dressed " in a riding habit of stone-coloured cloth, lined with rose colour, and frogs of the same, the collar being cut open at the neck." The man has the technical precision of a ladies' tailor. Henry Woodley decides to journey on the Continent.

James Spencer's letter in reply is short and business-like. Woodley is not to travel abroad. Spencer has thought out a scheme—a virtuous scheme, but he, too, cannot set it on paper at present. " As a man of fashion, Sir William Stanley would blush to be too attentive to his wife." He glories in delights which should inspire him with disgust, he gambles, he associates with ladies whose reputation is more than doubtful. J. Spencer is like every good young man as described by a woman's pen. He is a prig, and can seldom resist the inclination to moralise. He admits that he once joined in the follies and extravagances of the town. " Thank Heaven ! My eyes were opened before my morals became corrupt, or my fortune and constitution impaired." Julia is to be preserved from the dangers which surround her. " She is totally unhackneyed in the ways of men, and consequently can form no idea of the extreme depravity of their hearts."

The characters having been duly introduced the plot slowly meanders through a couple of volumes. The construction of the novel resembles the child's game known as " general post." Everybody writes to everybody else, and all the letters are identically phrased, sententious, high-flown, and wearisome. The only bright patches are little personal experiences which read naturally because they are the results of actual observation.

Julia describes the business of her day. She is surrounded by mantua-makers, milliners, and hairdressers. She has not a moment to call her own. She lives in " a continual bustle without having literally anything to do." Again the short phrase exactly fits the feverish life of Devonshire House.

" I have had a thousand patterns of silks brought me to make choice, and such colours as yet never appeared in a rainbow. A very elegant man, one of Sir William's friends I thought, was introduced to me the other morning. I was preparing to receive him as a visitor, when, taking out his pocket-book, he begged I would do him the honour to inspect some of the most fashionable patterns, and of the newest taste. He gave me a list of their names, as he laid them on the cuff of his coat. This you perhaps will think unnecessary, and that, as colours affect the visual orb the same in different people, I might have been capable of distinguishing blue from red, and so on ; but the case is quite otherwise ; there are no such colours now. " This your ladyship will find extremely becoming, it is *la cheveaux de la Regne,* but the *couleur de puce* is esteemed before it, and mixed with *d'Artois* forms the most elegant assemblage in the world ; the *Pont Sang* is immensely rich ; but to suit your ladyship's complexion I would rather recommend the *senile mort*, or *la noysette.*"

She is immensely shocked when she fiuds that her mantua maker is a man. Sir William laughs at her ridiculous scruples. " Custom justified everything. Nothing was indecent or otherwise, but as it was the *ton.*" She blushes at her stupidity to blush. " It is so immensely *bore* to blush," cries Sir William. She does not understand the meaning of the strange expression. " Ah ! quel savage ! " cries Sir William, shrugging his shoulders, and composing his ruffled spirits by humming an Italian air. He is tired of the gaucherie of his country wife.

Upon the day she is to be presented at Court she has much trouble over her dress. The French hairdresser, most sought after of his tribe, arrives at eleven in the morning, with a servant and a number of boxes. Sir William begs Monsieur, " for God's sake, to exert his abilities, as everything depends upon the just impression his wife's figure made." In a moment Julia is enveloped in a cloud of powder.

" What are you doing ? I do not mean to be powdered ! "

" Not powdered," repeated Sir William. " Why you would not be so barbarous as to appear without. It positively is not decent."

" I thought you used to admire the colour of my hair. How often have you praised its glossy hue, and called me your nut-brown maid."

" I can bear to see a woman without powder in the summer ; but now the case is otherwise. Monsieur knows what he is about. Don't interrupt or dictate to him."

At last the words are pronounced. " Vous êtes finis, madame, au dernier gout." Lady Julia advances to the glass.

" What with curls, flowers, ribbands, feathers, lace, jewels, fruit, and ten thousand other things, my head was at least from one side to the other full half an ell wide, and from the lowest curl that lay on my shoulder, up to the top, I am sure I am within compass, if I say three-quarters of a yard high ; besides six enormous large feathers, black, white and pink, that reminded me of the plumes which nodded on the immense casque in the castle of Otranto."

" Good God," I exclaimed, " I can never bear this."

She commences to unravel it. The Frenchman wants half a guinea for the dressing and four guineas for the feathers, pins, wool, false curls, *chignion* toque, pomades, flowers, wax fruit, ribbon. She refuses to pay for things she will never wear. " It was the same to him," he replies. " They were now my property. He had run the risk of disobliging the Duchess of D——,[1] by giving me the preference of the finest bunches of radishes that had yet come over, but this it was to degrade himself by dressing commoners."

The Frenchman was paid and pacified. The Welsh maid breaks the laces of her mistress's stays. " You might literally span me. You never saw such a doll. . . . My sides so pinched. But it is the *ton ;* and pride feels no pain. It is with these sentiments the ladies of the present age heal their wounds ; to be admired is a sufficient balsam."

To-day the only attraction of *The Sylph* is in such sidelights upon eighteenth-century life. Aphorisms, not very deep in themselves, give the moral tone of the period. " Marriage is now a necessary kind of barter, and an alliance of families, but little else," remarks one of the ladies of fashion.[2] The husband keeps a mistress from the

---

[1] There was only one Duchess of D—— in the peerage, and that was the author.

[2] In a novel entitled *Pompey the Little* the same thought was set out more explicitly. " His Lordship married for the sake of begetting an heir to his estate ; and married her in particular because he had heard her toasted as a beauty by most of his acquaintance. She, on the contrary, married because she wanted a husband ; and married him because he could give her a title and a coach and six." Well might Dr. Johnson write : " I believe marriages would in general be as happy, and often more so, if they were all made by the Lord Chancellor upon a due consideration of the characters and circumstances without the parties having any choice in the matter.'

first moment of marriage. " What law allows those privileges to a man, and excludes a woman from enjoying the same ? " asks another indignantly. She does not object to the husband's conduct, for " the conduct of a husband cannot discompose a lady of sense."

Husbands and wives gamble until they have lost every penny, and to be seen together is *mauvais ton.* " Whom God joined let no man put asunder is a part of the ceremony, but here it is the business of everyone to endeavour to put a man and wife asunder—fashion not making it decent to appear together."

The society comedies of General Burgoyne and Lady Eglantine Wallace reflect the same cynical sentiments. *The Sylph* may be dismissed with one final quotation which comes from the heart of the author. " While we feel ourselves happy we shall think it no sacrifice to give up all the nonsense and hurry of the *beau monde.*" That was the spirit of the Duchess of Devonshire in her saner moments.

CHAPTER XII

DURING one of her frequent visits to Bath the
Duchess made the acquaintance of an unfortunate
lady who was in bitter distress. The chance
meeting developed into the warmest friendship.
It has often been said that women are seldom good comrades,
one to the other. " I never yet knew a tolerable woman to
be fond of her sex," wrote Dean Swift. He did not look
far, for the suggestion is one of those innumerable libels on
womanhood which are not and never have been true. The
affection of the Duchess of Devonshire and Lady Elizabeth
Foster is a case in point.

In 1780, Lady Elizabeth Foster was twenty-one years of
age, two years younger than the Duchess. By birth she
was a Hervey, a brilliantly gifted family, famous, in the old
phrase, for the beauty of its women and the bravery of its
men. It was also notorious in other directions. Lord
Chesterfield once said that " at the beginning God created
three different species, men, women, and Herveys." The
Mordaunts were eccentric, the Townshends were mad. But
the Herveys moved upon a loftier plane of oddity. They
were neither eccentric nor mad, but simply Herveys. A
law to themselves they certainly did not bow to the laws of

Sir Joshua Reynolds pinxt   E. Bartolozzi sculpt.

LADY ELIZABETH FOSTER

God or recognise the laws of man. In trying to explain the actions of Lady Elizabeth we must remember the family into which she had been born.

The first Earl of Bristol, created Baron Hervey of Ickworth in 1703 and Earl of Bristol in 1714, was a country gentleman of Suffolk. Marlborough and his strong-willed Duchess procured his peerage chiefly on account of his zealous support of the Whigs and the Hanoverian succession. From the date of the patent of his earldom until his death in 1751 at the age of eighty-six he disappeared from public life. Being a dissentient Whig, and looking to Pulteney for leadership, he attempted to oppose Sir Robert Walpole, and Walpole was evidently too strong for him.

His first wife died soon after their marriage. Fifteen years after, in 1695, he married the daughter and co-heir of the third Earl of Suffolk, who was also Baron Howard de Walden. She presented him with eleven sons and six daughters. Thus the world was peopled with Herveys. Their curious ideas and actions were probably inherited from the first Countess, who was vivacious and eccentric, loving pleasure and high play. " The Countess has come out a new figure," wrote Lady Mary Montagu in 1723, " is grown young, blooming, coquette, and gallant. And to show she is full sensible of the errors of her past life, and to make up for time misspent she has two lovers at a time." At the age of sixty-five the Countess had a sudden fit in her sedan chair as she was being carried through St. James's Park. She was dead before succour could be found. The Earl died ten years later. He was " a judicious, dispassionate, just, humane, and thoroughly amiable man," according to his son, who did not speak in such flattering terms of his mother. Decidedly the Countess was responsible for the flaw in the Hervey brain.

The title passed to a grandson. The only son of the Earl's first marriage died in 1723. He was generally believed to be the father of Horace Walpole, whose paternity is an unsolved family mystery. Walpole himself was the only person who never appears to have heard the rumour, for he had an intense admiration for his father the Prime Minister, and he was the only member of his family who really loved that unhappy lady his mother. In any case the Hervey in question left no legitimate heirs, and the succession fell upon the shoulders of the eldest son of the second wife, the much gifted John, Lord Hervey, the bosom friend not only of Sir Robert Walpole but also of Stephen Fox.

Hervey was a clever degenerate. He was always ill, owing, said his father, to that detestable and poisonous plant tea, which had once brought him to death's door, and, if persisted in, would carry him through it. Epilepsy overshadowed his life. In 1742 Robert Walpole jokingly refers to his " coffin-face." Sarah, Duchess of Marlborough, described him as having " a painted face, and not a tooth in his head." He was probably the wittiest and most intelligent man at the Court of George II., and his memoirs are a valuable record of its political and social history. As chamberlain of the royal household he was a trusted friend of the Queen, and he married one of the maids-of-honour, " the beautiful Molly Lepell." Princess Caroline, the King's daughter, fell in love with him ; he quarrelled with Frederick, Prince of Wales, over another maid-of-honour, Miss Vane,[1] and Alexander Pope had words with " Sporus " concerning his attentions towards Lady Mary Wortley Montagu. Lady Molly Hervey was equally celebrated for her wit and charm. She was certainly the most beautiful woman of her time.

Her three sons were successively Earls of Bristol. The eldest died unmarried in 1775. " He was born to the gout from his mother's family, but starved himself to keep it off," was Horace Walpole's explanation. " This brought on paralytic strokes which have despatched him." As a Whig, and a member of the Grafton and North administra-

---

[1] The severest comment on these ladies is recorded by Horace Walpole. " There has happened a comical circumstance at Leicester House ; one of the Prince's coachmen, who used to drive the maids of honour, was so sick of them, that he has left his son three hundred pounds, upon condition that he never *marries* a maid of honour."

tions, he was enabled to secure several valuable appoint-
ments. In 1766 he accepted the office of Lord Lieutenant
of Ireland. Political complications compelled him to
resign before he could reach Dublin, but he managed to
collect his official salary of £16,000, together with a bonus
of £3,000 for " equipage," and also to elevate a younger
brother to the Irish Bishopric of Cloyne. The Herveys
were undoubtedly odd, but no one could call them mad.

Upon his death the second brother, Augustus Hervey,
then an Admiral in the Navy, succeeded to the title and
£20,000 a year. His life had been chequered. As a sailor
his actions were criticised. " He had performed offices
of extreme bravery, and on other occasions had had his
courage called in question," wrote Horace Walpole. " He
had no parts and but a very confused understanding . . .
a most servile and forward courtier." But his chief notoriety
arose from the fact of his marriage with Elizabeth Chudleigh,
who, as mentioned on an earlier page, had angled for the hand
of the Duke of Hamilton. She married the Duke of Kingston
whilst Augustus Hervey was still her husband, and her trial
for bigamy was taken before the House of Lords in 1776.
Augustus Hervey did not long survive the drama in which
he was such a prominent actor. He died in 1779.[1]

There then succeeded to the earldom the third grandson
of the first Earl, and the father of Lady Elizabeth. Frederick Augustus Hervey, born in 1730, was one of the most
extraordinary members of the family. At first he entered
the Inns of Court, but soon exchanged the Law for the
Church. That he had any spiritual inclination for that

[1] He was described as " an active member of Parliament, a candid
friend, and an active member of the Board of Admiralty," to which
an enemy added, " his moral character, his matrimonial transactions,
etc., excite our pity and contempt." The first does not contradict
the second. His union with his wife was dissolved by collusion, and
Horace Walpole said that he received £14,000 for his consent.
When the Duchess of Kingston was presented at Court " Augustus
Hervey chose to be there, and said aloud that he came to take one
look at his widow," quite a Herveyish touch. He quarrelled with
his brother, and alienated the income from the property not strictly
entailed.

calling can hardly be credited, but, as the younger son of a peer, it was likely to be more immediately lucrative than the Bar. His religious convictions were vague, and he can best be described as a thorough-going pagan in complete sympathy with the classical revival. Whilst waiting for preferment he travelled on the Continent, studied art and science, explored Italy and Dalmatia, and was seriously injured whilst investigating a volcanic eruption at Vesuvius. When his brother became Lord Lieutenant he was nominated to the Bishopric of Cloyne, and a year later translated to the much richer See of Derry.

Let us first look at the better side of this very complex individuality. As bishops went in the eighteenth century, he was a good bishop. He visited every parish within his charge, expended the revenues of the see lavishly upon public rather than ecclesiastical service, built roads and bridges, fostered agriculture, opened coalfields. When he became a member of the House of Lords he was an unprejudiced and fair-minded friend of the Irish Catholics, strongly in favour of a Catholic Relief Bill, for he advocated a relaxation of the penal laws, and consistently preached a doctrine of peace and goodwill. As an amateur architect he built great mansions at Downhill and Ballyscullion, which he adorned with the spoils of his Italian journeys. He made lavish gifts to Londonderry, and both that city and Dublin sought to honour him with their civic freedoms.

John Wesley, when at Londonderry, in 1775, met the Bishop, and wrote in his journal: " the Bishop preached a judicious, useful sermon on the blasphemy of the Holy Ghost. He is both a good writer and a good speaker, and he celebrated the Lord's Supper with admirable solemnity. A few days later the Bishop invited me to dinner. . . . The Bishop is entirely easy and unaffected in his whole behaviour, exemplary in all parts of public worship and plenteous in good works." Lord Charlemont described him as " a bad father, bad husband, a determined deist, very blasphemous in his conversation, and greatly addicted to intrigue and gallantry." Charles James Fox called him

" a madman and a dishonest one " ; Barrington found him " a brilliant but purely secular and most unscrupulous politician " ; whilst Jeremy Bentham, who met the Earl at Bowood in 1781, wrote him down " a most excellent companion, pleasant, intelligent, well-bred, and liberal-minded to the last degree. He has been everywhere and knows everything." Bentham truthfully described the fascination of the man, but Lord Charlemont read his character better than pious John Wesley.

At the age of twenty-two Mr. Frederick Augustus Hervey had married Elizabeth Davers, the daughter of a Suffolk baronet. The match was against the wishes of both families. Elizabeth Hervey was a woman of much sweetness of disposition, who was compelled to give way, throughout her troubled life, to the will of her obstinate master. Of this marriage five children were born, two sons and five daughters.[1] The eldest daughter was soon married to Lord Erne, the second, Elizabeth, was married before she was eighteen to a Mr. Foster.

Of John Thomas Foster, of Dunleer, we know very little. He was the son of a clergyman, a member of the Irish House of Commons for Ennis, County Louth, and nephew to Lord Oriel, last Speaker of the House of Commons in Dublin. A contemporary called him " a clownish sot," and that is the only light upon his personality that we have been able to find. The story of this unhappy marriage can be followed in a selection of letters published by the late Mr. Vere Foster, a grandson of Lady Elizabeth Foster, some sixteen years ago, in a volume entitled *The Two Duchesses*. Unfortunately the letters cease where the problem becomes a riddle extremely difficult to solve.

---

[1] The eldest son, Augustus, died in 1796, leaving one daughter, who married in 1798 Charles Rose Ellis, created in 1826 Baron Seaford. His wife died in 1803, and her son succeeded his maternal grandfather as Baron Howard de Walden. The second son, Frederick William, became fifth Earl and first Marquess of Bristol. The eldest daughter, Mary Caroline, Lady Erne, died in 1842 ; Elizabeth became Duchess of Devonshire ; and the youngest, Theodosia Louisa, married in 1795 the second Earl of Liverpool.

N

The marriage took place December 16, 1776. The Hon. Mrs. Hervey found her son-in-law of perfect character, and spoke of him in her letters as "monsieur le sage." The bishop's wife was a simple-hearted and trusting soul. She had no doubts about the happiness of the marriage. Some six months later she wrote to her daughter from Brussels : " I may in plain English tell you a plain truth, that I love you with all my heart, that I think of you continually, and that your whole conduct since your marriage has given me the most perfect satisfaction. . . . Assure Mr. Foster of my sincere affection. He loves you too well for me not to feel a true regard for him, and I flatter myself that a well-founded esteem and perfect harmony will subsist amongst us all as long as we live." In a second letter she repeats that she will never forget her son-in-law's constant and kind attention to her daughter.

In July, 1777, Mr. and Mrs. Foster visited Sheffield Park, in Sussex, the seat of Lord Sheffield. Edward Gibbon, the friend of all the Holroyds, had gone to Paris, and he did not meet Mrs. Foster until later. The Bishop, who had left his see for a prolonged tour on the Continent, sent his blessing to Mr. Foster, and Mrs. Hervey playfully referred to him as " little slimness.' "Assure him of my sincere affection," she told her daughter.

At the end of the year the Bishop settled in Rome. " 'Tis really a life of Paradise," he told Mrs. Foster. " The set of English, too, are pleasant enough, and have their balls, their assemblies, and their conversationes, and instead of riots, gallantries, and drunkenness, are wrapt up in antiquities, busts, and pictures." The news from Ireland was of a peculiarly domestic nature. On October 2, 1777, Frederick Thomas Foster was born, and Mrs. Hervey wrote pages of instruction and warning to her daughter. The Bishop was not so concerned. He was active in many directions. It was reported in England that he was negotiating with the Pretender ; he was certainly sending to the English Foreign Office all the news he could extract from the Irish exiles in Italy. In a letter written about this time by Mrs. Hervey we get a glimpse of the personality of Foster. She had been talking about him with Sir Robert Smyth, who spoke of the young Irishman with much kindness. " He (Smyth) said he was sure he would make a good husband, and I don't remember that we could find any fault, except a little too much reserve and gravity for a young man, but he swore to me that he had seen him at times lively, even to mixing humour very agreeably with his conversation."

The eldest sister, Lady Erne, was at Rome with her husband. Mrs. Hervey admitted that her daughter was far from happy. Lord Erne was a restless and discontented man, who hated society, and yet was dull without it.

The Bishop continued to write the tenderest letters to his daughter. In September, 1778, he was at Castel Gandolfo. "We all hope to winter in Ireland . . . but the poverty of the country is so extreme, rents have so entirely failed that the poor tenants are not able to pay even with daily labor, the bankers in Dublin are failing by dozens, famine stares the country in the face, providence itself seems to fight against us, and the crops threaten to be worse than ever. The pitiful concessions made to us by England will not compensate for a hundredth part of the losses which their multiplied blunders have brought upon us. In the meantime I advise your husband to live very frugally, since if the American war continues, it is almost impossible that Irish tenants in the north should pay above two-thirds of their rent." Mixed with domestic matters he continues to show an active interest in the political world. Lord Erne tries his wife " to atoms by his silly difficulties, and his endless irresolution. Great God, how ill she is matched ! Tell your husband, the antipode of t'other, that I should be much obliged to him for a list of the speakers in our house on the Popish bill, and the sum of the arguments against us." He, a bishop of the Established Church of Ireland, pledges himself, if the bill passes, to bring sixty thousand pounds into Ireland for the purpose of building Catholic cathedrals, churches, and chapels. He is all for

reciprocal toleration, " having seen the bad effects of in-
tolerance through all the great towns of Italy." Then he
sends " sincerest affection " to his son-in-law, and " every
protestation of the truest love " to his daughter. Mrs.
Elizabeth Foster was evidently sobering into a staid matron,
and her mother declared, in a letter from Rome, that she
too lost her wild, youthful spirits at the same age, but hopes
that Elizabeth will never become " grave," which does not
belong to her character.

Within a year everything had changed. The Bishop had
commenced his homeward journey. He wrote, rather
irritably, " What is your husband doing ? I never hear
from either of you." The relationship however remained
very friendly, for he was bringing two cameo rings, one of
Apollo for Lord Erne, the other of Plato, for " our philosopher, John Thomas."

A month later, Augustus Hervey died suddenly without
heirs, and the Bishop of Derry became Earl of Bristol.
And then, for a reason not disclosed in the letters, the perfect
son-in-law went to ruin. In August, 1780, Mrs. Hervey,
now the Countess of Bristol, wrote to her husband that she
is in hourly expectation of her son-in-law Foster, " who has
been more absurd and inconsistent than it is possible to
express . . . a ship totally without ballast, blown
about by every gust of passion, a very tiring companion,
and an insufficient and unsatisfactory friend." The letter
closes : " Colonel H. is on the road at last, and will perhaps
be here to-day or to-morrow, which I am glad of, for I think
f. [J. T. Foster] a——, and it may keep him in better order.
How could I be so mistaken in him ? Yet are not wiser
people than myself mistaken every day ? Adieu. Lady
Hervey still up. Poor Elizabeth better notwithstanding,
and eats a little." On December 6, 1780, her younger son,
Augustus John Foster, was born, and husband and wife
separated for ever.

There is no hint in the correspondence of the reason.
His wife, now, as the daughter of an earl, Lady Elizabeth,
was in monetary distress. At the solicitation of her mother,

Sir Charles Davers, her uncle, came to her aid. " As to the message which you have delivered to me from Mr. Foster, I should be surprised at it from anybody else," wrote the Countess indignantly to her daughter. " He cannot but recollect that I have mentioned the very sums for which he is engaged to me.' Evidently Mr. Foster had been borrowing from his mother-in-law. " I am sure that when he is cool enough to have his judgment operate, he cannot term a conduct severe which is only the steady performance of a very painful duty. He will recollect perhaps that I once consented to your reconciliation, and tried by uniting you under my own very eyes to promote your happiness : his return to me has been a conduct which I confess was the last I should have expected from him : but it has opened my eyes." Yet she advises Lady Elizabeth to give up the children " as they are boys, I advise you to make no opposition to his desire of having them."

" Never was a story more proper for a melancholy novel than poor Lady Elizabeth Foster's," wrote a cousin, Mrs. Dillon, in a letter to her husband dated 1781. " She is parted from her husband ; but would you conceive that any father, with the income her's has, should talk of her living alone on such a scanty pittance as £300 a year ! And this is the man who is ever talking of his love of hospitality and his desire to have his children about him ! Might one not imagine that he would be opposed to a pretty young woman of her age living alone. It is incredible the cruelties that monster Foster made her undergo with him : her father knows it ; owned him a villain, and yet, for fear she should fall on his own hands again, tried at first to persuade her to return to him."

Horace Walpole, always hostile to the Herveys, referred to the scandal, in a letter to Sir Horace Mann, dated December, 1783. The " Count-Bishop," as he describes the Earl of Bristol, after marrying his daughter to the nephew of the Speaker of the Irish House of Commons, became engaged in intricate political negotiations which he did not wish to compromise by a domestic squabble with a powerful faction.

Upon his return from Italy he did not immediately take a hand in the political tangle, but, at the great volunteer convention at Duncannon, in February, 1782, he publicly announced his intention of joining the Londonderry volunteers. His wealth was enormous, and his personal popularity unrivalled, for he received the ungrudging support of the Presbyterians, and the Catholics did not forget that he had always advocated the full franchise, which had hitherto been denied to members of that Church. As an Irish patriot he was worshipped by the democrats, and in England he was suspected of a leaning towards republicanism.

In 1773 he visited Dublin as delegate from County Derry to the national convention. His conduct was in itself a revelation of unbalanced pride and self-will. By his side was his nephew, the notorious " Fighting Fitzgerald." [1] Dressed in the purple robes of his ecclesiastical rank, with

---

[1] Cousin to Lady Elizabeth Foster. George Robert Fitzgerald was the eldest son of an Irish officer in the Austrian service and Lady Mary Hervey, sister to the " Count-Bishop." His life recalls the mad escapades of Lever's heroes. Educated at Eton, he became early notorious for duelling and gallantry. He ran away with the Duke of Leinster's cousin, heiress to £10,000, but she died soon after. In 1773 he was mixed up in a discreditable squabble over an actress at Vauxhall. He then married a second heiress, entered the world of politics, and preached the political independence of Ireland. On his estate in county Mayo he introduced hunting by night. The settlement of the family property brought about a complicated squabble with his father and brother, which he sought to solve by forcibly abducting the brother. For this, after some extraordinary adventures, he was committed to jail. The feud was gleefully taken up by the servants of the two parties, and one of his followers was arrested for wounding a certain M'Donnell belonging to the other camp. In revenge M'Donnell was beset by a hostile crowd of desperadoes, and, in the scuffle, a man was shot dead. Whether or no Fitzgerald fired the shot is far from clear, but he was recaptured, tried for murder, found guilty, and executed at Castlebar, July 12, 1786. When Mr. Creevey was dining with the Earl of Lonsdale, in August, 1827, the Earl said : " You have heard of Mr. Fitzgerald, who was called the Fighting Fitzgerald, whom I used to see a good deal of at Lord Westmoreland's. There was a man who bet a wager he would insult him ; so, going very near him in a coffee-house, he said—' I smell an Irishman ! ' to which the other replied—' You shall never smell another ! ' and taking up a knife, cut off his nose."

gold fringe and large gold tassels, wearing white gloves and diamond knee and shoe buckles, he paraded through the streets of Dublin in an open landau drawn by six beautiful horses in purple harness. He was escorted by a troop of light cavalry, splendidly dressed and accoutred, and mounted on the finest chargers that he could procure. Amidst cries of " Long live the Bishop," and the sound of trumpets, he made an almost royal progress, " never ceasing to make dignified obeisances to the multitude," towards his seat amongst the delegates in the Rotunda. " His ambition for popularity obviously knew no bounds, and his efforts to gain that popularity found no limits."

Horace Walpole's bitterest comments were reserved for " that mitred Proteus, the Count-Bishop, who, I dare to say, would be glad of a red hat, and whose crimes you are infinitely too charitable in not seeing in the blackest light ; nor can they be palliated, but by his profligate folly." Politically, he told Mann, the two Houses of Parliament would not endure a congress of delegates from an armed multitude, and " announced a resolution of maintaining the King's title with their lives and fortunes." In the same letter he spoke scathingly of the Earl as a man. " His immorality, martial pretences, and profaneness, covered him with odium and ridicule. Blasphemy was the puddle in which he washed away his episcopal Protestantism."

In the midst of these excitements Lady Elizabeth's troubles were disregarded and forgotten. Her position was public gossip which Walpole did not allow Mann to forgo. " You may add, that though the daughter of an Earl in lawn sleeves, who has an income of four or five and twenty thousand a year, he suffers her from indigence to accept £300 a year as governess to a natural child. Last year he let his own house in St. James's Square for the usurious rent of £700 a year, and without acquainting his Countess, who is a very respectable woman." Sir Horace Mann was British Resident in Venice, and the " Count-Bishop " was supposed to be in correspondence with the Pretender. " I tell you these things for your information, and for your private ear, that you may keep an eye on the negotiations of such a detestable character."

Lord Bristol's conduct can only be explained by a continuous weakening of brain control accelerated by the publicity which he so evidently enjoyed. At first a good husband and a good father, the letters of his family prove that he gradually became neither one nor the other. And the extraordinary proposals he made relating to his son's marriage, which must be referred to in a later chapter, are a further indication of the traditional madness of the Herveys.

In June, 1782, the Countess of Bristol wrote to Lady Elizabeth Foster from the house in St. James's Square. Lady Erne, the eldest daughter, was much better, and there was a plan for both sisters to live together in retirement to save expense. Lady Elizabeth was staying in Bath with Lady Erne, and a new name suddenly appears in their mother's correspondence. " The Duchess of Devonshire's behaviour on this occasion is heavenly, and your distress will have been I hope at this hour that I am writing, relieved by your father's £100. I am so hurried and agitated that I don't know what to say. Adieu ! my dear children. Is it possible that I am so near having you both with me again, and may I look forward to a degree of comfort and happiness for you this summer ? My blessing on this dear woman."

Whether the little circle spent its summer months together cannot be said. There is no record. But Georgiana, Duchess of Devonshire, was taking a real interest in the affairs of Lady Elizabeth Foster, and discovered a curious method of increasing her new acquaintance's limited income. The *liaison* between the Duke of Devonshire and Miss Charlotte Spencer had resulted in a daughter, mysteriously known as " Miss W." The Duchess exercised a sympathetic control over her husband's child, a fact which speaks volumes for the largeness of her heart and freedom from feminine prejudice and jealousy. Lady Elizabeth Foster was appointed governess to " Miss W.," and, although Horace Walpole imagined it derogatory to her rank to chaperone an illegitimate piece of humanity, the Earl of Bristol did not object so long as it saved his pocket.

In the last days of 1782, Lady Elizabeth and her charge left London for Nice. The child was delicate. On January 5, 1783, the Countess of Bristol wrote from Ickworth Park : " I saw your Duchess several times before I left Town. She behaved like an angel in everything, supported her loss with fortitude and felt it with the utmost tenderness, was warm and interested about you to the smallest trifle, and infinitely kind to me on your account. I rely on her for the first possible tidings of you, but I am quite vexed that she should have found a way of writing to you which I did not, and reproach myself for your being solitarily at Dover with a comfort less than I could have given you."

These few lines reflect not only the love between mother and daughter, but also the strong feeling which had so suddenly grown up between the young Duchess, the most brilliant member of the great world, and the Irish girl, who had been deserted by her husband and robbed of her children.

Her domestic worries had not yet been terminated, for a curious incident is related in the same letter. Lady Bristol had called at Devonshire House to see the Duchess. Whilst there a letter had been delivered addressed to Lady Elizabeth, which indicates that she had already taken up her residence in Piccadilly. The Countess recognised the handwriting. It was that of her son-in-law, Mr. J. T. Foster. She opened it to save postage. There was a reference to a remittance already sent and a receipt to be given. Mr. Foster was beginning to support his wife again. Then came a paragraph which Lady Bristol transcribed. " I would ask you," wrote Mr. Foster to his wife, " if it should not appear to you as a question of idle and impertinent curiosity, whether, since I saw you, you have ever received any pecuniary assistance from either of your parents : if it appears to you in the light I have stated you have only to be silent ; if otherwise, you will give me an answer.—J. T. F." Lady Bristol added a short comment : " This is so extraordinary that I should advise you to answer him by asking leave to answer his question by a question, how he thought you had been maintained for the eight months he had left you without a shilling."

The letter throws a light upon the sufferings of Lady Elizabeth, and makes some of her subsequent actions easier of explanation.

Lady Bristol had her own trials to bear. The " Count-Bishop " was a changed man. " I am sorry that my situation has sat so heavy on your mind," wrote mother to daughter. " I can give you no comfort on that subject except by assuring you that my mind is quite above and out of the reach of the oppression I receive and the insults which accompany it, and that I have pride enough to bear being told that my advice is presumption, and that I am a being so made up of vanity and ostentation as not to be capable of co-operating in so laudable a plan without feeling the least humbled by it ; and even my resentment is softened down into compassion for the frailties of human nature, and for the wreck which warring passions bring upon it."

" My own happiness has long been an empty sound." The despairing cry corroborates Walpole's criticism of the clever man whose brain had given way under the sudden accession of great wealth and a commanding position. The Countess and her remaining daughter were ejected from their home in St James's Square. " The house in town is let for three years to Lord Paget for £700. I have sent servants up to-day to prepare for his coming in. God knows what is your father's plan . . . I must write a line or two to your dear Duchess. Adieu, my dear Bess."

Lady Elizabeth Foster was absent from London for eighteen months. Lady Bristol wrote constantly to Nice. The Earl had taunted her for her vanity and levity of character, two weaknesses which are certainly not revealed in her correspondence. " I own I have never condescended to answer these accusations," she wrote. " I leave my whole life to do so. . . . In the meantime I have accounts from time to time of his great spirits and happiness in everything that is going on in Ireland, and he seems quite unconcerned at having placed me here without a plan, view, object, or improvement of any sort to occupy a mind so much harassed; but I thank God I have objects that are out of his reach, and from which my mind receives such daily comfort that I hope you will not be uneasy for me."

In the same letter " the dear Duchess " is not forgotten. " Your heavenly friend is every day more and more the object of my admiration and love. What a note! from a person apparently absorbed by every worldly pursuit and gratification." Lady Bristol had asked the Duchess to gain the interest of the Duke of Portland for a *protégé*. " Her humanity to him, condescension and real attention to his affairs have been beyond any possible description, as I learn from himself."

Another letter followed in March. The Countess desired her daughter to live in strict retirement whilst at Nice. She was to receive none but a few intimate friends. " Something decisive in your conduct was necessary to make an impression, and to put you upon a new footing." Lady Elizabeth replied that her spirits were low. Her residence in Nice was exile. Then, as her health recovered, her mother asked if she kept a good house, did not study too deeply, and what her expenses were.

" Your father, in his last letter to me, says he intends to add £50 a year to your income, and perhaps £100 if you conduct yourself prudently. I beg you will be very cautious in speaking of him to others, how you throw any blame on him on my account. I leave him to Heaven, and to those thorns that in his bosom lodge to prick and sting him."

" My poor child," cries the afflicted mother, " I have always said that you was made for domestic happiness and duties.'

The Duchess of Devonshire was still in their thoughts. " What you tell me of the Duchess goes to my heart, and will, I hope, be a real comfort to yours. You have done well, most certainly, to leave your interest in her hands; for where could it be so well? But I am pleased at your growing indifference to those matters, and do not doubt but that your affairs will be made easy in some way or other. The Duchess and I do not correspond, but we write sometimes occasionally. She is vastly obliging to me, and treats me like your mother, and I love her as your friend, and beside that, am charmed with her disposition and character."

The two ladies exchanged portraits. Lady Bristol added some advice. A " dangerous Italian " had been referred to in one of Lady Elizabeth's letters. " Avoid him by all means—their whole composition is intrigue." Lady Craven was at Nice. " You must have no intercourse at all there. She is quite undone, and has not an atom of character left."

The " pupil " was mentioned rarely. " I hope Miss W. will answer to all your care and their hopes, and then it will be a pleasant circumstance between you ; but I am sorry she requires strictness : that is against the bent of her indulgent governess, but perhaps even that may have a good effect, and give to a soft heart a firmer texture."

In April Lady Bristol was still troubled about her daughter's health. " Is it that we have been so unlucky as to choose a wrong climate. . .   Or is it still the effects of your long journey and the scene you went through : or a wound that is still festering, though you think it healed ; or the absence from your friends ; or the severe judgment you are passing on yourself ? "

What fault had Lady Elizabeth committed that she should pass " a severe judgment " upon ? In an earlier letter Lady Bristol wrote : " Appease the reproaches of your own mind on the uneasiness you have given me (which I confess has been great) by reflecting that you have it still in your power to make me amends for it. For thou art the sheep that was lost and is found again, and I will rejoice over thee.' Had Lady Elizabeth in any way contributed to the estrangement which had wrecked her home ?

There is no hint to be discovered, but undoubtedly she went to Nice in order to retire from the London world. A suggestion was made that she should take Miss W. to Italy. " I confess it is one thing to care her with you for health to a place of retirement, and another to act as a mother to her all over the world," was Lady Bristol's comment.

Further remarks in these letters suggest more than we can explain. Despite her troubles, Lady Bristol admitted that she had reason for contentment. " You, my dearest child, make a great part of this, for I cannot but flatter myself that you are getting into port again, though the current may be a little against you, and oblige you to work for some time at the oar ; but I do earnestly beg of you not to be discouraged, and to endeavour to steer safely between two dangerous points of too much confidence and too much fear and distrust of yourself. The one would make you imprudent and careless, and the other too anxious and unhappy. You have, I trust, a solid principle on which to form your conduct ; you have now, some experience on which to rectify your sentiments, and I think you have good sense and steadiness enough to lay down the coquette without adopting the prude, and to give an example of a reform which may set your character in its true light and give it all the dignity of virtue, without the severity which would be necessary to a heart viciously inclined, but which is totally improper for yours."

The sentences are long-winded, and, although written in excellent spirit, obscure. They give rise to the obvious thought that Lady Elizabeth could not have been asked to reform if she had been entirely free from accusation or blame.

Lady Bristol acknowledged her daughter's desire " to throw a drop of comfort into my bitter cup." But she added : " When I see you borne away by the defects in your character, or blinded by your own approbation acting so as I think will provoke the censure of the world, I must tell you of it. I hope it is not with *aigreur*, but I own it is with strong feelings, because I see you in a situation in which you have everything against you. I am grieved to say your father's very extraordinary conduct has given rise to many ill-natured reflections on the whole family."

The Duchess of Devonshire is spoken of in many of the letters, and always with affection. " What heavenly good-

nature and attention she shewed you in that £20 ! " writes
the mother. Mr. Foster has sent a letter to his wife. " I
long to hear whether that letter of Mr. F. to you is to
produce anything."

In the autumn of 1783 Lady Elizabeth Foster travelled
with her charge through Italy, arriving in Rome during
November. Despite her retirement she met the most distinguished visitors, the Emperor Alexander I. of Russia
and King Gustavus of Sweden, whilst Cardinal Bernis, one
of her father's old friends, showed her the utmost kindness.
From home the Countess of Bristol had much news to send.
The " dear Duchess " gave birth to her first child, a daughter
named Georgiana Dorothy. Her father, Earl Spencer, died
rather suddenly, leaving his affairs much involved, for he
had been a heavy gambler in late life.[1] Lady Elizabeth's
father-in-law, Dr. Foster, the Rector of Dunleer, also died.
He had been a good friend and his death was regretted.
" I know you will be very uneasy about the poor boys.
. . . As to what you ask me about your father and Mr.
Foster, I suppose they have quarrelled, for I wrote to him
when he was in Dublin to beg he would get your settlement

[1] The third Earl Spencer, in his recollections, quoted Lady Jones
as saying that his grandfather was " the noblest man that ever
existed." The family opinion was more guarded, and Lord Spencer
went on to write : " My mother has also told me that my grandfather's
manners, when he wished to please, were so fascinating that it was
scarcely possible to resist his influence ; at the same time, she
mentioned many instances which proved that he had no command
of temper whatever. From what indeed is notorious, he must have
been a man who never put any restraint upon himself. He succeeded
to an enormous property in money, as well as land, before he was of
age ; and he died at forty-nine years old, very much in debt. He
spent extravagantly large sums in contested elections, and endeavoured to obtain great parliamentary influence, without, as far as
I am aware, ever having been at all eager as a politician ; and
he played very deep. I believe that he was a man of generous and
amiable disposition, spoiled by having been placed, at too early
a period of his life, in the possession of what then appeared to him
inexhaustible wealth ; and irritable in his temper, partly from the
pride which this circumstance had produced, and partly from almost
continued bad health." Duchess Georgiana assuredly inherited
much of her character from her father, although no one ever accused
her of bad-temper.

registered, and his answer was that he would have nothing more to do with Mr. F."

Lady Bristol was becoming inured to the vexations of life. She could not leave Ickworth as she had no town house. She could not even drive out, for the Earl had taken away all the horses without notice. She preached resignation. " Do not let your imagination be too busy, for our real evils are enough and more than we can well cope with. . . . I am well and calm, though I live in a storm."

Lady Elizabeth Foster returned to England in the early months of 1785, and the Duchess arranged that she should take up her permanent residence at Devonshire House. " Miss W." drops out of the story, and the poor child of seven must have been placed in the hands of a less exalted governess.

CHAPTER XIII

The Westminster Election, 1784—Fox and George III.—the East India Company—Lord Hood and Sir Cecil Wray—a tax upon servant girls—the " honest mob "—kissing and canvassing— the Devonshire House party—" Madame Blubber " and " Diana of Hatfield "—the poets intervene—Sam House—attacks upon the Duchess—scenes at Covent Garden—announcement of the poll—enthusiasm of the Foxites—Rowlandson's cartoons —the High Bailiff and the scrutiny—a debate in the House— curious parallels.

THE year 1784 was a period of considerable activity and excitement at Devonshire House. The Duchess had securely established her position as a leader of society, but her political ambitions had scarcely been realised by the world outside the great gates in Piccadilly. She belonged to a family which was hereditarily predisposed to meddle in the affairs of the State. Her friends, in the intervals of their pleasures, devoted themselves whole-heartedly to the business of the nation. The atmosphere in which she moved was thus strongly political. In 1784 the dissolution of Parliament afforded an opportunity for direct intervention. She and her associates were eager for notoriety. For a few weeks they displayed an enthusiasm which would have been commendable had it not been accompanied by an exhibition of high spirits and a lack of restraint which scandalised the more strait-laced members of an older generation.

The election of 1784 differed from many of its predecessors. It was the culmination of George III.'s personal dislike of Charles James Fox, the antipathy every unconsciously dull man feels towards his keener witted neighbour.[1] The

[1] The King believed that Fox had alienated the Prince of Wales from his parents. A contemporary wrote that, being at Court when

Coalition Administration, which included Fox and North, had not proved happy. Fox was amiable, and his ability was unquestioned. Lord North was sweet-tempered, with a considerable sense of humour. Good temper may be a political asset, but a statesman with a sense of humour can never hope to be taken seriously by the body of the electorate. North and Fox, old personal friends of long standing, had been outwardly political adversaries. The tangle of party intrigue brought them together in the same cabinet. Their united efforts were not appreciated. Frankly the country abominated them both, and the Tories determined to wreck the combination at the first favourable complication.

We are not concerned with the merits of Fox's scheme of Indian reform, which naturally aroused the bitter resentment of the East India Company. " Carlo Khan," as the cartoonists named him, succeeded in passing through the House of Commons a measure which threatened to extinguish many of the privileges enjoyed by the great trading corporation. But although the Coalition could command a servile majority in the Commons, it had no control over the upper house. At the direct wish of the King the Lords rejected the Bill. The prerogative of the Crown and the privilege of the House clashed. On March 15, 1784, the Commons dissolved, and the contest was transferred to the people. George III., backed by large secret funds, conducted the operations of the Court party. " Only think, Sir,' said Dr. Johnson. " It was a struggle between George the Third's sceptre and Mr. Fox's tongue." The power and wealth of the East India Company were also directed against Fox.

The verdict was disastrous to the Whigs, and the King's nominees were carried to victory. The country, distrusting North and his coalition, was determined to have a complete change of government. Fox and his party were wholly submerged beneath a flood of hostile influence.

Fox kissed hands, " he observed George III. turn back his ears and eyes just like the horse at Astley's when the tailor he had determined to throw was getting on him." This was before the overthrow of the Coalition.

o

Horace Walpole tells us that " the gold of the East India Company, that nest of monsters," had not a little to do with this disconcerting result. He was honest enough, however, to admit that the old Whig families " have lost all credit in their own countries ; nay, have been tricked out of seats where the whole property was their own ; and in some of these cases a *Royal* finger has too evidently tampered."

As the elections went against the party it became evident that in the City of Westminster Fox would barely retain his seat. In the old parliament the representatives had been Fox and Sir Brydges Rodney. The candidates in 1784 were Lord Hood, a rear-admiral of the Blue, Fox, and Sir Cecil Wray. Hood represented the Court and his return was certain. Wray also came forward as a nominee of the royal interests. The Whigs rallied to preserve their champion from defeat. At their head was the Duchess of Devonshire. Behind her stood George, Prince of Wales. After a campaign which raged like a madness for over six weeks Fox was placed second on the poll, and the Duchess had achieved a fame which extended from Land's End to John o' Groats.

It was an age of youth. Fox, who was first elected a member of the House of Commons when only nineteen, was now thirty-four. His opponent, the younger Pitt, was twenty-five. Sheridan was thirty-three. The Duchess was twenty-seven. The Prince of Wales had not reached his twenty-second birthday. Youth thirsts after fame, and yet fame was not altogether the impelling motive of Fox's friends. With a somewhat frothy affection of patriotism there was a spice of devilry in their attack. They fought for the joy of battle, and were ready to make use of any trick which might turn the scale in their favour.

The women became hero-worshippers. In March, 1784, the Duchess went to the Opera. " I had several good political fights. The Duchess of Rutland said D—— Fox, upon which Colonel St. Leger with great difficulty spirited up Lady Maria Waldegrave to say D—— Pitt."

The Foxites had the advantage of a leader who exercised

a most potent fascination. In Burke's telling phrase. Fox was " a man to be loved."

The Westminster poll was opened at the hustings in Covent Garden on April 1st, a not inappropriate date. Until the close of the poll on May 17th the west end of London continued to groan through an orgy of drunkenness, riot and confusion, " fighting, drumming, screaming, singing, marrowboning, hooting, hurrahing." Charles James Fox, " the Man of the People," directed operations from St. James Street, unabashed by the growing evidence of the elections in all parts of the kingdom that the people wished to have very little to do with him. He denounced the iniquities and extravagance of the East India Company, whilst remaining more firmly in the grip of the Jews and the money-lenders than any member of the Surface family.

King George and his household were equally energetic. Every change in the state of the poll was immediately carried to the monarch. Voters were alternately threatened and rewarded by the members of the royal household. The Prince of Wales, eager to show his contempt for parental authority, rode through the streets wearing Fox's " true blue," the colours of the American Independents. The Heir Apparent spent hours discussing the details of the contest at Devonshire House, where it was broadly hinted the attraction was as much personal as political.

The bitterest venom of the Whigs was expended upon the unfortunate Sir Cecil Wray. Once he had been a Whig and a good friend of Fox. Now he had turned coat and joined the Court. Promptly he was entitled Judas Iscariot, the man who betrayed his master. No accusation was too scurrilous to be used against him. A scheme he had fathered for the better organization of Chelsea Hospital was described as a trick to defraud poor soldiers of their pensions. A discarded proposition to levy a tax upon maid-servants was revived with unscrupulous skill. Fox was not conspicuous for an exalted standard of moral conduct. His friends could hardly be called prudish. But this sug-gestion to tax the poor serving girl froze them with a well-simulated horror. It was an unabashed incentive to vice, a " bounty for bachelors," as Sheridan told the House of Commons. No employer could afford to pay such an imposition. The wretched girls would be discharged from their situations. They would be cast in misery upon the streets. Wray wanted to starve them. Unfeeling monster ! They would be forced in their thousands to join a profession which was old though not respectable. This argument probably had some influence upon the smaller tradespeople of Westminster. Election cries of the same character have been advanced in a modern and more highly educated age. They have always a success, of sorts. The average intelligence of the average voter is to be measured in millimetres.

More forcible arguments were quickly introduced. A large number of sailors from Admiral Hood's ships were imported into the constituency. The Foxites asserted that they were not true mariners, but hired ruffians disguised in sailors' slops. Whatever their original occupation they were undoubtedly desperadoes of the most savage description. And they served their purpose to prevent Whigs attending the polling-station to register votes in favour of Fox. For four days Covent Garden and its neighbourhood lived through a reign of terror. An attempt was made to wreck Fox's local headquarters, the Shakespeare Tavern, and in a pitched battle the sailors were beaten off by the inmates. Then Fox's friends organised " the honest mob," chiefly recruited from the hackney chairmen of St. James's Street. Devoted to Fox and his fellow clubmen, and Irish in nationality, they were even rougher vagabonds than the sailors. A series of running combats between Covent Garden and Piccadilly rendered the streets unsafe for peaceful pedestrians. The sailors endeavoured, in what might be called a " cutting out " expedition, to capture and burn the chairs in St. James's Street. They would have been successful, but the Guards were called out to repel them. These simple soldiers had a personal interest in the election. For the King had ordered 280 to march in a body to the hustings for the purpose of tendering their votes.

The sailors returned to Covent Garden followed by the chairmen with their poles, butchers with their cleavers, brewers and draymen, all the scum of the city. In a second battle the sailors were again defeated. Special constables were enrolled to guard the committee rooms of Hood and Wray. The Justices of the Peace for Westminster were members of the Court party. The constables they appointed were good Tories who did not scruple to goad the Whig voters to a fresh fury. The "honest mob" armed itself anew, and, in the heat of the fray, one special constable inadvertently knocked down and slaughtered a member of his own squad.

Canvassing was not neglected. Fox's election agent approached the expectant voter in a sporting mood.

" I'll lay you five guineas, and stake the money in your hands, that you will not vote for Fox,' he cried.

" Done ! " replied the patriotic householder, who went to the polling-booth and won the bet and the bribe. But a few months earlier the House of Commons had been serenely discussing a bill to suppress bribery at parliamentary elections. Said one member—" the laws against bribery are already too severe. They were repugnant to the general tenour of the constitution." They were certainly repugnant to the general temperament of the electorate, and, it is hardly necessary to add, the bill did not become law.

Fox was less politic on his visits. He called upon one freeholder, a saddler, and asked for his support. " All I can give you, sir, is a halter," said the man impudently, for he was pledged to the Court. " Thanks," replied Fox. " I have no wish to deprive you of what is doubtless a family relic."

Argument and force were not sufficient to win so closely contested a fight. Another form of persuasion was brought into play. Votes were exchanged for kisses. When Pitt's cousin Grenville, " young, genteel, and handsome," visited the poet Cowper at Olney soliciting his interest (this also was in 1784), he kissed the ladies in the parlour, " kissed likewise the maid in the kitchen, and seemed, on

the whole, a most loving, kissing, kind-hearted gentleman."
And Grenville not unnaturally headed the poll for Buckinghamshire. In 1783, John Scott, the young barrister who
became Lord Eldon, was contesting the borough of Weobly
in Herefordshire. " When I got to Weobly, I enquired what
was the usual mode of proceeding there, and I was told that
I was to go first to the house that contained the prettiest girl
in the place, and give her a kiss. This I thought was a
very pleasant beginning. I did so, and then went to the
different voters." He attended the hustings, and addressed
the constituents. " My audience liked the speech, and I
ended as I had begun by kissing the prettiest girl in the place ;
very pleasant, indeed." And young Scott was given the
same reward as young Grenville. Weobly gave him the
first lift on the journey that led to fortune and the Lord
Chancellorship.

Fox proceeded on the same lines, but kissed by proxy.
An old elector once described the lost glories and delights
of the Westminster contest. " Lord, sir, it was a fine sight
to see a grand lady come right smack to us hardworking
mortals, with a hand held out, and a ' Master, how-dye-do,'
and a laugh so loud, and talk so kind, and shake us by the
hand, and say ' Give us your vote, worthy sir, a plumper
for the people's friend, our friend, everybody's friend,'
and then, sir, we hummed and hawed, they would ask after
our wives and families, and, if that didn't do, they'd think
nothing of a kiss, aye, a dozen of them. Lord, sir, kissing
was nothing to them, and it came all natural."

The Westminster Election was by no means the first
occasion upon which the ladies attempted to influence the
British elector. Indeed politics have always had a most
unholy fascination for the female mind. ' Indeed, my dearest
Mary, *I am sick* of the mischief of politics," wrote Mrs.
Delany to Mrs. Port. " They tear asunder the very vitals
of friendship ; set families and friends at variance." But
nobody took the wise old lady's advice. At the Westminster
election of 1774 the Duchess of Northumberland was busy
on behalf of her son Lord Percy. Mrs. Delany said the

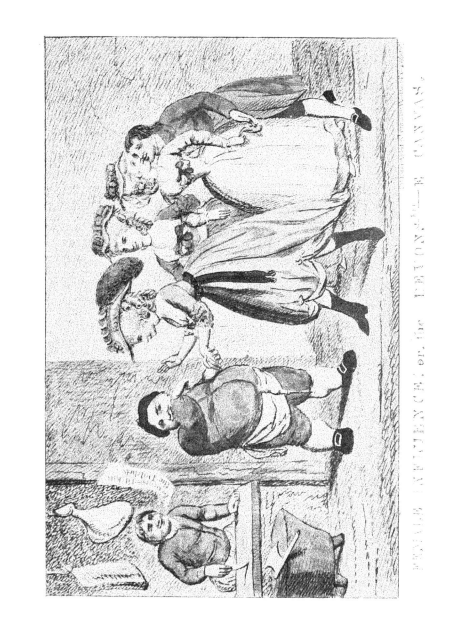

FEMALE INFLUENCE, or the REFORMED GAMBLER.

performance was extraordinary. The Duchess was of the bluest blood. She enjoyed seven baronies in her own right. But she was every day on the hustings, "haranguing the populace." Horace Walpole was disgusted, and pictured her "sitting daily in the midst of Covent Garden. She puts me in mind of what Charles the Second said of a foolish preacher who was very popular in his parish. 'I suppose his nonsense suits their nonsense.'" The Duchess's nonsense suited Westminster, for Lord Percy was returned triumphantly.

Innumerable instances can be collected from the correspondence of the time proving what a valuable aid women were to their political friends. Wrote Sir William Musgrave to Lord Carlisle in 1767 : "I am told Lady S. Bunbury is an indefatigable canvasser in favour of Sir Charles, and with the greatest success. For the greater expedition she undertakes one district while he goes into another, and the other day she alone secured 94 out of 100 voters. I am only surprised how those remaining six could withstand so charming a solicitress."

Lady Strathmore's methods in 1777 were more exciting. The election was at Newcastle. "Her ladyship" (said Mrs. Montagu) "sits all day in the window at a public-house, from whence she sometimes lets fall some jewels or trinkets which the voters pick up, and then she gives them money for restoring them—a new kind of offering bribes."

Fox had many female friends, and, when it became evident that the voting was going against him, he mobilised them all for active service. The Devonshire House *coterie* was eager for the fray. First came the Duchess, then her sister Lady Duncannon, another relation in Lady Carlisle, Lady Beauchamp, Mrs. Crewe, Mrs. Damer the sculptress, Mrs. Bouverie and the three beautiful ladies Waldegrave.[1] Never were such batteries of grace levelled in action against

[1] Westminster was divided into three districts. The Duchess took charge of one, Mrs. Crewe of another, and Mrs. Damer—who was a Whig by conviction—of the third. C. J. Fox was a nephew of Mrs. Damer's brother-in-law, the third Duke of Richmond.

a stolid electorate. Other ladies joined with them in the common cause. Poor " Perdita " Robinson, the wife of a lawyer's clerk, who was mistress to the Prince of Wales, and had indeed been one of Fox's many flames, canvassed energetically for her former lover. That mysterious person Mrs. Armistead, who was probably living with Fox at the moment (for she certainly kept house for him shortly afterwards until they were married eleven years later), was also busily co-operating with the Duchess, although her position was equivocal and she had only shortly before been acting as lady's maid to Perdita. But she was clever, charming, amiable, and devoted to the interests of Fox. These ladies assiduously flattered the electors, who, in their turn, attempted to prove themselves gallant gentlemen.

" Your eyes are so bright, my lady," said an Irish labourer to the Duchess, " that I could light my pipe at them." She never forgot the admiring compliment, which she valued more highly than any she had been paid in the course of her life.

On his side Sir Cecil Wray enlisted his friends to give their aid. The best known of his supporters were Mrs. Hobart (Lady Buckinghamshire), and Lady Salisbury. Lady Buckinghamshire, of " Picnic " fame, a relation of Pitt's, was good-humoured but portly. The Whigs genially referred to her as Madame Blubber. " Diana of Hatfield " could not rival the roguish eyes of Georgiana of Devonshire. As a cynic remarked, with such supporters Wray had little chance.

Undaunted by the frantic abuse of the " Morning Post " and " Morning Advertiser," the Whig ladies continued their labours. Fox needed all their help. It was evident that Hood would head the poll, and the fight narrowed between Fox and Wray for the second seat. The voters came forward slowly. Sir Nathaniel Wraxall describes in his Memoirs the methods of Devonshire House. " The party was driven to new resources, and the Duchess of Devonshire restored the fates of the Whig champion. The progress of the canvass thenceforward is amusing. The centre of the voters for

J. K. Sherwin delt. et sculpt.

MRS. ROBINSON

Westminster having been exhausted, the only hope was in exciting the suburbs. The Duchess instantly ordered out her equipage, and with her sister, the Countess of Duncannon, drove, polling list in hand, to the houses of the voters. Entreaties, ridicule, civilities, influence of all kinds were lavished on these rough legislators ; and the novelty of being solicited by two women of rank and remarkable fashion took the popular taste universally. The immediate result was that they gallantly came to the poll, and Fox, who had been a hundred behind Sir Cecil, speedily left him a hundred behind in return. An imperfect attempt was made on the hostile side to oppose this new species of warfare by similar captivation, and Lady Salisbury was moved to awake the dying fortunes of the Government candidate. But the effort failed ; it was imitation, it was too late ; and the Duchess was six-and-twenty, and Lady Salisbury thirty-four ! These are reasons enough, and more than enough for the rejection of any man from the hustings."

The poets of the hustings came to the same conclusion as Wraxall :

> A certain lady I won't name,
>   Must take an active part, sir,
> To show that Devon's beauteous dame
>   Should not engage each heart, sir.
>
> She canvass'd all, both great and small,
>   And thunder'd at each door, sir
> She rummaged every shop and stall—
>   The Duchess had been before her.

According to the *Cornwallis Correspondence* the Duchess was indefatigable in her canvass for Fox, visiting " some of the most blackguard houses in the Long Acre " by eight o'clock in the morning. Walpole did not neglect to chronicle the current gossip. " Mr. Fox has all the popularity in Westminster ; and, indeed, is so amiable and winning that, could he have stood in person all over England I question whether he would not have carried the parliament. The beldams hate him, but most of the pretty women in England are indefatigable in making interest for him; the Duchess of Devonshire in particular. I am ashamed to say how coarsely she has been received by some worse than tars. . . . During her canvass the Duchess made no scruple of visiting the humblest of the electors, dazzling and enchanting them by the fascination of her manner, the power of her beauty and the influence of her high rank, and sometimes carrying off to the hustings the meanest mechanic in her own carriage."

Whilst Rowlandson gave his pencil to Hood and Wray, Fox claimed the aid of some of the cleverest rhymesters of the moment, including that clever writer of *vers de société* Captain Morris. One of the most enthusiastic supporters of " Carlo Khan " was a licensed victualler known as " honest Sam House." Because his figure offered itself as an easy butt for the caricaturist Sam House became almost as celebrated as the Duchess herself.

> Brave bald-headed Sam, all must own is the man,
>   Who does canvas for brave Fox so clever;
> His aversion, I say, is to *small beer and Wray* !
>   May his bald head be honour'd for ever, for ever !
>   May his bald head be honour'd for ever !

The doggerel does not reach any exalted inspiration, but it was bellowed through the streets by the heated partizans of Fox, who were ready to make away with any kind of beer—strong or small. In one of Rowlandson's caricatures Sam House is shown in the boudoir at Devonshire House drinking afternoon tea with Fox and the Duchess. " Lords of the Bedchamber " is the title, and on the wall of the apartment hangs Sir Joshua's portrait of the Duke.

Rowlandson's charming drawings are of greater artistic value than the floods of insipid verse inspired by Fox's gallant little band. The Tories denounced the ladies in terms which surpassed the most imaginative outbursts of Billingsgate. The calumnies hurt the Duchess. She told Lady Spencer that she was unhappy beyond measure, and abused for nothing, but that her friends insisted that she must continue the canvass having once commenced. " I am really so vex'd at the abuse in the papers that I have no heart left."

The Whig poetasters compared her to all the goddesses of antiquity.

> Let slander with her haggard eye,
> No more blaspheme with hideous cry
> Th' indefatigable dame.

But slander did blaspheme when it became known that she had given a butcher a kiss in exchange for his vote. Mr. W. T. Whitley, in his valuable *Life of Gainsborough*, refers to this well authenticated tradition. In a circumstantial account of the incident discovered in a contemporary journal the Duchess is said to have kissed not one tradesman but seven. The correspondent affirmed it to be true from his own knowledge. The Duchess heard that seven friends of Lord Hood, the opposition candidate, were to dine at the house of one of their number in Henrietta Street. The dinner was at three, and at half-past four, when the bottle was circulating freely among the company, the Duchess's coach drew up at the door. The fair visitor was shown in, and after having " in her easy way removed the awkwardness of the master of the house," without further ceremony placed herself at the head of the table. A toast was proposed, and drunk in Irish whisky punch, to which the Duchess was unaccustomed, and after the toast she proceeded at once to business by asking the company to vote for Mr. Fox. The tradesmen declared that they would do nothing unless they were bribed—a kiss was proposed and the lady kissed each man in turn round the table. " And now," said the Duchess, " you will all vote for Mr. Fox to-morrow ? " " Not to-morrow," replied the host, " because we have already voted for Lord Hood to-day, but we will vote for Mr. Fox at the next election." " And have I then been imposed upon ? " said the indignant lady. " Have I been kissing seven dirty tradesmen for nothing ? " The men, now angry in their turn, declared that they could give the kisses back, and proceeded to do so, and the Duchess had a hard matter to escape into the street, where she found her carriage surrounded by a noisy and abusive mob, whose members by this time had become acquainted with the whole story of her adventure.   Against this strange story must be set a statement in another journal that the supposed Duchess who went about endeavouring to gather votes for Fox was " a painted girl with a due share of impudence for the undertaking, dressed up and put into a genteel hired equipage with a ducal coronet and a servant in livery, who assumed the name and rank of a celebrated lady, and in that manner boldly drove about the town."

This was a slander the poets neglected.   But the veritable duchess did not confine her approval to a single trade, if we are to believe another poet, who wrote :

" Devon's fair kiss seduced a blacksmith's vote."

Her conduct was criticised and approved in every metre :

Her mien like Cytherea's dove,
Her lips like Hybla's honey ;
Who would not give a vote for love,
Unless he wanted money ?

The voter who held out was probably rewarded by both. Another author was less classical :

Hail, Duchess ! first of womankind,
Far, far you leave your sex behind,
With you none can compare ;
For who but you, from street to street,
Would run about a vote to get,
Thrice, thrice bewitching fair !
Each day you visit every shop,
Into each house your head you pop,
Nor do you act the prude ;
For ev'ry man salutes your Grace,
Some kiss your hand, and some your face,
And some are rather rude.

The ladies who assisted in the canvass were not forgotten :

Fair Devon all good English hearts must approve,
And the Waldegraves (God bless their sweet faces),
The Duchess she looks like the sweet Queen of Love,
And they like the three Sister Graces.

The Whigs declared that though their cause was assaulted by all the power of the Court, it was defended by Virtue and Beauty. The Tories became sarcastic when the failure of " Diana of Hatfield " and Madame Blubber became apparent.

See modest Duchesses, no longer nice
In Virtue's honour, haunt the sinks of Vice ;
In Freedom's cause, the guilty bribe convey,
And perjur'd wretches piously betray :
Seduced by Devon, and the Paphian crew,
What cannot Venus and the Graces do ?—
Devon, not Fox, obtains the glorious prize,
Not public merit, but resistless eyes.

Early in May it was evident that Fox was safe. But the excitement increased rather than abated. The fair canvassers were determined and redoubled their efforts.

Then come, ev'ry free, ev'ry generous soul,
That loves a fine girl and a fine flowing bowl,
Come here in a body, and all of you poll
'Gainst Sir Cecil Wray.

C. P. Moritz, a German tourist from Berlin, was visiting the sights of London in May, 1784. In his journal he gives a comical picture of the antics of an electioneering cockney crowd.

"While I was in London, what is called ' hanging day ' arrived. There was also a parliamentary election. I could only see one of the two sights, and therefore, naturally, preferred the latter, while I only heard tolling at a distance the death-bell of the sacrifice to justice. Mr. Fox is one of the two members for Westminster ; one seat was vacant, and that vacancy was now to be filled. Sir Cecil Wray, whom Fox had before opposed to Lord Hood, was now publicly chosen. The election was held in Covent Garden, a large market place, in the open air. In the area before the hustings immense multitudes of people were assembled, of whom the greatest part seemed to be of the lowest order. To this tumultuous crowd, however, the speakers often bowed very low and always addressed them by the title of ' gentlemen.' The moment Sir Cecil Wray began to speak, this rude rabble became all as quiet as the raging sea after a storm—

only every now and then rending the air with the parliamentary cry of ' Hear him ! hear him ! ' Even little boys
clambered up and hung on the rails and on the lamp-posts ;
and, as if the speeches had been addressed to them, they
also listened with the utmost attention, and they, too, testi-
fied their approbation of it by joining lustily in the three
cheers, and waving their hats. At length, when it was nearly
over, the people took it in their heads to hear Fox speak and
everyone called out, ' Fox ! Fox ! ' I know not why, but
I seemed to catch some of the spirit of the place and time,
and so I also bawled ' Fox ! Fox ! ' and he was obliged to
come forward and speak. When the whole was over, the
rampant spirit of liberty, and the wild impatience of a
genuine English mob, were exhibited in perfection. In a
very few minutes the whole scaffolding, benches, and chairs,
and everything else were completely destroyed, and the mat
with which it had been covered torn into ten thousand long
strips or pieces, with which they encircled multitudes of
people of all ranks. These they hurried along with them, and
everything else that came in their way, as trophies of joy :
and thus in the midst of exaltation and triumph, they
paraded through many of the most populous streets of
London."

All this is the purest Eatanswill. There is little difference
between the behaviour of Fox, Wray, and Hood, in the
Westminster Election of 1784, and the antics of Horatio
Fizkin and the Honourable Samuel Slumkey in their efforts
to capture the representation of the borough of Eatanswill
some forty years later. Dickens has been accused of fantasti-
cally exaggerating and caricaturing the social life of England
in the early nineteenth century. But the more we learn of
the real England of the Georgian age the more we realise
that Dickens drew from the life, and was, in the broadest
sense, a realist. There is little difference between Moritz's
account of the children of Covent Garden, and that picture
in the *Pickwick Papers*, of a member of Slumkey's committee, speaking from a back window of the Town Arms
to an assemblage of six small boys and one girl, "whom he

PROCESSION TO THE HUSTINGS AFTER A SUCCESSFUL CANVASS.

dignified at every second sentence with the imposing title of ' men of Eatanswill,' whereat the six small boys aforesaid cheered prodigiously."

During the progress of the poll both parties professed themselves well satisfied. Pitt wrote to Wilberforce: " Westminster goes on well, in spite of the Duchess of Devonshire and the other women of the People." But the women of the people, who were also the most beautiful ladies of Mayfair, redoubled their efforts. On May 17 the polling-booths were closed, to the great relief of the more respectable and quieter inhabitants of the ancient city. Hood was elected with 6,694 votes ; Fox came second with 6,233 ; Wray, the defeated candidate, was not far behind with 5,998. The Duchess and her friends had undoubtedly turned the scale. They had not been strong enough to place Fox at the head of the list, but they saved him from defeat. We know that Fox and his friends with all their assurance were not certain of victory, for the Man of the People had taken the precaution of standing for the Scottish constituency of Kirkwall.

The verdict of the electors was greeted with a frenzied enthusiasm by the Foxites. A hostile critic, a certain John Robinson, whose comments are quoted in one of the Reports of the Historical Manuscripts Commission, wrote that Fox, after the declaration of the poll, was drawn in his chariot " by a low mob of about one hundred to Devonshire House, but what will astonish you is that Colonel Stanhope, Mr. Hanger, and Mr. O'Byrne were on the coach box, and that Mr. George North, Mr. Adam, and a third person stood as footmen behind. How disgraceful ! "

That was the opinion of the Court party which recognised a heavy defeat. Earl Russell gives an ampler description of the wild proceedings after the announcement of the poll. " At the end of the election there was an immense crowd collected for the chairing of Mr. Fox. He mounted a car ; an immense procession followed, which was closed by the state carriages of the Duchesses of Portland and Devonshire, drawn by six horses each. Mr. Fox descended from the car at Devonshire House, where the Prince of Wales and the Duke and Duchess of Devonshire were assembled on a temporary platform to receive him.   He dined at Willis's Rooms, where he made a warm speech on the subject of the election.   On the same day the Prince of Wales, after attending the King at a review at Ascot, rode up St. James's Street in his uniform, and afterwards went to dine at Devonshire House wearing Mr. Fox's colours and a laurel branch for victory.   On the following day more festivities took place. The Prince of Wales gave a grand breakfast which lasted from noon to six o'clock in the evening."

The Memoirs of Mrs. Papendick give a detailed chronicle of the rejoicing. " The procession was conducted in the following manner : bands of music, cat-call noises of all kinds, emblems of every insignia of a fox, twelve carriages of commoners and gentry, with their best liveries and every possible decoration, twenty-four horsemen, dressed in blue coats and double brass buttons, waistcoats and shorts of buff kerseymere with the same buttons, silk stockings, dress shoes, yellow or gold shoe and knee buckles, buff Woodstock gloves and cocked hats ; the horses handsomely caparisoned, and ornamented with fox tails and heads, flowers, etc., and buff and blue ribbons.   These made a dashing appearance.   Then came Fox in a decorated chair, with a good brass band preceding him, and immediately following the chair were twenty-four gentlemen of the Prince of Wales's household, of whom George Papendick was one and my cousin Hugh, page of presence, was another, in the same dress, Quentin bringing up the rear on a beautiful horse, strikingly ornamented with appropriate designs. Then six of the carriages of the nobility in state costume. The Devonshires last, with four footmen behind, two at each door, and a groom at the head of each of the six horses, the five other carriages having each their complement of attendants.   Last of all came the state carriage of the Prince with the full equipment of horses, men, dress, etc.   The procession of course began from the hustings, St. Paul's, Covent Garden, from whence it went three times round the square or market, down King Street and Bedford Street, just round Mrs. Clay's corner into the Strand. At the corner of Cockspur Street and Pall Mall, all the barrels for refreshment were put ready by the brothers Harry and Sam House, the great spirit merchants of the day, the former of whom had expended on the election £25,000, and the latter £15,000. Then on went the procession to the courtyard of Carlton House, which it went round three times, the Prince and his friends being at the windows to cheer Fox ; then down Pall Mall, up St. James's Street to Devonshire House, where a platform had been erected against the wall in Piccadilly, within the courtyard, for the Prince and others to receive Fox, and whither they had arrived in private carriages through back streets. The Duke would not permit anyone to enter his gates save the member himself, although he had allowed his Duchess to waste his property and degrade herself. After shouts of welcome the day's sports ended there. At the public-houses it finished with the needful."

Other remembrances of the tumultuous riot are equally interesting. From Fox's chariot floated a large banner bearing the words " Sacred to Female Patriotism." Colonel Hanger, who acted as coachman, was dressed in coachman's coat, hat, and wig. Colonel North was not less successful in acting as footman. Unfortunately, North, despite his Foxite predilections, was comptroller to the household of Queen Charlotte. When his royal mistress heard the story of the day's doings North was dismissed from his office. " I do not covet another person's servant," was the bitter remark.

Wraxall is a valuable eye-witness of the jubilation. He had been an active participator in the election, although his account was not written until many years later. " The Whigs " (he said) " were not to be disappointed of their ovation. The exultation of those gay times forms a strange contrast to the grim monotony of our own. Fox, after being chaired in great pomp through the streets, was finally carried into the courtyard of Carlton House. The Prince's plume was on his banners in acknowledgment of princely partisanship."

" The carriages of the Dukes of Devonshire and Portland,

each drawn by six horses, moved in procession, and Fox's own carriage was a pile of rejoicing Whiggism. On its boxes and traces, and where they could, sat Colonel North, afterwards Lord Guilford ; Adam, who but a few years before wounded the patriot in a duel ; and a whole cluster of political friends, followers, and expectants. The prince came to the balustrade before the house to cheer him ; with a crowd of fashionable people. Fox finished the triumph by a harangue to the mob, and they in return finished by a riot, an illumination, and breaking Lord Temple's windows.

" But the festivities were scarcely begun. The prince threw open his showy apartments to the nobility, and gave them a brilliant *fête* in the gardens, which happened to be at its height just when the king was passing through St. James's Park in state to open the new parliament. The rival interests were within a brick wall of each other, and their spirit could not have been more strangely contrasted than in their occupations. But nights and days to those graceful pursuers of pleasure and politics alike knew no intermission. On that evening the celebrated beautiful and witty Mrs. Crewe gave a brilliant rout, in which ' blue and buff ' were the universal costume of both sexes ; the buff and blue were the uniform of Washington and his troops, and imprudently adopted by Fox to declare his hostility to the Government. The prince himself appeared in the party colours. At supper, he toasted the fair giver of the feast in the words ' True Blue and Mrs. Crewe ! ' The lady, not unskilfully, and with measureless applause, returned it by another, ' True Blue and all of you.' "

The most pleasing relics of this famous election are the drawings and cartoons of Rowlandson. In " Liberty and Fame introducing Female Patriotism to Britannia " the Duchess, representing " Female Patriotism " is escorted by a bevy of typical Rowlandson nymphs to Britannia, who extends a wreath of laurels to the fair lady, whilst the lion looks on in surprise—as well he might at such an apparition of beauty. " She smiles, Infused with a Fortitude from Heaven," is the somewhat inept quotation from Shakespeare

Fox's Cotillon in St James's Market.

to explain the simpering grace of the Duchess. Then follows a panegyric on the " Man of the People."

> Let envy rail and disappointment rage,
> Still Fox shall prove the wonder of the age !
> Triumph and Fame shall every step attend
> His King's best subject and his country's friend.

So far as it concerns the Duchess the history of the Westminster Election is now closed. She had become the popular idol of the London mob, and one of the ruling spirits of a powerful political clique. Fox, however, was not able to take his seat as the elected representative of the city of Westminster for nearly a year, although he sat in the House of Commons as member for Kirkwall. For Westminster Sir Cecil Wray demanded a scrutiny, and, giving this as a reason, the High Bailiff of Westminster, a good Tory, withheld the return to the writ.

Notwithstanding repeated motions in the House, which were defeated by the ministerialists, the matter was allowed to stand in abeyance for eight months. Soon after the meeting of Parliament in 1785 the High Bailiff was called to the bar of the House and examined, when he gave evidence that the scrutiny would probably last more than two years. Mr. Welbore Ellis, a Whig, moved that the Bailiff should be commanded to make a return to the writ, but an amendment to the contrary effect was carried by 174 votes to 35. Motions and counter-motions were repeatedly brought forward with similar results, until on March 3 the Pitt party was beaten by 162 to 124. The direction to the High Bailiff was then issued, and he was compelled to make his return that Hood and Fox had been elected ten months previously. Fox then brought an action in the Court of Common Pleas against the High Bailiff for not returning him in the first instance, laying his damages at £100,000. The action was tried before Lord Loughborough, and the jury gave Fox the verdict with damages of £2,000. This sum Fox allotted to the Westminster charities.

The scrutiny occupied two months, and cost £18,000. Fox was confirmed in his seat. Feeling ran high in the House of Commons. Although far more serious questions required the urgent attention of the legislators, long nights were wasted over petty wrangles between Fox and Pitt and their respective followers.

"Base and shuffling tricks had been practised at the election," cried Lord Mulgrave in the small hours of one excited debate. The assertion was true, and applied with equal force to both parties. But Fox was immediately on his feet to repel the charge. From the official reports can be extracted the following sample of his parliamentary manner.

"The noble lord held a language which no gentleman, no man of honour, which no man of feeling, and which no man fit to be received into the company of gentlemen ought to hold; indeed he trusted every gentleman, every man of honour, and every man of feeling who heard him, would have been ashamed to have held such language."

An almost exact parallel to this style of oratory will be found in Mr. Chadband's address to the Snagsby family. The preacher built up his resounding periods with the same careful economy. Pointing to Jo, he described the wretched urchin as a brother "devoid of parents, devoid of relations, devoid of flocks and herds, devoid of gold, of silver, and of precious stones. . . . My friends, may I so employ this instrument as to use it to your advantage, to your profit, to your gain, to your welfare, to your enrichment.'

Lord Mulgrave was not smashed so utterly as the poor law stationer. But Lord Mulgrave was touched. There was no personal meaning in the words, he explained rather lamely, "no ill will to the Right Honourable gentleman as an individual. Everything he said had been said by him merely on a public view of the question."

Again the pages of Dickens furnish a parallel. In the first chapter of the transactions of the Pickwick Club we are told that Samuel Pickwick's theory of tittlebats aroused the envy of Mr. Blotton of Aldgate. Pickwick referred to the vile calumnies of a disappointed haberdasher amidst the loud cheers of his partizans. Mr. Blotton repelled the hon. gent.'s false and scurrilous accusation with profound contempt. " The hon. gent. was a humbug."

" The Chairman felt it his imperative duty to demand of the honourable gentleman, whether he had used the expression which had just escaped him, in a common sense.

" Mr. Blotton had no hesitation in saying, that he had not—he had used the word in its Pickwickian sense. (Hear, hear.) He was bound to acknowledge, that, personally, he entertained the highest regard and esteem for the honourable gentleman ; he had merely considered him a humbug in a Pickwickian point of view. (Hear, hear.)

" Mr. Pickwick felt much gratified by the fair, candid, and full explanation of his honourable friend. He begged it to be at once understood that his own observations had been merely intended to bear a Pickwickian construction. (Cheers.) "

Dickens had not sat in the Press Gallery of the House of Commons in vain. His satire is in many instances scarcely distinguishable from actual fact.

CHAPTER XIV

Fashionable activity—the Duchess harshly criticised—dinners and breakfasts—men of the World—drink—the passive Duke— his appearances in the House of Lords.

THE Westminster Election represented but one side of the life of the Duchess. To write the biography of a woman of society is difficult, if not impossible. Her days are taken up by innumerable occupations of the moment which in themselves are of the slightest consequence. In the memoirs and newspapers of the period are a thousand references to the doings at Devonshire House and the public appearances of its mistress. We read of great concerts in the state rooms of the Piccadilly mansion, attendances at the masquerade balls of the Pantheon and Ranelagh, water *fêtes* given by the Savoir Faire club. Horace Walpole complained that he would have to relinquish the joys of polite life, professing to find the pleasures of the town dull and unentertaining. But the ladies of the *monde* found a peculiar zest in a daily round which was not a common task.

The Duchess was always before the public. She won the election for Fox, and then left London for her usual visit to the country, Althorp, Chatsworth, and the other palaces in the north. But in November she was back again within the Bills of Mortality, and, when Blanchard, the Frenchman, went up in a balloon from Park Street, Grosvenor Square, she and Mrs. Crewe held the retaining cords and gave the signal to " let go."

Her critics never agreed in discussing her character. Walpole told Mason that " you may bear to have filth thrown at you, when it is at the Duchess of Devonshire and at the youngest and handsomest women in town. It is a polished, sweet-tempered age." Walpole worshipped at the shrine although he had not high belief in female virtue or wisdom.

In 1781, Miss Burney was talking to an old friend, Mr. Crutchley. " Among other folks, we discussed the two rival duchesses, Rutland [1] and Devonshire. ' The former,' he said, ' must, he fancied, be very weak and silly, as he knew that she endured being admired to her face, and complimented perpetually, both upon her beauty and her dress ' : and when I asked whether *he* was one who joined in trying her,

" ' Me ! ' cried he, ' no, indeed ! I never complimented anybody ; that is, I never said to anybody a thing I did not think, unless I was openly laughing at them, and making sport for other people.'

" ' Oh,' cried I, ' if everybody went by this rule, what a world of conversation would be curtailed ! The Duchess of Devonshire, I fancy, has better parts.'

" ' Oh yes ; and a fine, pleasant, open countenance. She came to my sister's once, in Lincolnshire, when I was there, in order to see hare-hunting, which was then quite new to her.'

" ' She is very amiable, I believe,' said I ; " for all her friends love and speak highly of her.'

" ' Oh yes, very much so ; perfectly good-humoured and unaffected. And her horse was led, and she was frightened ; and we told her *that* was the hare, and *that* was the dog ; and the dog pointed at the hare, and the hare ran away from the dog ; and then she took courage, and then she was timid ;—and, upon my word, she did it all very prettily ! For my part I liked it so well, that in half an hour I took to my own horse, and rode away.' " Crutchley fell under the personal charm of a pretty woman, but found her prattle tiring.

To understand the characters of men and women we must know the petty details of their daily life. " Tell me

[1] Mary Isabella Somerset, 1756–1831, wife of the 4th Duke.

when a man rises, and I will tell you what he is " may be suggested for the consideration of all future biographers. Men and nations plan the twenty-four hours in different ways, and the varying methods of apportionment are the result of personal and racial temperament. Watts sneered at the sluggard, quite forgetting that in all probability the wretched man's desire for more slumber was based upon physiological necessity.

> Early to bed and early to rise
> Makes a man surly and gives him red eyes.

Sir Richard Burton says that most barbarians sit deep into the night in the light of the moon and a camp fire, and will not rise until nearly noon. In the East they wholly disregard a proverb ever on the lips of those who believe that, as truth is only to be found at the bottom of a well, virtue can seldom be attained after breakfast.

Our great-grandparents were not early risers—at least not in London. In 1782 breakfast was rarely served before ten o'clock, and often not earlier than eleven. The afternoon, from three to six, was devoted to shopping and visiting. Dinner became later and later. During the reign of Queen Anne the hour was usually two. When George III. was a young man many of the nobility dined at four or five. In 1790 the Marquis of Landsowne sat down soon after six, and at the end of the century the fashionable hour was between six and seven. Lord Eldon mentions that the Duchess of Gordon invited Pitt to dine at eight. The minister begged to be excused as he had accepted an invitation at a slightly advanced hour to sup with the Bishop of Lincoln. Probably the Bishop belonged to a conservative school and dined early, forgetting, in the lines of Pope,

> The family that dines the latest
> Is in our street esteemed the greatest.
> But latest hours must surely fall
> 'Fore him who never dines at all.

The Duchess had hours of her own. In 1777, according to Lady Sarah Napier, " the pretty Duchess of Devonshire, who by all accounts has no fault but delicate health in my mind, dines at seven, summer as well as winter, goes to bed at three, and lies in bed till four : she has hysteric fits in the morning, and dances in the evening ; she bathes, rides, dances for ten days and lies in bed the next ten : indeed I can't forgive her, or rather her husband, the fault of ruining her health." Mrs. Sheridan, in Bruton Street, retired to rest about three, and breakfasted at two in the afternoon.

After dinner the men and the women of the fashionable world sought the real interest of the day. Many went to the theatre, where the performances commenced about seven and concluded between eleven and twelve. After the drama and opera came balls, masquerades, parties, receptions, and social pleasure. At an assembly no one dared to arrive until eleven, wrote Lady Coke, who fixed six o'clock as the only proper dinner time. Walpole, always querulous, complained that the fashionable hour at Vauxhall became later and later, for no man of the world could appear before eleven or half-past.

The House of Commons regularly sat all night. When the Speaker left the chair, the members refused to go home, and settled down in the clubs along St. James's Street. The Duke of Devonshire spent most of the night at Brooks's, and was known as "a pillar of the Club." His rubber of whist ended, a hot supper of boiled mackerel, while in season, constantly awaited His Grace at four o'clock. Then he strolled up the hill to Devonshire House, and passed a cobbler who had his stall at the corner of Jermyn Street. " Good night,' said the Duke on his way to bed. " Good morning, your Grace," replied the shoemaker, taking down his shutters.

Most of the men were incapable of intelligent speech at such an hour. When Creevey dined with Sheridan he told his wife that they both " got a little bosky." This was a private festival in honour of Bacchus. Public manners were no better. Sir Gilbert Elliot (afterwards first Earl of Minto), writing also to his wife, March 8, 1787, tells her, that from the opera he went on to Mrs. Crewe's, " where there was a large party and pleasant people, among them, for example, Tom Pelham, Mundy, Mrs. Sheridan, Lady Palmerston, etc., besides all which were three young men so drunk as to puzzle the whole assembly." One was a Bridgeman, the second a Greville, the third a Gifford, and, if their conduct " puzzled " the ladies if does not appear to have disgusted them. In the same letter Sir Gilbert continued : " Men of all ages drink abominably. Fox drinks what I should call a great deal, though he is not reckoned to do so by his superiors, Sheridan excessively, and Grey more than any of them, but it is in a much more gentlemanly way than our Scotch drunkards, and is always accompanied with lively clever conversation on subjects of importance. Pitt, I'm told, drinks as much as anybody."

Some of these men enjoyed their hectic careers. But the majority suffered from a chronic ennui. The legendary " spleen " of the travelling Englishman of the wealthier classes dates from this period of extravagance and idle excitement. " Prince " Boothby, one of the best known members of the Devonshire House set, at last became so tired of everlastingly dressing and undressing that he shot himself in despair. Another, Fitzpatrick, said with truth of his associates :

> Whate'er they promised or professed
> In disappointment ends—
> In short there's nothing I detest
> So much as all my friends.

They bored each other, and were bored by themselves. The wise drank heavily in order to sparkle " on subjects of importance." The foolish drank to escape solitude. For, left to themselves, they were,

> In the remotest wood and lonely grot
> Certain to meet that worst of evils, thought.

This verse cannot be applied to the fifth Duke of Devonshire, who remained a silent man living very much in a world of his own.

A friend wrote that his most striking characteristic was an " unambitious passiveness." Nothing disturbed him. A curious instance was related by Miss Monckton to Miss Burney. " The Duke of Devonshire was standing near a very fine glass lustre in a corner of a room, at an assembly, and in a house of people who were by no means in a style of life to hold expense as immaterial ; and, by carelessly lolling back, he threw the lustre down and it was broke. He showed not, however, the smallest concern or confusion at the accident, but coolly said, " I wonder how I did that ! " He then removed to the opposite corner, and to show, I suppose, he had forgotten what he had done, leaned his head in the same manner, and down came the opposite lustre ! He looked at it very calmly, and with a philosophical dryness, merely said, " This is singular enough ! " and walked to another part of the room, without either distress or apology."

This action was a combination of shyness and good manners. The Duke was as celebrated for the one quality as the other. " His modesty produced in him such an habitual shyness as to make him renounce every degree of action that required an effort," wrote Sir Robert Adair in the memorial appreciation printed by the second Duchess. " There can be no apter illustration of this defect in him than the abilities he discovered whenever he fairly put himself forth ; but this so rarely happened that the proofs we have of them stand rather as desultory instances of what he could perform, than as the systematic exertions of the Statesman and the Patriot."

Horace Walpole asserted that the Cavendishes considered the office of Prime Minister in any Whig administration as one of the perquisites of their family. But, if Walpole admired the Duchess, he did not worship the Cavendish clan and was hostile to its political influence. Although the Duke was admitted to all the inner deliberations of the party he seldom actively advanced the cause. As late as 1804 the Prince of Wales, in writing to Croker, refers to a " kind of cabinet with whom I used to consult. They were the dukes of York, Portland, Devonshire, and Northumberland, Lord Guilford (that was Lord North), Lords Stormont, Moira,

and Fitzwilliam, and Charles Fox." But the Duke was
certainly a silent member.

He spoke but twice in the House of Lords, and the first
occasion has a certain interest in modern politics. Lord
Shelburne moved to enquire by whose advice His Majesty
had dismissed the Earls of Carmarthen and Pembroke from
the lieutenancy of their respective counties. These peers
had annoyed the Crown by their voting in the House.
Such degradations were not infrequent. In 1798, at a
meeting of the Whig Club, the Duke of Norfolk gave as a
toast : " Our Sovereign—the People. The People—our
Sovereign." He was immediately dismissed by the Crown
from his office of Lord-Lieutenant of the West Riding of
Yorkshire. Fox gave the same sentiment, and Pitt struck
his name off the list of the Privy Council.

The Duke protested against such actions. " He spoke
with a firmness and facility which seldom accompanies a
first essay in Parliament, and with a moderation, and an air
of sincerity, which seemed to gain the hearts of those without the bar, while an universal silence reigned within. He
said that he had hitherto been silent on all the political
questions on which he had voted, because speaking in public
was not agreeable to his temper ; but he observed that such
was the deplorable situation of his country that he should
think himself base, degenerate, and unworthy the name and
character of a man who had its interests at heart, if he
remained any longer without an express and unequivocal
declaration of his sentiments."

This speech was made in 1780. The Duke was a young
man, only thirty-two years of age, in the plenitude of his
powers, admittedly a man of considerable intellectual
ability. Territorially and politically he was in a position
to move vast forces into action. The condition of Great
Britain became more deplorable as time passed on. In
1781 Benjamin Franklin sportingly offered Edward Gibbon
materials for writing a history of the Decline of the British
Empire, and the only comment Horace Walpole could make
was that the historian would be overburdened with facts.

England called for the aid of every son.   Yet eighteen years elapsed before the Duke of Devonshire rose to deliver his second and last speech in the House of Lords.   His friends said that he was diffident of his powers.   Had he not been born in the purple a rougher word would more justly have been applied to his inaction.

CHAPTER XV

Edward Gibbon and the Cavendishes—his early love—life in
Bentinck Street—nights at the Pantheon—" Sappho " of
Welbeck Street—Gibbon at Devonshire House—Lady Elizabeth
Foster—" A bewitching animal "—Gibbon dreams of marriage
—his proposal to Lady Elizabeth.

THE author of the *Decline and Fall of the Roman
Empire* had long been a welcome visitor to Devonshire House.   Dr. Johnson died in the last month
of 1783, and Gibbon easily succeeded to his place
as the chief representative of literature in the Piccadilly
salons.   Every coterie possessed its author.   Wrote Walpole
cynically, " every woman has one or two authors planted in
her house, and God knows how they water them." [1]   But
Gibbon was not a tender plant, and needed little care.   The
former captain in the Hampshire Militia was a gentleman of
some property in the south of England.   His political
friends gave him a share in the spoils, and, to quote a bookseller, the guinea volumes of his history sold across the
counter like threepenny pamphlets.

He was nearly forty when the first volume of the *Decline
and Fall of the Roman Empire* established his reputation.
At forty a bachelor is least manageable.   A younger man
can usually be snared in matrimony by the expert fowler,
but at forty the hardened bachelor has generally learned how

[1] Walpole did not love authors.   " You know in England we read
their works, but seldom or never take any notice of authors.   We
think them sufficiently paid if their books sell, and of course leave
them to their colleges and obscurity, by which means we are not
troubled with their vanity and impertinence."   This feeling is
reflected in the Duke of Cumberland's greeting of Gibbon.   " Well,
Mr. Gibbon.   Still, scribble, scribble, scribble ? "

to preserve a cool head and firm foot in the midst of enticing traps and pitfalls.

With both Georgiana Cavendish and Elizabeth Foster Gibbon could boast an early acquaintance. In March, 1763, writing to his stepmother from Paris, he recounted a chance meeting with old Mrs. Poyntz, the grandmother of the future Duchess. Mrs. Poyntz had been the bosom friend of the elder Gibbon's second wife, told the boy that she adored his new parent, demanded answers to a hundred questions, and revealed to the youth all the secrets of her family. Mrs. Poyntz was a gossipping and not wholly discreet matron. But she was good company, knew everybody in Paris, including the daughters of Louis XV., and Gibbon admitted that after an evening with the " most impertinent old brimstone," Madame Geoffrin, he was delighted to renew his conversations with his cheery fellow-countrywoman.

The Herveys he had met even earlier. In 1758, soon after his twenty-first birthday, he wrote from New Bond Street to his father respecting a suggested introduction to the drawing-room of the beautiful Molly Lepel, mother of three successive Earls of Bristol and grandmother of Lady Elizabeth. Her assembly was an excellent one for a young man to frequent. There was no card playing, he explained to his father, but very good company and very good conversation. In these bright surroundings the future historian probably saw the little Elizabeth in the arms of her nurse.

Rousseau said that Gibbon was too cold-blooded a young man for his taste. During the twenty-five years which elapsed between 1758 and 1783 Edward Gibbon passed through a variety of experiences which formed a character distinctly interesting to any woman. He had suffered from " a spiritual malady " which he contemplated afterwards with the complacency of a convalescent. Living in semi-exile in Lausanne he had met Rousseau and dined at the table of Voltaire. He had fallen in love, and scrambling to the bank, found himself permanently chilled but otherwise uninjured. A man who has loved once and then renounced the sex for ever is a standing challenge to all womankind. They examine him with the eye of a physician in the presence of an abnormal case. They compare diagnoses. And naturally they do their best to effect a cure.

> Tôt ou tard il faut aimer,
> C'est en vain qu'on façonne ;
> Tout fléchit sous l'amour
> Il n'exempte personne.

The verse is not startling, but it was the best the boyish Gibbon could offer to Suzanne Curchod. In an age of sentimentalism Gibbon wallowed in the excess of his feelings with as much self-congratulation as Rousseau himself. He implored Mademoiselle Curchod to fly with him to the altar. He wandered about Lausanne, stopping the peasants, and demanding, at the point of a naked dagger, whether a more adorable creature than Suzanne Curchod existed. Suddenly he became jealous. The minister's daughter was smiling upon other admirers. He would accept no excuse. " Infidelity is sometimes a weakness, duplicity is always a vice," he wrote sententiously in his diary. The phrase might have been conceived by Rousseau. At least it was good imitation. " She has opened my eyes to the character of women. Her action will preserve me for a long while from the seductions of love." Suzanne Curchod crushed her affection for the Englishman, and married the banker Necker, soon father of the woman who became famous as Madame de Staël. Gibbon was not absolved from blame. Rousseau criticised his behaviour. The youth left Lausanne for London, and, in course of time, fathered the *Decline and Fall of the Roman Empire*.

In 1773 Gibbon entered into possession of a house in Bentinck Street, Manchester Square. " My little Palace is absolutely the best house in London," he cried with glee. Madame Necker had been married nine years. Gibbon was too engrossed in his studies to think of marriage. He sat in his snug library at the back of the house and defied Cupid to break in. He did not disdain the amusements of the frivolous, and left his folios to attend those gatherings in the ballrooms of the Pantheon which were frequented by " peers, peeresses, honourables, and right honourables, jew-brokers, demi-reps, lottery insurers, and quack doctors." Walpole called the show " Balbec in all its glory;" Gibbon wrote that " in point of Ennui and Magnificence it is the wonder of the Eighteenth Century and the British Empire." He was keenly interested in the frail beauties who forced their entrance into these glittering halls, by the aid of the swords of their friends. Holroyd was told in a gossiping letter that the proprietors had decided to exclude " all beauty unless unspotted and immaculate." But many gentlemen were " friends and patrons of the Leopard Beauties. Advertising challenges have passed between the two Great Factions, and a bloody battle is expected Wednesday Night." The philosopher, having disposed of Christianity in the fifteenth and sixteenth chapters of his book, laid down his pen and walked through Cavendish Square to the Pantheon in Oxford Street. The great mind unbent to a passing sensation which employed his fellow-authors, the rival poets of the town.

Said Elegance in the dialogue:

> I glory to keep on a *virtuous course*,
> And hate the very name of a *divorce ;*
> Besides the *Managers* admit none in,
> That e'er were known to have committed sin ;—
> The needy dame, who makes of love a trade,
> These *Realms of Virtue* must not dare invade ;
> The company's selected from a class
> Too chaste to suffer *demi-reps* to pass.

Reason retorted :

> But, *Elegance*, before more time you waste,
> Inform me, pray, are all these Ladies chaste ?

The reply is decided :

> Chaste l surely yes.—The Managers admit
> None but chaste Ladies in their virtuous set ;
> Besides, if any one a slip hath made,
> A *Title* hides it with oblivious shade.

These verses passed from hand to hand, and although the " demi-reps " were never excluded, the reputation of the

Q

Pantheon did not decline.   Lunardi gave a special ball in honour of the Duchess of Devonshire.

The historian frequented the other fashionable masquerades of the town, including the notorious gatherings conducted by Mrs. Theresa Cornelys at Carlisle House in Soho Square. " A gay varied scene," he tells his stepmother, adding : " there will be another next week, at the Haymarket, and yet *we* have had no Earthquake,"—this soon after the terrible upheaval at Lisbon.

The years fled rapidly, but Gibbon remained a bachelor and man of the town.   His friends wished to see him married. There was some talk of a Miss Fuller, known to the circle as " Sappho."   " Ah ! my Lady, my Lady," he wrote to Mrs. Holroyd in 1773.   " What rumours have you diffused in the regions of Bath relating to Sappho and your Slave." Sappho came up to town, and lodged in Welbeck Street, the next street to Bentinck Street.   It was a case of siege. " Sappho is very happy," wrote Gibbon.   Sappho's uncle refused to allow her to attend a masquerade at the Pantheon arranged by Boodle.   Gibbon was a member of Boodle's Club, and probably offered an escort.   In 1774 the affair was becoming desperately earnest.   " You see how serious I am in this business.   If the general idea should not startle Miss, the next consultation would be how, and where the Lover may throw himself at her feet, contemplate her charms, and study her character.   After that we may proceed to other more minute enquiries and arrangements."   The letter was ominously signed " Benedict Gibbon," and " Sappho " never reigned over the house in Bentinck Street.

In 1774 Georgiana Spencer became Duchess of Devonshire, and in the same autumn, Gibbon was elected Member of Parliament for Liskeard.   Three years later the Countess Spencer told her daughter that " Mr. Gibbon is more the fashion than ever Hume was," maternal advice of the deepest importance to an ambitious lady who desired to collect all the celebrities of the town under her roof.

Although his grandfather was a tradesman there was not much doubt concerning the historian's gentility.   For

amongst his ancestors was that Lord Saye and Sele of whom
Shakespeare speaks in "Henry VI." And of his perfect
manners and the charm of his conversation there could be no
question. He had not been educated at Lausanne in vain. His
talk was like his dress—rich, refined, and in the best of good
taste. The Duchess was able to compare the member for
Liskeard with the old sage of Fleet Street. Dr. Johnson was
a professional conversationalist. Gibbon, commencing as
a gifted amateur, reached an equal perfection in a different
manner. "Johnson's style was grand, and Gibbon's elegant;
the stateliness of the former was somewhat pedantick,
and the polish of the latter was occasionally finical. Johnson marched to kettledrums and trumpets; Gibbon moved
to flutes and hautboys; Johnson hew'd passages through
the Alps, while Gibbon levelled walks through parks and
gardens." George Colman, the author of this criticism,
also spoke of their clothes. Johnson clad himself in a suit
of rusty brown and black worsteds. Gibbon strutted about
in flowered velvet with a bagwig and a sword. Gibbon was
often light and playful. Johnson was never light, and his
playfulness was elephantine in its graces. Gibbon smirked,
smiled, tapped his snuffbox, "rounded his period with the
same air of good-breeding. . . . His mouth, mellifluous as
Plato's, was a round hole, nearly in the centre of his visage."
Gibbon was ugly. That was an additional recommendation
to the goddesses at Devonshire House. Beauty never objects
to shine with an increased brilliancy in the presence of the
poor Beast.

"Le petit Gibbon was not only a man of merit and a
good historian, but, far more, amiable, a talent for conversation, and amusing." So wrote Madame du Deffand.
Let the being who wishes to bask in the good graces of
Madame du Deffand's successors note her careful distinction.
We are all men of merit, and some of us dream that we are
capable historians. But we are not all amiable, and few of
us are amusing; whilst the talented conversationalist is a
pearl amongst diners-out.

The earliest reference to the Duchess in the Gibbon

correspondence will be found in a letter addressed to Colonel Holroyd in September, 1779. The Duchess, her mother, and her sister, were returning from Spa. At Ostend they embarked on a sloop bound for Calais. During the short voyage the boat was attacked by two French cutters. The ladies, according to Gibbon, behaved like heroines during the engagement, in which the enemy were successfully beaten off. Such events were to be expected in the course of foreign travel. Gibbon himself, in crossing from Dover to Calais, had to wait until the Channel was free of an American privateer waiting in the Downs for English shipping. Writing from Dover to his friend Holroyd, May 6, 1777, he complained of his detention at that port. " Last night a small Privateer, fitted out at Dunkirk, with a commission from Dr. Franklin, attacked, took, and has carried into Dunkirk road, the Harwich Pacquet. The King's Messenger had just time to throw his despatches overboard ; he passed through this town about four o'clock this afternoon on his return to London. As the alarm is now given, our American friend will probably remain quiet, or will be soon caught ; so that I have not *much* apprehension for my personal safety.' Gibbon had a serene conviction that the British Navy was equal to its task. Patiently he waited in his inn at Dover until the seas were declared clear. " Our American friend," the *Surprise*, commanded by a Captain Cunningham, and carrying four guns and ten swivels, did remain quiet. Gibbon crossed to Calais in peace, and went on to Paris. But the incident shows that Continental travelling in the eighteenth century was attended by a real danger, although the French and American sailors never murdered passengers in the ships they attempted to destroy.

There is no reference to Devonshire House and its inmates in Gibbon's letters from 1779 to May, 1782. Then Gibbon abruptly tells his stepmother about Lady Elizabeth Foster. He mixes her up with a number of other matters. The Board of Trade has been suppressed. That is a disaster, for he has lost his appointment. There is not less work to do, for the office was a sinecure. But the income was

£800 per annum. He bears his loss with philosophy,
" I enjoy health, friends, reputation, and a perpetual fund of
domestic amusement." He is heartily tired of the House of
Commons, and casts a longing eye towards the delights of
the season at Bath. Then he adds : " Are you acquainted
with Lady Eliza Foster, a bewitching animal ? You have
heard of my Gouts, they are vanished, and I feel myself
five and twenty years old. . . . Next Wednesday I conclude my forty-fifth year, and in spite of the changes of
kings and Ministers, I am very glad that I was born."
Artless philosopher. Did he imagine that his stepmother
could not easily penetrate his childish screen of subterfuge,
his House of Commons and Board of Trade, his gout and
a season at Bath ? " I am very glad that I was born. . . .
I feel myself five and twenty years old." That is to say
exactly two years older than the bewitching animal. The
bachelor who had jilted Suzanne Churchod, and forgotten
the Sappho of Welbeck Street, had at last been caught.
The poor Beast had fallen in love.

In 1782 Lady Elizabeth Foster's separation from her
husband was but recent. Gibbon, who had frequently met
her in the company of " the dear Duchess " at Devonshire
House, and also during the season at Bath, knew the full
story. When he suggested to his stepmother a visit to
that fashionable resort he was probably dreaming of Lady
Eliza, for she was at the wells with her sister Lady Erne in
the summer of that year. Early in 1783 she was at Nice
with " Miss W." Ten months later Gibbon, writing from his
retreat at Lausanne, reminded Lord Sheffield of " your
later flame, and our common Goddess, the Eliza." In
1784 he wrote to Lady Sheffield : " should you be very much
surprised to hear of my being married ? Amazing as it
may seem, I do assure you that the event is less improbable
than it would have appeared to myself a twelvemonth ago."
He evidently considered that he was still a marriageable
man.

On her way home from Italy, in October, 1784, Lady
Elizabeth rested at the town on the shores of Lake Leman.

Gibbon reported that she was " poorly in health, but still adorable (nay, do not frown !), and I enjoyed some delightful hours by her bedside."

At this moment can be dated an incident which shows how fascinated Gibbon had become. " The whole story is probably an invention," says Dr. Birkbeck Hill, who could not allow that Gibbon was ever in an undignified position. The modern biographer is only content if he can invest his subject with a halo. The attitude represents the difference between biography and autobiography. The official biographer will not admit that his idol possesses any faults. But in autobiography the vain adventurer loves his readers to understand that in odd moments if he has not actually broken all the commandments he has at least cracked the tables of stone. Rousseau set the example in his notorious and untrustworthy Confessions.

" Cette malheureuse passion m'a toujours fait une peine infinie," wrote Gibbon once. Who was the lady who fluttered his heart ? Madame de Genlis said it was Madame de Crousaz. But Madame de Crousaz, who married the Baron de Montolieu in 1786, protested publicly in the "Gazette de Lausanne." She did not deny the story, but she denied that she took a part in the little comedy. Many years later Lady Elizabeth, when in Rome, told the Chevalier Artaud. And in 1843 a correspondent to the *Gentleman's Magazine*, who signed himself " J. R." and evidently was closely connected with the Herveys, made the following communication :

" One of the anecdotes obtained from the Duchess (of Devonshire) by direct information to M. Artaud (" C'est de sa bouche que l'a entendue de cet article ") places our eminent historian, Gibbon, in rather a ludicrous position. While yet Lady Elizabeth Foster, and her first husband still living, she accompanied her predecessor in the higher title, the mother of the present Duke of Devonshire, on a continental tour, and in June, 1787, spent some time at Lausanne, where Gibbon, a fixed resident, formed a welcome part of their society. Beautiful in person, fascinating in manner, still under the age of thirty, and wholly unsuspicious of all amorous intentions from a man of the mature years, ungainly figure, and love-repelling countenance of her learned countryman, she checked not the exuberance of her admiration of his genius. She had unconsciously, however, made a deep impression on his imagination, and one morning, more especially, just as he had terminated his elaborate performance, and fully elated with the achievement, as he so glowingly describes the sensation in his life, he invited the seductive lady to breakfast, when, in a bower fragrant with encircling acacias, he selected for her perusal various attractive passages of the concluding sheets. Enchanted with the masterly narrative, her ladyship complimented him on the completion of his task, with a charm of language and warmth of address which the author's prurient fancy, much too licentiously indulged, as his writings prove, converted into effusions of tenderer inspiration. Falling on his knees, he gave utterance to an impassioned profession of love, greatly to the surprise of its object, who, recoiling from his contact, entreated him to rise from this humiliating posture. Thus recalled to cooler feelings, but prostrate and helpless from his unwieldy form, he vainly sought to regain his feet ; and the delicate female, whose first astonishment soon yielded to irrepressible laughter at the ridiculous scene, was equally powerless at affording relief ; until, at length, with the aid of two robust women, he was reseated in his armchair, from which, it was pretexted, he had accidentally slipped. Thus, " Solventur risu tabulæ ; " a laugh at once dissolves the lover's enchantment, and with it evaporated the lady's anger, genuine or simulated. For, with the Duchess, this demonstration of the Promethean puissance of her charms, which could quicken into vivid emotion such a mass of seemingly inert matter, was, on reflection, felt rather as a homage than an offence, and, though unfruitful of effect in evoking, as in the opera of *Zémir et Azor, or Beauty and the Beast*, a responsive flame, it, in no sense, interrupted her friendly intercourse with Gibbon."

The story was widely spread. Lord Brougham said the

lady was Suzanne Curchod, which was absurd, for Madame Necker was in love with Gibbon. The only error is in the date. Madame de Genlis spoke of Madame de Crousaz, but she became Madame de Montolieu in 1786. The affair must have occurred in 1784, for there were good reasons why Gibbon could never dream of going on his knees to her after her permanent settlement at Devonshire House.

Madame de Genlis recites her anecdote with malicious wit. "I hear from Lausanne," she wrote, "that Mr. Gibbon, who has established himself there for some time, is very successful and extremely well received. He is (so I am told) much stouter, and so prodigiously large that he has much difficulty in walking. With that strange figure and face so well known as belonging to him, Mr. Gibbon is infinitely gallant, and he has fallen in love with a very amiable person, Madame de Crousaz. One day, finding himself alone with her for the first time, he wished to seize so favourable a moment, and suddenly threw himself on his knees, declaring his love in the most passionate terms. Madame de Crousaz replied in a way to remove from him all temptation to re-new this pretty scene. Mr. Gibbon's face bore an air of consternation, yet he remained kneeling in spite of repeated invitations to resume his seat ; he was motionless and silent. " But, sir," Madame de Crousaz repeated, " pray get up." " Alas ! Madame," at length replied this unfortunate lover, "*je ne peux pas.*" In fact, the size of his body prevented his rising without help. Madame de Crousaz rang, and said to the servant who came : " *Relevez M. Gibbon.*"

" Poor man ! " was the comment of a sympathetic heart. " Had he gone down on his knees to me I would not have been so cruel."

Dr. Hill is sure that if Gibbon was really rejected by Lady Elizabeth Foster he would never have talked to her about his gout. There is no conviction in such an argument. Surely if a man reveals to a goddess the pain in his heart he may also explain to her the pain in his toes. The two remained fast friends. " We call her Bess," he writes in 1792.

" As seducing as ever," is the judgment of 1793. " I now sigh for your return to England, and shall be most bitterly disappointed if I have not the pleasure of seeing you in that happy island—yourself and the most amiable of Duchesses, before the end of the autumn. . . . Excuse brevity, and address a classic prayer in my behalf before some statue of Mercury, the god of travellers." This was written at Lausanne on the eve of his journey to London. He gave up all thoughts of marriage. " At fifty-four a man should never think of altering the whole system of his life and habits."

Gibbon was a very likeable man in a drawing room. He was " perfectly modest " which Walpole, who was not modest, considered a quality. He was also—like all modest men—rather vain ; vain, cried Walpole in disgust, " even about his ridiculous face and person." A clever man who suffers from vanity is generally acceptable in the boudoir where vanity usually stands at the elbow. Drunkards are flattered when a wise brain gives way to the bottle.

CHAPTER XVI

Marriage of Lord George Cavendish—birth of Lady Georgiana—
Lady Elizabeth Foster and the Duchess—readings in history—
Ferdinand Christin's story—a curious position—*Les Liaisons
Dangereuses*—Rousseau—his vogue in England—a woman's
author—the return to nature—*La Nouvelle Héloise*—Julie
and Saint Preux—the effect of *Emile*—the Cavendish
nursery—Fanny Burney's observations—Gibbon's admiration
—"tout comprendre c'est tout pardonner"—public life and
private morals.

IN one of George Selwyn's gossiping letters to Lord
Carlisle, extraordinary mixtures of an Anglo-French
jargon which embraced all the current small talk of the
town, a few lines dated May 21, 1781, cast a new light
upon the domestic problems at Devonshire House. " Lord
G. Cavendish is to be married to Lady Eliz. Compton.[1]
it being agreed that the Cavendish family must be continued
from his loins. *M^e la Duchesse fait des paroles, mais non
pas des enfans.* I hear that she has won immensely *et avec
beaucoup d'exactitude, ce qui n'est pas fort ordinaire aux
dames.*"

Upon the surface there does not appear to be any link
between the two items. But few secrets could be kept from
the eyes and ears of " Bosky " and his associates. The first
sentence dealt with the contemplated marriage of the Duke's
younger brother, which Anthony Storer also reported to
Lord Carlisle ; the second, to the Duchess's notoriety at
the gambling-tables of Mayfair. Selwyn passed easily and
without explanation from one subject to the other as naturally interrelated. The marriage was probably postponed

[1] Elizabeth (1760–1835), only daughter of Charles Compton,
seventh Earl of Northampton.

owing to the death of Lord Richard Cavendish in September. In the February of 1782 Selwyn incidentally remarks that " Lord G. Cavendish is to be married to-morrow, and at St. George's Church, as I am told, and they go to Chiswick to perpetuate the race of Whigs and Cavendishes." Unfortunately there is a long gap in the correspondence for 1783, and we cannot give Selwyn's announcement of the birth of a daughter to the elder branch of the ducal house.

The Duchess's eldest child, Georgiana Dorothy, was born July 12, 1783. Of her joy at the event there can be no doubt. Lady Duncannon's first child had been born August 31, 1781. The Duchess was at Plymton at the time, and, in her own words, wanted to elope to see the brat, envying her sister's happiness, even wishing to take the place of the servants who nursed the babe. When she became a mother, her disposition showed no change. She was annoyed when the Duchess of Portland suggested that though Georgiana was a very pretty child she was too much of a Cavendish to be a handsome woman. She wrote a gushing letter of affection and friendship to her " dearest angelic Bess," Lady Elizabeth Foster, describing the christening. A second daughter, Harriet Elizabeth, was born August 29, 1785. The heir came five years later, May 21, 1790.

During the whole of this period, with the exception of some absences abroad, Lady Elizabeth Foster was living with the Duchess. The affection of these two ladies for each other was exceedingly deep and very sincere. They were drawn to each other by the bonds of a similar misfortune. The Duchess had passed through years of wretched unhappiness, which accounted for much of her erratic behaviour. In 1782 James Hare told the Earl of Carlisle that " the Duchess of Devonshire looks very handsome, and seems easier and happier than she used to be." The shipwreck of Lady Elizabeth's life has already been set forth. The Duchess was a woman of impetuous emotion, and a heart full of feeling. She found in the Irish M.P.'s wife the friend of her dreams, and offered her an unfailing welcome. In 1782 they were exploring the beauties of Devonshire, and reading together

Rousseau's *Confessions* and *Les Liaisons Dangereuses* by Choderlos de La Clos.[1] The Duchess described her companion as a poor little soul, the quietest little thing in the world. She said that Lady Elizabeth would sit in a corner of the room, or be sent out of the room, or do whatever one pleased with her. In 1784 they were at Chatsworth, and in September together entertained Dr. Johnson. In the autumn of 1786 they were again at Chatsworth with a gay party comprising Sheridan, Hare, and Fitzpatrick. A rubber of whist was made up of " Bess " and the Duke against the Bishop of Peterborough and Dr. Moore. At Christmas they were in Buxton, all " reading mad." Lady Elizabeth and the Duchess were engrossed in the Memoirs of Madame Maintenon and Pascal's *Provincial Letters*. The Duchess told her mother that she was half inclined to turn Jansenite, discusses the merits of the " grand Arnauld," dives into Madame de Sévigné, refers to Boileau, Lafontaine, and the Apocrypha. The Duke, who was with them, studied Cæsar, Plutarch, Vertot's *Histoire des revolutions arrivées dans le gouvernement de la république romaine*, and Richard Hooker's *Ecclesiastical Polity*. Imagine this eager little household conversationally ranging over every subtlety of human thought and conduct, weighing the crystal logic of Pascal, the wit of the mistress of the Hotel de Carnavelet, the massive Elizabethan prose of Richard Hooker, and the stern lessons of Plutarch's lives. And the party was in full youth—the best if not the only time to read great books. The Duke was thirty-eight, his consort twenty-nine, Lady Elizabeth Foster only twenty-seven.

That is the brighter side of the picture. There is another, and it can be best stated by simply quoting a portion of a lengthy letter written by Ferdinand Christin to the Princess Tourkestanow, and dated June 18, 1817. The letter is reprinted by Paul Lacroix from the *Archives russes*, published in Moscow about thirty-three years ago. The opening paragraph has already been referred to in an earlier

---

[1] Both fresh from the press, being published in the same year.

chapter, and the facts are open to criticism. But the remainder of the story fits in with the little other contemporaries have written, and we can agree with Paul Lacroix that
the history is substantially true.

"I knew the Duchess of Devonshire very well," writes
Christin. "Both before the birth of her son, and also in later
years when he was known under the title of Marquis of
Hartingdon. This Duchess was the prettiest, the most
amiable, and the most gracious of women. She had the
secret of attracting the adoration of everyone who knew her.
The birth of the young duke of to-day cost his father one
hundred and fifty thousand pounds sterling. I was a witness
of the business. Lady Spencer married her daughter against
her will to the Duke of Devonshire, without question the
first match in the three kingdoms for fortune as well as for
birth. The girl's tears were not able to prevent an engagement so advantageous. She loved, and was loved by the
Duke of Hamilton. That counted for nothing. She was
made Duchess of Devonshire. She obeyed, but she swore
to remain faithful to the man she had been compelled to
sacrifice. To carry out this vow from the moment of her
marriage she did what the Princess Galitzine, *née* Ismaïlow,
has done in more recent times. She refused all communication with her husband, and continued in this resolve for
several years. The Duke of Hamilton was not less faithful
or less romantic. He retired to his estates in Scotland,
allowed his beard to grow, like one of our moujiks, until the
day of his death, which was hastened by despair.

"In the meanwhile the young Duchess lived under her
husband's roof, and performed all the honours of his house.
The Duke was married, without having a wife, which did not
trouble him. In society one of the saddest and most frigid
of men, he was very different when his heart was touched.
Unable to conquer the caprice of his wife, he was consoled
by a friend named Lady Elizabeth Foster, and they had
several children. The Duchess knew of the matter, and saw no
wrong. She was Lady Elizabeth's best friend, and one never
visited Devonshire House without finding them together.

The secret of this singular household was soon public knowledge.   Doctor Farquhar educated the children of the Duke
and Lady Elizabeth under fictitious names.   It was generally
believed that the illustrious house of Cavendish would be
extinguished in the legitimate line.

" Happily, the young Duchess, wearied by the emptiness
of her life, devoted herself whole-heartedly to gambling.
In one winter she lost £100,000, or, what would be equal
to-day to two millions and a half of roubles.   Frightened
at her position, she confessed everything to Lady Spencer,
her mother, and to her brother Lord Spencer, then a minister
of State.   They did all they could to save her, collected every
penny at their disposal, but did not succeed in making up
half the sum she required.   A disclosure to the husband
became unavoidable.   Lady Spencer went to him, and, after
a long preamble about the goodwill of the family, she revealed
her daughter's debt, and the need for the husband's assistance
to meet payment.   The Duke very phlegmatically asked
what was the total amount.   ' One hundred thousand
pounds,' was the answer, ' It is much,' he replied.   ' But
I will pay it, without your help, upon the condition of
becoming my wife's husband.'   The Spencers were tired of
the Duchess's attitude for so many years.   They found the
Duke's attitude exceedingly generous, and his conditions
reasonable and legitimate.   They hastened to write to the
Duchess, who, during the negociation, had gone to Spa
to escape the Duke's anger.

" She was told that an advantageous treaty had been
concluded, but that she would have to return to ratify it in
person.   However the Duke very gallantly desired to carry
the letter himself.   He paid up every outstanding creditor,
and, appearing at his wife's lodgings at Spa, placed in one of
her hands the receipts for her debts and in the other the
letters from her family.   I cannot tell you whether she
acceded to the treaty with repugnance or with good grace.
But this I do know.   When she returned from Spa, to the joy
of her husband and family, there were hopes of a heir to
the house of Cavendish.   Unfortunately, a daughter was

born, and the Duchess returned to her former mode of life.

" Her fellow gamblers, who found her profitable, and were possibly this time in league with her husband, enticed her afresh in pharaon. Again she lost to the tune of £50,000. Her husband undertook to become responsible for this sum, upon condition that the treaty of Spa was renewed permanently. The result of the fresh alliance was the young man we know to-day. These facts were told me by his mother, and in far greater detail by his grandmother Lady Spencer, and his aunt Lady Bessborough. The poor Duchess died quite young, and her husband did not long survive her, but he married Lady Elizabeth Foster before he died."

Paul Lacroix, in his edition of the letters of Madame de Coigny, sums up this peculiar situation in a few telling sentences which cannot be improved. " Lady Elizabeth Hervey fut en même temps la maitresse du duc de Devonshire et la plus fidèle amie de la femme de son amant, sans que cette situation équivoque ait jamais altéré leur amitié mutuelle. Elles vivaient, côte à côte, dans la même maison, comme deux inséparables. La célèbre et belle duchesse de Devonshire, loin d'être jalouse de sa rivale, lui savait gré de la délivrer ainsi de ses devoirs de femme mariée. Rien ne troublait donc la bonne intelligence des trois intéressés, dans cette étrange association. . . . On voit, dans les lettres qui lui sont adressés par la marquise de Coigny, que le monde aristocratique s'était accoutumé à tolérer ce qu'il y avait d'anormal dans la position de Lady Foster entretenant un commerce illégitime avec le duc de Devonshire au su et au vu de la duchesse, qui semblait l'approuver et l'autoriser."

The French author suggests one reason for the tacit acknowledgment by society of the equivocal position. There was no high standard of morals in the age immediately before the Revolution.[1] Every community is ruled by its

[1] Every generation deplores the decadence of its younger members. Mrs. Delaney was aghast at the manners of her juniors, which were, however, distinctly an improvement upon those of fashionable society during her youth. But there was nothing to boast of during the first period of George III.'s reign. Mrs. Montagu wrote to

own social code, and humankind is seldom strong enough in its units to rise above the average of the many. " Oh, Lud ! you are not going to be moral, and forget that you are among friends," cried Lady Sneerwell to Joseph Surface. The Duchess and Lady Elizabeth were women of considerable intellectual ability. They had both studied Jean Jacques Rousseau, and submitted to his influence. He, who taught that the outward appearance of virtue is one of the first duties of woman, also suggested that virtue itself could only be found in a state of nature. To follow, rather than to subdue one's passions, is a seductive doctrine, particularly when preached with the convincing eloquence of a Rousseau. It does not excuse the error of this household, but it affords a plausible and very probable explanation.

The Duchess had the grace to apologise to her mother for reading Choderlos de la Clos. Even to-day *Les Liaisons Dangereuses* is not sweet, and can well remain upon the index. But Rousseau's *Confessions* impressed her, and she sought to defend the author. In its pages could be traced his great and burning genius, she said. The principles of Madame De Warens might surprise, but, being odious and ridiculous, could not entice or mislead. Rousseau's character displayed romantic sincerity and candour. He admitted all his faults. His ideas of honour were of the highest. He had a horror of deviating from them. He confessed every deviation. His language and sentiments were enchanting. The Duke had read it with the greatest pleasure and marked all the pages. Everybody was reading it. The influence of Rousseau was supreme, and in many cases his readers allowed their moral purpose to be warped by his special pleading.

The Duchess thought that a very young unmarried person ought not to read Rousseau. But every girl in England

Mrs. Robinson, December 29, 1779 : " Our town amours present us with everything that is horrible. Women without religion or virtue, and men, void even of a sense of honour. Never till now did one hear of three divorces going forward in one session, in which the ladies of the most illustrious rank and families in Great Britain are concern'd."

was acquainted with his books. In 1778, Lady Louisa Stuart, then aged twenty-one, wrote to her friend Lady Caroline Dawson : " We (Lady Louisa Stuart and Lady Mary Lowther) both read the same book, and it furnished us with a great deal of conversation ; it was *La Nouvelle Héloïse*, with which I am charmed, perhaps more than I should be, yet I do not think I feel the worse for it, though Rousseau says in his preface, ' Toute fille qui en ose lire une seule page est une fille perdue ; ' and indeed I believe it might be very dangerous to people whose passions resembled those he describes. But I have nothing to do with love, so it is safe for me, and I do think it, notwithstanding several absurdities, the most interesting book I ever read in my life."

Jean Jacques Rousseau was a dangerous author, and there was reason enough for Samuel Johnson's withering denunciations. The fascination of Rousseau's eloquence was irresistible. His ideals were of the noblest. He gazed on the stars—with his feet in the gutter. No man had a profounder knowledge of the heart, or a keener insight into the tangled warfare between right and wrong which surges over our soul. Yet this inspired genius could mingle the purest wisdom with the strangest rubbish. Many of his truths were only half-truths, and his readers were not clever enough to discriminate. The first sentence in the *Contrat Social* rings clear as the call of a bugle. " Man is born free, and everywhere he is in chains." Such a thought is calculated to arouse our most generous instincts. We wish to rise in our might and strike away the shackles. But reflect ! Is any man born free ? Is not life compulsion from birth to death ? Our fetters are the duties we owe to our neighbour, and the chains are as heavy, or as light, as we care to make them.

Rousseau, however, excites the warm emotion first, and the sober reflection, the reaction, does not come until later—may not, indeed, come at all. His books were read by the whole world. His ideas were accepted without hesitation. Probably no author ever possessed so unchallenged

R

a dominion over the minds of his readers. Girls could be excused for becoming fascinated by the teaching of *La Nouvelle Héloïse* when clear-headed Necker, banker, husband of Suzanne Curchod and father of the future Madame de Stael, could write to the author : " Ah, how close the tender, humane, and virtuous soul of Julie has brought me to you. How the reading of these letters gratified me ! how many good emotions did they stir and fortify ! how many sublimities in a thousand places in these six volumes ; not the sublimity that perches itself in the clouds, but that which pushes everyday virtues to their highest point."

Rousseau was essentially a woman's author, not the author of the illiterate members of the sex but rather of the educated and fashionable such as Duchess Georgiana and Lady Elizabeth Foster. Alternately he praised women and denounced them.[1] Both attitudes are flattering. If one cannot be a saint there is some satisfaction in being a criminal. Angrily, Rousseau insisted that French gallantry had given universal power to women, which, like much of what he wrote, was only partly true, and yet pleasant to be told. " Everything depends upon women, and nothing is done save by them and for them. Olympus and Parnassus, glory and fortune, are equally under their laws. Books sell, authors are esteemed, only as it pleases women. They decide authoritatively concerning the highest matters of knowledge no less than the most agreeable. Poetry, literature, history, philosophy, even politics—one can see from the style of all books that they are written to amuse women. In affairs they are in a good way to obtain what they demand, a natural ascendancy over their husbands, not as husbands, but as men. For it is understood that a

---

[1] Jules Lemaïtre, in his study ot the master, suggested that Rouseau was not feminist. " He was even anti-feminist. Probably because he had greatly loved women. He thought, or felt, on that point like Michelet, like Sainte Beuve, like all who, greatly attracted by feminine nature, would have liked not to attenuate, but, on the contrary, to cultivate, and even to accentuate the differences between the two sexes."

man must refuse nothing to a woman—even if she is his
wife."

No woman can read these lines without mentally deter-
mining that Rousseau was a man of sound sense. Yet,
when he veered to another point of the compass, attacked
his own argument and destroyed his own creation, the
verdict of every sensible woman remained unaltered. Woman, he declared, ought not to be in the ascendancy. Such a
state of things was the destruction of all virility, tending to
inaugurate a reign of effeminacy. Women should be ruled
by men.[1] Rousseau used the plural, but the world, when it
discusses itself, thinks only in the singular. Women should
be ruled by man. What more did any woman ask for—
in the eighteenth century?

Rousseau advocated a return to nature. Beautifully
ignorant of the smallest knowledge of ethnology—a science
that hardly existed in his day—he believed that the aboriginal
races of the earth were patterns of innocence. Therefore
to regain our lost simplicity we must retrace our steps
towards savagery. Again he appealed for and won the
sympathies of the sex which has never wholly been conquered
by civilization. Man has been drilled into a passive obedi-

[1] He put it rather crudely in another place. " Dependence is the
natural state of women. . . . Women are always to be subject either
to a man, or to the judgments of men, and must never be allowed to
put themselves above those judgments." Lady Louisa Stuart,
who had studied Rousseau in her youth, evidently was of the same
opinion in her old age, for she wrote, in a letter dated 1830:
" The truth is, woman has a natural dependence on man, which,
do what she will, she never can quite shake off. I believe (in earnest
believe) it was part of the curse originally laid on Eve. ' Thy
desire shall be to thy husband, and he shall rule over thee,' which
she can by no means elude by taking no husband, or surviving one,
or keeping her heart free from a tyrannical passion. A son or a
brother takes the reins, or a clergyman, a lawyer, a physician, becomes
her governor. If she can escape all and stand quite alone, quite
independent of man, *tant pis pour elle*, it only renders her existence
uncommonly forlorn and desolate. I have seen a woman forced
to endure treatment from her butler that would have been held just
cause of complaint against a husband. However unpleasant it may
be, therefore, it is wise to view early and steadfastly the necessity of
submitting to our fate and not to exasperate the evil by exerting
what we call spirit in opposing it."

ence to and respect for law. Women obeys law when it coincides with personal fancy. A doctrine of nature supreme, and the right of every individual to an untrammeled expression of personality, has many attractions for the undisciplined. The root of woman's opposition to " man- made law ' is in reality an objection to law itself.

La Nouvelle Héloïse is not known by the present generation. Julie, the daughter of the Baron d' Etange, was placed under the care of a tutor named Saint Preux. They fall in love, and Julie, in a moment of passion, slips into what Rousseau terms " an abyss of ignominy." Cries the heroine : " We have sought pleasure, and happiness has fled far from us." When the Baron discovers the truth he compels his daughter to marry De Wolmar, a wealthy Russian. Saint Preux goes to Paris, and, after some insignificant adventures, travels round the world with the Englishman Anson. Twice he is cast away on desert islands. When he returns to France De Wolmar invites him to Clarens.

" Though we do not yet know one another I am com- missioned to write to you. The wisest and most beloved of women has just opened her heart to her happy husband. He believes you worthy to have been loved by her, and offers you his house. Innocence and grace reign here. Under her roof you will find friendship and hospitality, esteem and confidence. Consult your heart. And, if there is nothing which alarms you, come without fear."

Saint Preux, who was a pinchbeck hero, and deserved neither esteem nor confidence, settled down at Clarens with his former mistress and her husband. " Embrace your sister and friend," cries Wolmar, as Julie comes for- ward to greet him. Then, to prove his confidence and to test his rival, De Wolmar quits Clarens and leaves wife and lover together. Saint Preux is quite ready to resume the old relationship with the mistress of the house, but Julie's stronger nature prevails, and he admits himself conquered.

Very roughly outlined, this is the unedifying and to

modern ideas very tedious story of *La Nouvelle Héloïse*
The first part has been called the glorification of passion.
Julie is so touching in her weakness that her virtue gains by
reason of her sin.   " To sin, and to repair sin by repentance,
is the fundamental idea of Julie's history," wrote Saint
Marc Girardin.   The thought is fascinating ; it was at
least an excuse for a lax standard of social morality, as well,
possibly, as being an explanation.

For although passion was conquered by law—in the
novel—passion often rose superior to moral law in the
chronicles of eighteenth century society.   All the men
considered themselves to be Saints Preux and De Wolmars,
and most of the clever young women based their conduct on
that of Julie.   But, if the men were not quite so contemptible
as Saint Preux or so silly as De Wolmar, not all of the
women had the strong mind of Julie.   Hence came disaster.

Rousseau's doctrines were responsible for a tidal wave
of false sentiment and emotion.   Like Julie the women
dissected, and discovered most of the symptoms of disease
before they were ill.   The story of Julie and Saint Preux
is an interminable conversation upon the subject of virtue.
Now virtue is not a safe topic to ponder over, because
virtue is strength and mortals are generally weak.   Rousseau
inferred that as we are controlled by the laws of nature
weakness is natural.   Perhaps he was not altogether wrong.
But many of Rousseau's disciples found themselves able to
imitate Julie's glorification of passion, but were unable to
rise to the heights of Julie's obedience to the call of duty
and her triumph over temptation.   Thanks to *La Nouvelle
Héloïse*, the fashionable society of that day, as Jules
Lemaitre so well expresses it, began to love nature and
country life—which was excellent, and to cultivate feeling—
which might be good, and also to encourage sentimentality
disguised as virtue—which was dangerous.

How seriously Rousseau was accepted may be proved
by an account of the effects of his novel *Emile*, which
helped to revolutionise the old ideas upon education.   We
know that the Duchess brought up her own children upon

the lines set forth in that extraordinary pedagogic fiction. " Rousseau's eloquence excited women to an inordinate pitch of enthusiasm for the duty of suckling their infants," writes Lord Morley in his famous study. Arthur Young, in his travels on the Continent, noticed that women of the first fashion in France were ashamed if they did not nurse their own children. At the opera, during the intervals, the babes were brought to their mothers in the boxes. In this respect Rousseau was triumphantly successful in inducing his disciples to return to nature, although " his contemptuous denunciation of the gaieties of Paris could not extinguish the love of amusement."

The new movement was bitterly satirised, particularly in London. One of the characters in Burgoyne's play *The Heiress* drew an indignant picture of some of the most unpardonable infringements of the decencies of high life. " More than one Duchess has been seen in the same carriage with her husband—like two doves in a basket in the print of ' Conjugal Felicity,' and another has been detected ! I almost blush to name it——"

" Bless me, where ? and how ? and how ? "

" In nursing her own child ! "

" Oh, barbarous ! For Heaven's sake let us change the subject."

This criticism was undoubtedly directed against Duchess Georgiana. In some ways her example had not been one of the best. In her nursery she revealed the brighter side of her character.

Whatever her faults of character, the Duchess became a model mother. Lady Sarah Napier wrote to Lady Susan O'Brien in 1783 : " the Duchess of Devonshire is taken up with nothing so much as the prospect of nursing her child herself, which she talks of with so much eagerness as if her whole happiness depended upon succeeding. I do hope she will go on successfully." Of her scrupulous attention to her children we may read in the pages of Fanny Burney and the hurried correspondence of George Selwyn.

In 1790, when the young Marquis of Hartington was three

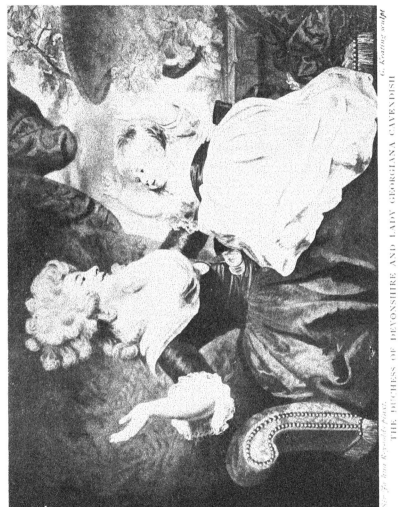

months old, George Selwyn was a guest at Devonshire House. He recites to Lady Carlisle his visit to the heir. " The Marquis was above, and there *M^e la Duchesse lui donna à dîner.* I was determined upon an audience, and found *l'heure du berger.* He received me *avec un sourire le plus gracieux du monde,* and I was obliged to present my address of compliments. But I think that the nurse is a bad *physiognimiste* if she did not see that what I said, and what I thought, were not *d'accord.* He is like the Duke if he is like anything, but a more uninteresting countenance I never saw—fair, white, *tâtè, sans charactère."*

In 1791 the author of *Evelina* was at Bath, and, meeting Lady Spencer, was introduced to the Cavendish nursery. Lady Spencer was an acting manager of the new Sunday Schools and Schools of Industry for poor children. " It was a most interesting sight," writes Miss Burney. " Such a number of poor innocent children, all put into a way of right, most taken immediately from every way of wrong, lifting up their little hands, and joining in those prayers and supplications for mercy and grace, which, even if they understand not, must at least impress them with a general idea of religion, a dread of evil, and a love of good ; it was a sight to expand the best hopes of the heart."

Then Miss Burney was taken to see the little Cavendishes. The young Marquis of Hartington " has a home of his own near the Duke's and a carriage entirely to himself ; but you will see the necessity of these appropriations, when I remind you he is now fourteen months old.

" I have neglected to mention, in its place, that the six poor little girls had a repast in the garden, and Lady Georgiana earnestly begged leave to go down and see and speak with them. She applied to Lady Spencer. ' Oh, grandmama,' she cried, ' pray let me go ! Mama says it all depends upon you.' The Duchess expressed some fear lest there might be any illness or disorder amongst the poor things : Lady Spencer answered for them ; and Lady Georgiana, with a sweet delight, flew down into the garden, all the rest accompanying, and Lady Spencer and the Duchess soon following. " It was a beautiful sight, taken in all its dependencies, from the windows."

Rousseau's ideas upon the rearing and education of young children were by no means novel or original. But they were based upon sound common-sense, and Rousseau's own genius put them into general currency. But when Emile and Sophie grew up their creator was not so fortunate. Some of his suggestions were monstrous. He was clever enough to recognise this himself. Staying at Strasburg in 1765, a man waited upon him with the introduction : " You see before you, Monsieur Rousseau, a man who has educated his son according to the principles he was happy enough to find in your *Emile*." " So much the worse for you and your son," was the philosopher's reply. Had any man or woman told Rousseau that in obeying their passions they had followed the example of Julie and Saint Preux, Rousseau might truthfully have made an answer in the same sense.

For the example was at once an excuse and a justification. To cast aside convention was to be in the movement, and the snare was an easy trap for persons who when free from this evil influence could boast of lofty ideals and carefully cultivated intellects.

The sequel must be given in a few bare facts. Lady Elizabeth Foster's first child was a daughter, christened Caroline Rosalie Adelaide St. Jules, born in 1786. Caroline was a favourite name in the Cavendish family, for a Lady Bessborough, eldest daughter of the third Duke, had been a Caroline, and Lady Duncannon's daughter, niece to the Duchess, and also born in 1786, received the same designation. In 1788, on May 26, a second child was born, who received the name of Augustus Clifford. Augustus was the name of Lady Elizabeth's father. The Duke had inherited the Barony of Clifford from his mother. Christin's remark that the children were given fictitious names is thus scarcely correct. The Doctor Farquhar who (according to his account) looked after their education was Walter Farquhar, a Scotch apothecary who became the most fashionable physician of his time, and, having been appointed physician in ordinary to the Prince of Wales, was created a baronet in 1796.

Sir Nathaniel Wraxall writes in his Memoirs that Lady Elizabeth " long constituted the object of the Duke's avowed attachment, and long maintained the firmest hold of his affections." To this " G. E. C.," in his *Peerage*, comments : " It has indeed been said that she (and not the Duke's first wife) was in 1790 the mother (exchange being made of two infants of different sexes) of his successor." This story is more elaborately given by " Grace and Philip Wharton," who were writing in the lifetime of the sixth Duke, and were able to collect their materials from contemporaries of his father. Political adversaries asserted that the little marquis was illegitimate. The report assumed several shapes, at one time pointing to the intimacy with Fox, at others to the close friendship with the owner of Carlton House. But these rumours were preposterous. " Another story also obtained credit, and never died away. This was, that at the time when the Duchess was confined, Lady Elizabeth gave birth to a son, the duchess to a daughter, and that the children were changed ; that the late Duke (the Marquis of Hartington) entered into a contract with his uncle, the late Lord George Cavendish, never to marry, in order that his lordship's children might have an undisputed succession at his Grace's death."

Such gossip was certainly baseless.[1] The details of Selwyn's visit to the nursery contradict it. In *The Great Governing Families of England*, by J. Langford Sanford and Meredith Townsend, the authors speak of the Marquess of Hartington, afterwards sixth Duke of Devonshire, as " a true Cavendish in every instinct, magnificent, accomplished, and dissolute, pursued through life by a story which asserted that he was a changeling, bound by a family compact not to marry. He did

---

[1] Lady Elizabeth Foster was at the opera with Lord St. Helens on the night of the birth of the Marquis of Hartington. See the *Jerningham Letters*, vol. 2, page 121.

not marry, and he did dip the estates ; but in those two facts lay the only evidence in support of a charge probably based on the tale of some discarded waiting-maid. There is scarcely a noble in England whose title is not assailed by some such rumour, though it more generally takes the form of a secret or Scotch marriage by some half forgotten ancestor."

Caroline and Augustus did not share the nursery of their little half-sisters and brother, although such a proceeding was not uncommon at the time.[1] But, as soon as they reached the fitting age, Augustus Clifford and the Marquess of Hartington were sent to school at Harrow, where their close relationship was no secret. In the *Correspondence of Sarah Spencer, Lady Lyttleton*, published in 1912, the paternity of Clifford and his sister is definitely stated for the first time in a collection of letters authorised by the family.

There was never any real mystery about the household at Devonshire House. When Gibbon referred " to the good Duchess of Devonshire and the wicked Lady Elizabeth Foster," his phrase carried its own meaning. George Selwyn, writing to Lady Carlisle in 1790, speaks of a dinner at the great mansion in Piccadilly. " We were to-day at dinner ten, besides the Duke ; Madame de Boufflers,[2] the

---

[1] In other noble houses things were arranged differently. Lord Cholmondeley, a member of the Devonshire House set, " a man who has lost the sense of moral rectitude," according to a contemporary, liked to have all his family round him. Thomas Raikes noted in his journal that " Lady Cholmondeley (a daughter of the Duke of Ancaster) was good nature personified. Besides their three children, there were at that time two beautiful girls in the house, who found a father's care and affection in Lord Cholmondeley." The elder went by the name of Miss Cholmondeley, and was probably his daughter but " others say General Keppell's." The younger, Miss Seymour, was the daughter of the notorious Mrs. Elliott. She was the child of George Selwyn, or Charles Windham, or the Prince of Wales. Miss Cholmondeley married Lord Durham, and Miss Seymour Lord Charles Bentinck, a son of the Duke of Portland.

[2] Countess de Boufflers-Rouvrel. She was the friend of Rousseau, and Dr. Johnson was very gallant to her when she visited him in Fleet Street, even escorting her to her coach. " La Reine des Aristocrates réfugiés en Angleterre," according to Selwyn.

Duke and Duchess of Devonshire, M. de Calonne,[1] The Fish,[2] Thomas,[3] Mie Mie,[4] and myself. I had liked to have forgot Lady E. Foster, *que l'on oublie pas souvent, dans cette partie au moins.*" Calonne talked to the Duchess, " and sat at dinner between her and Lady E. Foster, *avec qui je faisois la conversation*; the Duke over against us on the other side of the table, *comme la Statue dans le Festin de Pierre*, never changing a muscle of his face."

The following year, when Fanny Burney was in the dowager Lady Spencer's company at Bath, the footman announced two visitors. " Presently followed two ladies. Lady Spencer, with a look and manner warmly announcing pleasure in what she was doing, then introduced me to the first of these, saying, ' Duchess of Devonshire, Miss Burney.' She made me a very civil compliment upon hoping my health was recovering; and Lady Spencer then, slightly, and as if unavoidably, said, ' Lady Elizabeth Foster.' "

Miss Burney's friends at Bath had nothing good to say of the ladies. " Poor Mrs. Ord is quite in dismay at this acquaintance, and will believe no good of them, and swallows all that is said of evil." But the gentle novelist brushed aside all criticism with the remark that it was " utterly misinformed." And she gave a description of the Duchess which must be quoted without an omission.

" I did not find so much beauty in her as I expected, notwithstanding the variations of accounts; but I found far more of manner, politeness, and gentle quiet. She seems by nature to possess the highest animal spirits, but she appeared to me not happy. I thought she looked

---

[1] Charles Alexandre de Calonne, French courtier, politician, and comptroller-general of finance, 1783–87.

[2] " Fish " Crawford, always welcome at Devonshire House. A typical eccentric and man about town.

[3] Perhaps a Mr. Thomas Jones, " that very popular man."

[4] Maria Fagniani, the daughter, or adopted daughter, of George Selwyn. " Old Q," the fourth Duke of Queensberry, left her a fortune, as he believed himself to be her father. There were other claimants. She married the third Marquis of Hertford (Thackeray's wicked Marquis of Steyne) and was probably the mother of Sir Richard Wallace.

oppressed within, though there is a native cheerfulness about her which I fancy scarce ever deserts her.

" There is in her face, especially when she speaks, a sweetness of good humour and obligingness, that seem to be the natural and instinctive qualities of her disposition ; joined to an openness of countenance that announces her endowed, by nature, with a character intended wholly for honesty, fairness, and good purposes.

" She now conversed with me wholly, and in so soberly sensible and quiet a manner, as I had imagined incompatible with her powers. Too much and too little credit have variously been given her. About me and my health she was more civil than I can well tell you ; not from prudery but from its being mixed into all that passed. We talked over my late tour, Bath waters, and the King's illness. This, which was led to by accident, was here a tender subject, considering her heading the Regency squadron ; however, I have only one line to pursue, and from that I can never vary. I spoke of my own deep distress from his sufferings without reserve, and of the distress of the Queen with the most avowed compassion and respect. She was extremely well-bred in all she said herself, and seemed willing to keep up the subject. I fancy no one has just in the same way treated it with Her Grace before ; however, she took all in good part, though to have found me retired in discontent had perhaps been more congenial to her. But I have been sedulous to make them all know the contrary." [1]

Of Lady Elizabeth she said little. Perhaps she was afraid of being drawn against her will into the power of this fascinating woman. Her own opinion she did not give, but she wrote down the opinions of others. " Lady Elizabeth has the character of being so alluring, that Mr. Holroyd told me it was the opinion of Mr. Gibbon no man could

---

[1] Miss Burney had only recently retired from her appointment of second keeper of the robes to Queen Charlotte, for whom she had a great regard, being an enthusiastic member of the Court party. The King's sufferings were his frequent mental breakdowns.

withstand her, and that, if she chose to beckon the Lord Chancellor from his Woolsack, in full sight of the world, he could not resist obedience."

Gibbon's heart was always softly inclined towards Lady Betty. In his letters to Lord Sheffield he usually speaks of " the good Duchess," and the " wicked," or the " seductive " Lady Elizabeth. Of the affection of the two ladies there is much evidence. " All my possible hopes of friendship are concentrated in you," wrote the Duchess to her friend. "Without you the world is nothing to me. If you would forsake me I would not bear to live, or living should never think of any other creature." These words, although reflecting more or less the emotional outbursts of Rousseau's Julie, ring with sincerity. Yet in 1786 the rift between the Duke and the Duchess had become so acute that Sheridan was called in to make peace. If it were not for many proofs to the contrary we might imagine that the birth of Caroline St. Jules had been the cause of the quarrel.

" Tout comprendre c'est tout pardonner." That was the judgment of the men and women who visited Devonshire House, and it must have been a just verdict. The situation was accepted by all the allied families, the Spencers, the Herveys, the Fosters. The law of expediency is sooner obeyed than the Ten Commandments. Many years later Creevey noted that the " moral creed " of some great ladies was, to use his own word, " droll." He had been visiting Lady Grey. " It was just after Lady T— had left us ; so, being alone, she said to me :—' I *like* Lady T— : she is always good-humoured, and she amuses me ; and as she never says anything to offend me or those belonging to me I don't feel I have anything to do with Mr. Thompson or any other of the lovers which she has had. The same with Madame de Dino and the Duchess of B—— ; they are always very good-humoured and are very agreeable company ; and as they never say anything to offend me, I have nothing to do with all the different lovers they are said to have had. I take no credit to myself for being different from them :

mine is a very lucky case.   Had I, in the accident of marriages, been married to a man for whom I found I had no respect, I might have done like them, for what I know.   I consider mine as a case of luck ! '

" Droll, wasn't it ? " is Creevey's comment.   Droll maybe, but quite intelligible.   Society had its personal code of morals, and it was not that sanctioned by canonical law. There is a story of Lord Melbourne which illustrates a point of view very common to the higher ranks of that age. Lord Melbourne's wife was a niece of the Duchess of Devonshire, and his brother married Caroline St. Jules.   He himself had disturbed the peace of households.   One Sunday he accidentally found himself the unwilling listener to a rousing evangelical sermon upon sin and its consequences.

" Things have come to a pretty pass when religion is allowed to invade the sphere of private life," was the disgusted criticism of Queen Victoria's first Prime Minister.

Lady Macleod very naturally asked Dr. Johnson if no man was naturally good.

" No, madam.   No more than a wolf."

" Nor no woman, sir ? " interjected Boswell.

" No, sir ! " was the stern answer.

This short conversation sums up and explains everything.

CHAPTER XVII

THE Marquis of Hartington was born in Paris on May 21, 1790. Selwyn told Lady Carlisle that the Duchess presented the child to Marie Antoinette, and " the Queen kissed his hands twice." The Duke and Duchess had been spending much time on the Continent. In July, 1789, they were in Paris, but, owing to the political disturbances, thought it prudent to leave the city. They must have travelled at once to Spa, for Dutens notes their arrival, in his *Memoirs of a Traveller*, shortly after the fall of the Bastille.

Spa was crowded by the greater part of the French nobility, who had already begun the emigration. Amongst the visitors at the fashionable watering-place were the Lavals, the Luxembourgs, the Montmorencies, and many other famous families. Their spirits were unaffected by recent events. They were dancing with all the gaiety possible, writes Dutens, while their castles in France were being pillaged and destroyed. But the Duchess returned to Paris, and remained there until shortly after the birth of her son. Then came a short rest in London. In 1792, despite the unsettled state of France, she was again across the Channel and living in Marseilles and Aix.

The close friendship between the two aristocracies of France and England towards the close of the eighteenth century might form the subject for a fascinating study. Its origin is to be found in the love for foreign travel which distinguished the well-to-do classes of Great Britain, a trait in our national character already mentioned in an earlier chapter of this volume. Every youth of good family had to make the grand tour before his education could be considered finished. Women of rank travelled with their servants and without a chaperone with complete freedom and safety. English *milords* journeyed in their huge *berlines*, and with the retinue and luggage of a small army, to the furthermost cities of Italy.

A trip to Paris, despite the inconveniences of the passage, was an ordinary incident in the life of a man of wealth. Families went to Spa for the season as readily as to Bath. Nice was a favourite resort, especially for invalids. Pisa was a city to winter in, and Florence a permanent place of residence. There was generally a crowd at Lausanne. In 1792 Lord Cloncurry met in the Swiss town the Dukes of Sussex and Leeds, the Duchesses of Devonshire and Ancaster, and Lords Morley, Morpeth, Cholmondeley, and Annesley, besides untitled English people of fortune, French royalist *émigrés*, and some repudiated revolutionary patriots. Many of the English made their homes abroad, like the Marquis of Ailesbury, who lived in Brussels, and Sir Horace Mann, who refused to leave Venice.

In the small grand-ducal courts of Germany and Italy there was a ready welcome for the Englishman of rank. Lady Bristol, in her letters to Lady Elizabeth Foster, gives pleasing pictures of these international amenities. In Germany the princelings were closely related to the English royal house. At Pyrmont and Brunswick the Bishop of Derry (not yet Earl of Bristol) was most hospitably received by the reigning sovereigns. In 1777 the future Countess speaks without fear of a proposed journey by carriage from Frankfort to Rome by way of Darmstadt, Mannheim, Spiers, Stuttgart, Ulm, Augsbourg, Munich, Innspruck, Trente, and Verona. In these days of wagon-lits and restaurant cars such an itinerary provokes a shudder for those who have not the love for adventure.

The " Prince-Bishop " described his existence in Rome with considerable satisfaction. " 'Tis really a life of Paradise. The sett of English, too, are pleasant enough, and have their balls, their assemblies, and their conversationes, and instead of riots, gallantries, and drunkenness, are wrapt up in antiquities, busts, and pictures."

These pilgrimages across Europe were made in the usually short intervals between great military campaigns. Of the hundred years between 1700 and 1800 France and England were at loggerheads for nearly forty. Yet there was no real animosity between the French and the English until after the executions of Louis XVI. and Marie Antoinette. Generations came into being and accepted their neighbours as natural enemies. But the ill-feeling was more political than personal, and between the recurring conflicts there was much respect from one foe to the other.

In literature, art, and the drama a constant interchange continued between Paris and London, or rather London was always ready to import the latest novelty from Paris. Every English man of letters went to France, and French authors visited England more freely in the seventeenth century than they did in the eighteenth. Dr. Johnson's opinion of France and the French were not the considered judgments of his contemporaries. " The French are a gross, ill-bred, untaught people," odd remark from a man who himself needed education in a school of manners. " A Frenchman must be always talking whether he knows anything of the matter or not ; an Englishman is content to say nothing, when he has nothing to say." Johnson's idea of an entertaining conversation was a big-drum monologue—by Johnson. He put himself out of court by agreeing with Meynell's observation, " For anything I see, foreigners are fools ? "

A more pleasing and intelligent view is revealed in a letter by Hume to Sir Gilbert Elliot of Minto. Sir Gilbert, like many other British fathers, placed his two boys in a

s

French " pension militaire." Hume, being in Paris, visited the two young Scots, and had a talk with the abbé who superintended their education. " He told me that whenever his young pupils arrived, he called together all the French gentlemen, who are to the number of thirty or thirty-two, and he made them a harangue. He then said to them that they were all men of quality, to be educated to the honourable profession of arms, that all their wars would probably be with England, that France and that kingdom were Rome and Carthage, whose rivalry more properly than animosity never allowed long intervals of peace ; that the chance of arms might make them prisoners of arms to Messrs. Elliot, in which case it would be a happiness to them to meet a private friend in a public enemy ; that he knew many instances of people whose lives were saved by such fortunate events, and it therefore became them, from views of prudence and from the generosity for which the French nation was so renowned, to give the best treatment to the young strangers, whose friendship might probably endure and be serviceable to them through life. He added that the effect of this harangue was such that, as soon as he presented your boys to their companions, they all flew to them and embraced them, and have ever since combined to pay them all courtship and regard, and to show them every mark of preference."

In practice this sensible and chivalrous attitude worked admirably. War was conducted by gentlemen for gentle-men. During the campaigns the opponents exhibited a punctilious courtesy, and slaughtered each other with the utmost politeness. There was the historic example of Fontenoy, May 10, 1745. Lord Charles Hay advanced in front of his regiment towards the French, and drank to them. " Gentlemen of the French Guard, fire ! " he cried. To which the Comte D'Auteroche replied, as he raised his sword and saluted the enemy : " Fire yourselves, gentlemen of England, we never fire first ! " Another anecdote in the same *genre* is equally charming and not so well known. In 1758 Lord Frederick Cavendish, uncle by marriage to

Duchess Georgiana, accompanied the Duke of Marlborough
as aide-de-camp upon an unsuccessful expedition against
St. Malo. Lord Frederick was captured, and offered his
parole. At first he refused, on the ground that if he returned
to England his duty as member of parliament for Derbyshire would force him to vote further supplies to continue
the war against France.

"Do not let that prevent you," said the Duc d'Aiguillon,
the French commander, as he over-ruled young Cavendish's
objection. "We should no more object to your voting in
parliament than to your begetting children lest they one
day should fight against France."

Such graceful acts sweetened war—if war can be sweetened.
The code of manners suggested the ball-room rather than the
open field. These gentlemen were pleased to continue their
acquaintance when the statesmen had patched up a peace.
Owing to the number of Irish and Scottish exiles and soldiers
of fortune serving in the French armies men of the same stock
often confronted each other. When they met their cousins
during peace, or on neutral ground, the result was sometimes quaint. The "Count-Bishop" wrote from Rome
in 1778: "Mr. Dillon,[1] brother to our nephew, and colonel
of a regiment in the service of France, is here with some other
officers who had all received orders for their immediate
departure to join their corps." France was about to declare

[1] Arthur Richard Dillon, colonel of Dillon's regiment in the French
army. He was son of the eleventh Viscount Dillon. He fought
against the British in the American War of Independence, and also
in the West Indies. During the peace of 1783 he visited London,
and was received at Court. He became deputy for Martinique in
the National Assembly. In 1792 he was given command of the army
of the North, and fought against the Prussians in Champagne and the
Argonne. Replaced by Dumouriez, he was imprisoned by the
Comité du Salut Public, and guillotined in 1794. Amongst those
who were on the scaffold with him was a Miss Browne, a relative of
Lord Kenmare's. When Sanson beckoned to her she shuddered.
"Je vous prie, M. de Dillon, passez avant moi." "Je n'ai rien à
refuser à une dame," he replied, passing to his death with the cry,
"Vive le roy." His second wife was cousin to Mlle. de la Pagerie,
afterwards the Empress Josephine. One of his daughters, Fanny,
married General Bertrand, and accompanied her husband in
Napoleon's suite to Elba and St. Helena.

war upon England, and the English ambassador had been recalled from Paris. Wrote Lady Bristol to Lady Elizabeth Foster : " Many jokes pass between him and your father about the invasion of Ireland. The Colonel promises to be careful of the Palace, your father to be indulgent to the prisoners." Harmless persiflage on the eve of a war destined to continue without intermission for five years.

The ladies of the two nations were also well disposed. Even war did not altogether prevent the Paris fashions making an appearance in London. Rose Bertin regularly dressed the puppets which carried the latest mode from the Rue St. Honoré to the mercers on Ludgate Hill and in the Strand. Dutens, speaking of Duchess Georgiana, said that " everybody endeavoured to imitate her, not only in England but even at Paris." Small children were taken by their mothers to France for education. Young men borrowed mistresses, and old ladies sent packets of tea. " Dally the Tall," the notorious Mrs. Elliott, was equally at home in London or Paris, peace or war. In 1780, during the campaign which continued from 1778 to 1783, Lady Spencer told Duchess Georgiana that she had succeeded in getting a letter and some tea through to a friend, Madame de Bussy of Paris. Madame de Bussy had replied hoping that an early peace would soon reunite them all in the French capital. At that moment the French and Spanish fleets were cruising in the Channel, and England was under arms awaiting an immediate invasion.

There was little bitterness although the issue was quite undecided and both nations were acutely suffering. " We continue to take and destroy French frigates, convoys, etc. ; we certainly have had a long course of little successes," wrote Eden to the Carlisles. " I live, however, in hourly apprehensions that the balance will be struck by accounts of some thumping loss." Both sides longed for a decisive victory, particularly in England, which was still bleeding under the strain of the fight against the American colonists. The poor were beggars, and the rich had no funds. James Hare told Lord Carlisle, who was at Dublin Castle in 1781, that there was nothing to regret in being out of London during that terrible winter. " The complaint of its dullness is general, and is imputed to a very natural cause—the poverty of all ranks of people." But directly peace was signed the English flocked to Paris to renew old friendships and buy the seductive millinery of Mademoiselle Bertin.

The invasion of England by the French aristocracy did not begin in any marked degree until George, Prince of Wales, commenced to reign over his gay little court. Philippe of Orléans and his dissolute following were seen in Mayfair, and the ladies, whose mothers had welcomed Rousseau, now entertained Choderclos de La Clos, the Duke's secretary and author of the very doubtful *Liaisons Dangereuses*. The respective ambassadors were appointed because of their wealth and rank, not for any diplomatic ability. London had the Duc de Guines, who brought in his train Tessier, an earlier Coquelin. English society flocked to the French embassy to enjoy his witty acting. D'Adhémar, who came in 1783, was a most successful representative of France. He had " wit, talent, and a handsome face, could sing agreeably, played comedy well, and made pretty verses." Great Britain reciprocated in kind, and did not go to the extreme folly of exporting brains. The gay Duke of Dorset became British ambassador in Paris. His encouragement of the Parisian ballet was the amazement and envy of his age. He himself confessed to an ambassadorial expenditure of £11,000 a year. " He had been from early youth a devotee to pleasure," wrote Wraxall. " The celebrated Nancy Parsons was one of his mistresses. She made way for the Countess of Derby, who in her turn was eclipsed by the Baccelli, one of the most attractive dancers of our time." When La Baccelli came to London the Duke asked Duchess Georgiana to do what she could for his *protégée*. " I don't wish you to do anything for her openly, but I hope *que quand il s'agit de ses talens* you will commend her."

Never had the two countries been linked together so closely. In London the French nobility were welcomed for their grace and wit. In Paris the English were received with a warm hospitality ; the women considered delightful and unconventional, the men strange eccentric beings but good fellows at heart.   When Selwyn, who had a morbid taste, went to Paris in 1757 to witness the torture and execution of Damiens, the executioner inquired the name of the gentleman in the crowd who was so deeply interested in the proceedings.   " Un monsieur de Londres," was the reply. " Monsieur de Londres,' repeated " Monsieur de Paris," and immediately asked him to take a seat near the scaffold, mistaking the grave Englishman for a fellow-professional whose visit upon such an occasion was indeed a compliment.

The links between Mayfair and the Faubourg St. Germain were many.   Mrs. Poyntz, grandmother of the Duchess, had known Louis XV. and his daughters—had even been allowed to prescribe for them when they were ill.   Lady Spencer continued the family intimacy with the French Court, and her daughter was undoubtedly presented to the Dauphine soon after the Austrian princess's marriage to the future Louis XVI.   Marie Antoinette became Queen of France only a few weeks before Georgiana Spencer was married into the House of Cavendish.   Whenever the Queen met members of the English colony in Paris, or received one of the frequent English visitors, she asked for news of the Duchess.   Lady Clermont, who was at Fontainebleau in 1776, said that she had been presented to the Queen at Choisy. " One of the first things she said to me was, why did you not bring the Duchess of Devonshire.   I said there was nothing you wished so much. . . . She is a delightful creature, and puts me very much in mind of your Grace."   A year later Lady Spencer was in Paris.   " The Queen talked a great deal about you, and said a thousand pretty things."   In 1783, at the birth of her first child, a royal present was sent to the mother, and other marks of Marie Antoinette's pleasure were displayed during the next few years.

The leaders of society in the two capitals were of an age. Marie Antoinette was only two years older than the Duchess. An exception was the Duc de Chartres, to be known and execrated as Philippe Egalité, who belonged to an earlier generation. His visits to England were frequent, and he gained an unfortunate influence over the young and impressionable Prince of Wales. The brothers of Louis XVI. came between the brothers and sons of George III. in age. The Comte d'Artois and the Duke of Cumberland could teach each other little in the ways of folly and dissipation, and their example to the younger men was thoroughly bad.

A letter from the Duke of Dorset to the Duchess of Devonshire gives a picture of Marie Antoinette in the gardens of the little Trianon at Versailles a few weeks before the scandal of the diamond necklace covered the sky with threatening storm-clouds, for the Cardinal de Rohan had not yet been condemned to exile. The Queen had been entertaining a party of thirty that day. After dinner their chief amusement consisted in throwing each other's hats into the lake. Lord George (probably Lord George Cavendish) was the only man who could punt a boat. So he was given the business of fishing the hats out of the water. Curiously, at almost the same time the Prince of Wales and his brothers were in company with Philippe of Orléans, and their romping took the form of pushing each other—and some ladies in addition—into an ornamental pond of an English park.

In another letter the Duke of Dorset tells the Duchess that De Grammont, a younger brother of the Duc de Guiche, is setting out for London. The Duke describes him as a very amiable young man who danced like an angel, but preferred stage dancing to the ball-room. An attempt had been made to arrange a little *fête* at Choisy, in which De Grammont, " Coigny," and La Baccelli were to have performed *un pas de trois*. Unfortunately La Baccelli had already gone. Perhaps De Grammont's journey to London was not unconnected with the fascinations of the *danseuse*.

" Coigny " was the young Marquise de Coigny, one of the most famous women in the society of Paris at that time. She was beautiful and arrogant, with a tongue notoriously sharp, a woman of heart and undeniable seduction. Harriet, Countess Granville, who met her afterwards in England when she had become one of the intimate friends of the Duchess and Lady Elizabeth Foster, describes her as " very clever and witty."[1]   She was a perfect type of the French gentlewoman of the pre-revolutionary period.

In 1775, at the age of sixteen, she had married the eldest son of the Duc de Coigny.   Her husband was only a couple of years older.   The Duke of Dorset had very truly told Duchess Georgiana that men and women married young in France. The Duchess had complained to the Ambassador that she was already seven and twenty years old.   " Consider what an age that is ? " To which the Ambassador replied that in France at seven and twenty a woman was considered elderly. " We marry our young folks at twelve and fourteen." [2]

The marriage was not entirely successful, and in some ways the Marquise's matrimonial position was similar to that of the Duchess.   Madame de Coigny did not enter the world of fashion until 1780, and her triumph was rapid. She conquered as rapidly as the Duchess had conquered across the Channel.   All the men adored her.   She selected one Armand Louis de Gontaut, Duc de Lauzun, and remained faithful to him until the day of his death on the guillotine in 1793.

Madame de Coigny was bold enough to challenge the supremacy of the Queen herself.   Marie Antoinette was at the height of her power in 1776, and from that date her dominion steadily declined not only over the people but also amongst the nobility of France.   The rise of Madame de Coigny completed the royal eclipse, and the mutual dislike of the two ladies became unveiled enmity.   Lauzun was one

---

[1] Lady Granville says that she was " a great friend of Marie Antoinette."   This was an error, Lady Granville evidently confusing the Marquise with the Duchesse de Coigny, second wife of Madame de Coigny's father-in-law.

[2] There was a general fear of growing old at this time.   At the age of twenty-nine Marie Antoinette gravely discussed the question with her *modiste* Rose Bertin.   " She would soon be thirty.   No one would dare to acquaint her of her increasing years.   Her idea was to change her manner of dressing, which inclined too much to that of extreme youth.   In consequence, she would wear no more flowers or feathers."

of the reasons. He had paid court to the Queen before he had transferred his attentions to Madame de Coigny. Marie Antoinette had retaliated with bitter words which were not forgotten. Frankly the princess was jealous of her rival. " I am the Queen of Versailles," she complained, " but Madame de Coigny is Queen of Paris." Madame de Coigny went over to the party of opposition and joined forces with the Duc de Chartres. Even Lauzun forsook Versailles and appeared in the salons of the Palais Royal.

The Duchess of Devonshire must have met Madame de Coigny during one of her many visits to Paris at this time, and the close friendship was probably cemented at Spa. It is somewhat surprising that the Duchess was able to hold the goodwill and sympathy of the Queen. Devonshire House and the Palais Royal had much in common. They both represented a spirit of liberalism and revolt. Both were centres of opposition to their respective courts. The *va et vient* between London and Paris gradually increased. The Marquis de Conflans, Madame de Coigny's father, became one of the most joyous companions of the Prince of Wales, although he was a much older man.

In 1783 Count Valentin Esterhazy wrote : " There are many French in London, amongst others the duc d'Orleans, the duc de Guines, and the marquis de Conflans, a man of much talent and wit, but who affects more vices than he possesses ; immoral by principle, and braving every pre-judice and convention ; a liar, yet not false ; a drunkard, without loving wine ; a libertine, without the tempera-ment." The character is not pleasing, and Conflans was not the best mentor for the heir to the British throne.

Madame de Coigny, although the daughter of a great family which belonged to the *noblesse d'épée*, was on the maternal side allied to the *noblesse de robe*. Between these two sections of French society—the military and the legal— there existed an unending rivalry. The *noblesse d'épée* despised the *noblesse de robe* as inferior, but never objected to marrying their sons into a connection which controlled most of the wealth of the country. The *noblesse d'épée* gathered round the Court ; the *noblesse de robe* ruled the capital. Antagonistic to the Queen, encouraged by the Palais Royal, Madame de Coigny threw herself body and soul into the cause of the coming revolution.

This attitude was an additional recommendation towards the goodwill of the Whigs at Devonshire House. From political inclination, as well as personal goodwill, the party under the leadership of Fox looked with much favour upon the forward movement in France.

The Fall of the Bastille was the—

> glorious opening, the unlooked for dawn
> That promised everlasting joy to France.

In England the news was received with acclamation. The Duke of Dorset wrote a glowing despatch from the British Embassy to the Duke of Leeds upon the events of July 14, 1789. " Thus, my lord, the greatest revolution that we know anything of has been effected with, comparatively speaking—if the magnitude of the event is considered—the loss of very few lives. From this moment we may consider France as a free country, the king a very limited monarch, and the nobility as reduced to a level with the rest of the nation." The Duke was evidently ready to forgo all the privileges of his rank.

He must have written in the same strain to the Duchess of Devonshire. Yet he warned those at home that the recent troubles made travelling unsafe. " I really think it necessary that some public caution be given to put those upon their guard who may propose to visit this part of the continent." As the situation became more complicated and uneasy the Duke resigned his position and returned to London. But he remained in communication with his former friends, continued to supply Marie Antoinette with English gloves, and, in August, 1791, sent her a cypher letter of advice from Edmund Burke. For a brief period Lord Robert Fitz-gerald acted as *Chargé d'affaires*. Then, in May, 1790, Earl Gower (afterwards Duke of Sutherland) presented Dorset's letters of recall and his own credentials. He was a dull young man with no qualifications for the task, writes a descendant, beyond the fact that he had been sent to Auxerre to study French by the advice of Edmund Burke. His earliest despatches drew attention to the danger for English visitors in Paris.

The Duchess of Devonshire never lacked courage, but why she should have remained in the French capital at this time is not clear. Exactly a month before the official entry of the British ambassador the Marquis of Hartington was born. Lord Gower's ardent democracy was quickly watered down by the events which followed each other during his term of office. Lady Gower was the only lady who dared to visit Marie Antoinette the day before the attack on the Tuileries. When the royal family were prisoners in the Temple she sent the clothes of her own little son for the use of the wretched Dauphin.

The English Whigs remained strongly attached to the revolutionaries. The chaplain to the British Embassy was the Rev. John Warner, a parson who had proved of considerable value to the Devonshire House *coterie* during some of their underground negotiations on the Continent. On August 23, 1790, he wrote to his friend Selwyn that war might be declared by France upon England at any moment. The Duchess had already left Paris. Warner, says one of his biographers, as a strong Whig in politics had sympathised with the destruction of the Bastille and, unlike a good many of his associates in politics, he did not allow the excesses that followed to have a material effect upon his opinions. Towards the close of October news came that he had been dismissed from his post. His Whiggism had been too strong for his employer. He had delivered from the pulpit of the embassy chapel in the Rue St. Dominique a sermon in which he justified the proceedings of the Revolution. When he heard that the royal family had escaped from their jailers he exclaimed : " Damn the miscreants ! Have they escaped ? Well, that they may be brought back to Paris before evening and be guillotined before tomorrow morning are the two wishes next to my heart." That he had the reputation of being a mild mannered man proves the strength of the passion and partisanship that dominated humankind during those stirring and dreadful days.

Madame de Coigny was amongst the last to leave France. The emigration commenced early in 1789, and London became one of the centres for the exiles to congregate in. Many of the nobility who had entertained the Duchess in the Faubourg St. Germain were now happy to receive her hospitality at Devonshire House. In September, 1789, Selwyn wrote, " I fancy there are very near as many French in London as English." They were soon sheltered. Madame de Boufflers visited Lady Egremont, Lady Dover, and Lord Palmerston. Selwyn did his best. " I went to Lady Lucan with whom I have tried to *ménager* some *petit petit* soupers for these poor distressed people.' But their position in London was strangely different from their old magnificence.

" When I left St. James', I went in search of M^e. de Boufflers, and found her at Grenier's Hotel, which looks to me more like a hospital than anything else. Such rooms, such a crowd of miserable wretches, escaped from plunder and massacre, and M^e. de Boufflers among them, with I do not know how many beggars in her suite, her *belle fille* (*qui n'est pas belle, par parenthèse*), the Comtesse Emilie, a maid with the little child in her arms, a boy, her grandson, called *Le Chevalier de Cinque minutes*, I cannot explain to you why ; a pretty fair child, just inoculated, who does not yet know so much French as I do, but understood me, and was much pleased with my caresses. It was really altogether a piteous sight. . . I said *tout ce qui m'est venu en tête de plus consolant.*"

D'Orléans came over and tried to raise funds, he, who had offered to lend money to the Prince of Wales under happier circumstances. Lauzun, now the Duc de Biron, paid flying visits to see Madame de Coigny. He, too, crossed the threshold of Devonshire House, an eighteenth century Bayard who could do no wrong, the most perfect type of the old-fashioned French nobleman. English society was pleased to have him, and leniently forgot that he had been to America with Rochambeau and given active support to General Washington's soldiers. England has never shewn animosity towards chivalrous enemies. Indeed at times we have been rather foolish in our confidence. There is a paragraph in one of Lady Susan O'Brien's letters which says : " j'ai vu le Marquis de Fayette in the Pit of the Opera, [he is] going to America to fight against us ; he stopped to see what sort of people [we] were, and to get what intelligence he could to make use of against us."

The Duchess and Lady Elizabeth Foster were busy on behalf of the emigrants. At the receptions at Devonshire House and the garden parties at Chiswick there were always many French guests. The children of the house had remembrances of " shoals of French *émigrés* surrounding Monsieur (Charles X.)." Chateaubriand dined at her table, as well as the Abbé Delille. French children lived in the house. At the breaking out of the Revolution the young Duc de Guiche and his two sisters, the mesdemoiselles de Grammont, were placed under her protection. At Devonshire House schemes and plots were formed to rescue Marie Antoinette, or at least the Dauphin, from captivity. Sheridan, Fox, the Duchess, and the Duke of Dorset were certainly engaged in one of these conspiracies, and their Paris agent may have been that mysterious Englishwoman, Mrs. Atkyns, of whom we know so little. Mrs. Crewe, who had many French friends, organised a school for *émigrés* at Penn in Buckinghamshire. Burke, who lived in the same county at Beaconsfield, had a special interest in this work.

From the first Madame de Coigny occupied a very prominent position in English society. Upon her arrival she took a house in Hertford Street, Mayfair. Her husband escorted her to London before he joined the army of Coblentz. She was in a more fortunate position than many of her compatriots, for the Marquis made her a monthly allowance of £100, and she was never short of funds. She remained an exile until 1801, when the Consulate allowed her to return to Paris.

Her friends said that she preserved in London the same

empire she had been accustomed to rule in Paris. Lord
Glenbervie thought her very clever and truly witty. But
he thought her wit was biting. She was to be seen almost
daily in the company of the Duchess and Lady Elizabeth.
She visited Brighton and Newmarket, and dined with
Mrs. Crewe at Hampstead. She was of such public interest
that Bennet Langton asked one of Mrs. Crewe's servants
at a Hampstead gathering to point her out. When Madame
de Coigny heard of this, she asked ; " In what light does his
curiosity consider me—as a handsome woman, a wit or a
spy ? " She was the first, and the second, but never the
third.

Lord Glenbervie mentions a party of twenty at Devonshire
House, at which there must have an awkward constraint.
There were present Lady Bristol and her two daughters, Lady
Elizabeth Foster and Lady Louisa Hervey. The Prince
of Wales was amiable to seventeen of the guests, but to
three he refused to speak—the Duke of Bedford, Charles
Greville, and Madame de Coigny. History does not relate
the Russell and Greville offences, but we can guess that with
Madame de Coigny the tongue had been in error.

" Est-il vrai, madame, que vous dites partout que je
suis plus bête que belle ?" asked Lady Asgill angrily to her
at Harrington House, where she sat " huddled up in a black
cloak and bonnet, the impersonation of the whole Faubourg
St. Germain."

" Pardon, miladi," was the crushing reply. " Je l'ai
souvent ouï dire, mais je ne l'ai jamais répété."

Her regard for the Duchess and Lady Elizabeth was deep.
In 1803, writing from Paris, shortly after the rupture of the
Peace of Amiens had again plunged the two nations into
war, she addressed Lady Elizabeth as " *Dear* Ennemie,"
and sent a " mille tendresses à la duchesse par excellence."
She hoped yet to entertain her former hostesses, and finished
her letter with a line of English. " Oh ! pray do come, and
believe me when I assure you that you shall be very welcome."
The death of the Duchess was a bitter sorrow. She told
Lady Elizabeth that she shared in the " tristesse de vôtre

GEORGE, PRINCE OF WALES
From a Hitherto Unpublished Pencil Drawing by John Smart, Jnr. (1807)
Presented by the Prince of Wales to the Hon. Mrs. Richard Walpole
In the Collection of Mr. Thomas Vade Walpole

âme " for a " dear and celeste creature." That is the last letter we have of her English correspondence.

She never returned to London, but she was not forgotten by the English who went to Paris. In August, 1815, Lady Shelley was in the capital. " We went to Madame de Coigny's. This is the most like the old French society of any I have seen. The only women present were Lady Kinnaird and Madame Girardin . . . After passing the Cour—where our hostess will not allow carriages to enter— we ascended a dirty, narrow, winding staircase, and on the fourth floor we were received by Madame de Coigny. . . . The whole arrangements struck me as mean and uncomfortable."

But Madame de Coigny was now growing an old woman. She had lived to see the Restoration, but her interest in life ceased when Lauzun laid down his life on the guillotine in 1793.

CHAPTER XVIII

The Duchess's poetry—*The Passage of the Mountain of St. Gothard*—days at Lausanne—did the Duchess write Byron's *Werner?*

SIR Isaac Newton described poetry as " ingenious nonsense." This description can be applied without undue harshness to the greater part of the Duchess's rhymes. In her letters to the Countess Spencer there is much occasional verse which is decidedly ingenious though certainly nonsense. These jingles have a gaiety and rattle characteristic of the author. When the Duchess became serious she was far less entertaining. Horace Walpole spoke of an " Ode to Hope " as " easily and prettily expressed, though it does not express much." The criticism is true of her other productions.

Fanny Burney, when amongst the " showy, tonish, people " of Bath in 1780, was allowed to see the same work. " I believe I told you that before I last left Bath the Bishop (of Peterborough) read to Mrs. T(hrale) and me a poem upon Hope, of the Duchess of Devonshire's, obtained with great difficulty from Lady Spencer. Well, this day he brought a tale called *Anxiety*, which he had almost torn from Lady Spencer, who is still here, to show to Mrs. Thrale ; and, as before, he extended his confidence to me. It is a very pretty tale, and has in it as much entertainment as any tale upon so hackneyed a subject as an assembly of all the gods and goddesses to bestow their gifts upon mankind, can be expected to give."

If the Duchess wrote fiction of any length, which, in the case of *The Sylph* is by no means unlikely, she published anonymously. There was an unwritten law, long since repealed unhappily, which forbade ladies of rank to enter into competition with the professionals of Grub Street. But even Duchesses have ambitions which cannot be suppressed by the etiquette of the strawberry leaves. Dr. Johnson said that no man but a blockhead ever wrote except for money. An author who does not dream of seeing his name and works in print is not an author at all. The Duchess's poem entitled *The Passage of the Mountain of St. Gothard* was far too big a venture to be ushered into the world without a sponsor, or to be handed round in the obscurity of manuscript by Bishops. So, with a dedication to her children, the short poem was printed in folio with luxuriant margins. A French translation by the Abbe Delille was issued in 1802.[1] Polidori [2] prepared the Italian translation of 1803, and a German version appeared in 1805. In 1816 a sumptuous edition was published by Lady Elizabeth Foster, together with the *Journey through Switzerland*, originally published in 1796. Had Walpole lived to witness such literary activity he would have regretted the omission of the name of Duchess Georgiana from his *Royal and Noble Authors*.

The poem was written in 1793. If not absorbing in itself the verse is interesting because it marks a forward step in the popularisation of Switzerland as a tourist centre. Early in the summer of 1792 Gibbon wrote to Lord Sheffield from Lausanne that " the good Duchess of Devonshire and the

---

[1] Jacques Delille was born a poor boy in Glenat, a tiny village between Aigueperse and Artonne in Auvergne (Puy-de-dôme). The present writer knows and loves that beautiful spur of the hills, which drops into the immense plain of the Limagne, with, in the distance, the peaks of the old volcanic craters of Auvergne and the dim mass of the mountains of the Forêt. Educated at Amiens and Paris, Delille visited London during the Revolution, met the Duchess, and translated *Paradise Lost*. He died in 1813, and, though forgotten to-day, was the first of poets in his own time, being declared by his contemporaries the equal of Virgil and Homer.

[2] Gaetano Polidori, a teacher of Italian in London, who had been secretary to Alfieri. His son acted for a short while as physician and secretary to Byron. A daughter, who married Gabriele Rossetti, was the mother of Christina and D. G. Rossetti.

wicked Lady Elizabeth Foster, who are on their march,"
had visited his retreat on the shores of the lake.   There was
always bright English company to be found at Lausanne.
When Fox travelled he usually managed to give the historian
a call.   " A great coxcomb," he told Samuel Rogers.   " His
portrait by Sir Joshua Reynolds is over the fireplace at
Lausanne, and he used to look at it as often as if it had been
his mistress's."   The ladies of Devonshire House had a
tender feeling for the clever little fat man.   They understood and forgave his vanity.   Besides, in the laurel walks
of his château was the beauty and the peace which Byron
in later years found such a sure inspiration.

> Clear, placid Leman l thy contrasted lake
> With the wild world I dwell in is a thing
> Which warms me with its stillness to forsake
> Earth's troubled waters for a purer spring.
> This quiet sail is as a noiseless wing
> To waft me from destruction : once I loved
> The ocean's roar, but thy soft murmuring
> Sounds sweet, as if a sister's voice reproved,
> That I with stern delights should e'er have been so moved.
>
> It is the hush of night, and all between
> Thy margin and the mountains dusk yet clear,
> Mellowed and mingled, yet distinctly seen,
> Save darkened Jura, whose capt heights appear
> Precipitously steep ; and drawing near,
> There breathes a living fragrance from the shore
> Of flowers yet fresh with childhood ; on the ear
> Drops the light drip of the suspended oar,
> Or chirps the grasshopper one good-night carol more.

This was the atmosphere of the lake as it appealed to
the great poet.   But, as Charles James Fox observed,
" Lausanne was a pleasant, cheerful place, independent of its
scenery."   And, judging from some of Gibbon's letters, the
English visitors were ready to amuse themselves with all
manner of innocent games.

Writing to the Swiss boy he adopted, Gibbon says in a
letter : " You have just received the cockade and the
feather, but you are still unaware of the gracious and solemn
manner in which they were remitted to me who have sus-

tained in this ceremony the character of your representative. My two sponsors, MM. Pelham and Robinson, led me towards the Duchess [of Devonshire], who was seated in an armchair. While advancing I made three bows and placed one knee on the ground before her. Lady Elizabeth Foster presented to her a large unsheathed sword which M. Pelham had brought from the Prussian Army. With this sword she gave me the accolade on both shoulders, and while she presented me with the cockade and the feather I promised in your name to fulfil all the duties of a brave and loyal knight. I swore it on kissing her hand. This ceremony is only a joke, but you can count upon the friendship of the Duchess, who is as genuine as she is good. She leaves in the early part of next week. As she no longer has a cook, I dine every day with her at the de Cerjats', twice at the Princess de Bouillon's, at Tissot's (yes, at Tissot's!) at St. Germain's, who never loses an occasion of expense, and at my house; to-day I have a great dinner of fourteen covers."

In September the Duchess and her friend (" we call her Bess," says Gibbon) were undecided as to their movements. At last they determined to go to Italy, instead of returning to London, and set off with the Duchess of Ancaster at the end of October. Gibbon felt lonely when they were gone. He told Lord Sheffield of Lady Elizabeth's skill as an artist. They were wintering in Pisa, and would not return to England for several months.

"We quitted Italy in August, 1793, and passed into Switzerland over the mountain of Saint Gothard. The third crop of corn was already standing in Lombardy." This is the first note to the poem, and explains the opening stanza.

> Ye plains where three-fold harvests press the ground,
> Ye climes where genial gales incessant swell,
> Where art and nature shed profusely round
> Their rival wonders—Italy, farewell.

One verse only need be quoted as a taste of the quality of the whole.

And hail the chapel !   Hail the platform wild !
    Where Tell directed the avenging dart
With well-strung arm that first preserved the child,
    Then wing'd the arrow to the tyrant's heart,
Where three Swiss heroes lawless force withstood,
    And stamp'd the freedom of their native land.
Their liberty requir'd no rites uncouth,
    No blood demanded and no slaves enchain'd ;
Her rule was gentle and her voice was truth,
    By social order form'd, by laws restrain'd.

It is not bad verse—indeed for a Duchess it is surprisingly
good. And it prompted another poet to sit down and
address an ode to her, which was published three days later,
December 24, 1799, in the *Morning Post*. The spirit of
S. T. Coleridge had been awakened.

Thenceforth your soul rejoiced to see
The shrine of social liberty !
        O beautiful !   O Nature's child !
'Twas thence you hailed the platform wild,
Where once the Austrian fell
Beneath the shaft of Tell !
O ! lady nursed in pomp and pleasure,
Where learnt you this heroic measure ?

We can easily imagine the Duchess and Lady Elizabeth
sitting in their room at Devonshire House on Christmas Eve,
and wondering where they did discover the secret of the
" heroic measure."

The Duchess wrote other poems. There are " Lines on
the Battle of Aboukir," but the couplets are too tripping
for the theme of a girl who has lost her lover in the fight.

I am wretched, past retrieving ;
    He is lost, and I'm undone ;
All my life will pass in grieving
    For the battle we have won.

Then came an ode on the death of poor James Hare, who
was sincerely mourned as " a lov'd companion." An
epigram on the peerage was touched with a slight venom.

When a Peerage they give to some son of the earth,
    Yet he still is the same as before ;
'Tis an honour if gained as the premium of worth,
    But exposes a blockhead the more.

What unlucky creation prompted this cannot now be said. But there was keen competition always for promotion to the Upper House. In 1834 Lord Grey told Creevey that he had received over three hundred applications for peerages, and the demands for baronetages were absolutely endless.

The whole circle was given to poetry. The Duke, Lord Spencer, Lord Melbourne, and Lord Carlisle were ready at short notice to write an ode, or preferably an epitaph. The Duchess was as gifted as any of the men, but it was not until a few years ago that it was asserted that she was the actual author of Byron's *Werner*.

The case for the Duchess was set forth by her grandson, the Hon. Frederick Leveson-Gower, in the *Nineteenth Century* for August, 1899. He was convinced that Byron did not write the play, which was the work of the Duchess. " My sister, Lady Georgiana Fullerton, told me many years ago that this was the case. Her statement was that the Duchess wrote the poem and gave the manuscript of it to her niece, Lady Caroline Ponsonby, and that she, some years later, handed it over to Lord Byron, who subsequently published it in his own name." The family tradition seems to have been widespread, and Lady Carlisle, the elder daughter of the Duchess, has left a letter in which she writes : " Did you know that my mother had written an entire tragedy from Miss Lee's tale, *Kreutzner, or the Hungarian ?* William Ponsonby sent it to me this morning, and I will, if you like, send it you when Lord G. goes to London." This was written in 1822.

Mr. Leveson-Gower proves that the Duchess wrote a tragedy based upon *Kreutzner*, and assumes that it came into the hands of William Ponsonby from his sister " Caro " Lamb, the friend of Byron. Lady Caroline had previously lent it to the poet who, in 1822, published the Duchess's poem as his own work. Such a course requires some very adequate reason, and this Mr. Leveson-Gower cleverly supplies. In 1822 Byron was making frantic endeavours to obtain money, not for himself, but to help the cause of Greece. " I am determined to have all the moneys I can, whether by my own funds, or succession, or lawsuit, or MSS, or any lawful means whatever." In 1823 he wrote to Mr. Douglas Kinnaird: " I presume that some agreement has been concluded with Mr. Murray about *Werner*. Although the copyright should only be worth two or three hundred pounds, I will tell them what can be done with them. For three hundred pounds I can maintain in Greece, at more than the fullest pay of the Provisional Government, rations included, one hundred armed men for three months. You may judge of this when I tell you that the four thousand pounds advanced by me to the Greeks is likely to set a fleet and an army in motion for some months."

If the two manuscripts could be compared, the point might easily be settled. The Duchess's play has been lost, and the only copy of *Werner* is in the handwriting of Mrs. Shelley. After all, sums up Mr. Leveson-Gower, Byron's motive was good, and he injured no one living. He was ready in order to promote the emancipation of Greece, a cause to which he had devoted his life, to give his name to a work which, to say the least, was not likely to add to his fame. . . . There may have been other motives also— his love of mystification, and some curiosity to see how far the public could be bamboozled.

Here then we have a very pretty literary problem. A poet's desire for money to further his ideals set against his own fame and reputation.

The first evidence against the authorship of *Werner* by the Duchess is that Byron dedicated the play to " The Illustrious Goethe." Byron may have had a wish to bamboozle the public, but he had too much pride in his own genius to dream of dedicating a stolen poem to the greatest poet in Europe. The second witness is an angry letter to Mr. Murray that if *Werner* has been published without a preface " you will have plunged me into a very disagreeable dilemma, because I shall be accused of plagiarism from Miss Lee's German tale, whereas I have fully and freely acknowledged that the drama is taken entirely from the story."

A charge of plagiarism is fatal to any author of standing— it means mental exhaustion and bankruptcy. Byron's accomplishment was unequal, but he never lacked the poetic afflatus.

Byron told Medwin that " *Werner* was written in twenty-eight days, and one entire act at a sitting." Mr. Ernest Hartley Coleridge attacks the suggestion of the Duchess's authorship by some " internal evidence," and compares passages from *Werner* with parallels in the *Age of Bronze, Manfred*, and *Childe Harold*. But Mr. Leveson-Gower is ready to admit that Byron probably altered and amended many of the lines.

" However improbable, it is not impossible that the MS. was accidentally included amongst Byron's papers," writes Mr. Coleridge. " And if we knew nothing about the composition of *Werner*, the theory that Byron entered into the Duchess's labours, instead of snipping and pasting for himself (from Miss Lee's novel) might possibly be taken into consideration. But the piecing together of *Werner* is not only sworn to by Byron himself, but is attested by numerous witnesses."

" *Did* Byron write *Werner* or was it the Duchess of Devonshire ? " asks Mr. Coleridge in his great edition of Byron's works. If we turn back a few pages and compare Byron's lines on Lake Leman with Duchess Georgiana's " heroic measure " upon St. Gothard there should be no difficulty at arriving at a conclusion. But the whole problem is excellent exercise for a literary idle day.[1]

[1] The authorities are " Did Byron write *Werner? Nineteenth Century*, August, 1899 ; a correspondence in *Literature*, August 12, 19, 26, September 9, 1899 ; and *The Works of Lord Byron —Poetry*, Vol. V., edited by Ernest Hartley Coleridge, 1901.

CHAPTER XIX

The strain of war—a change at Devonshire House—gambling in high life—Fox's faro bank—Lady Louisa Stuart's recollections the Duchess's huge losses—disappearance of the old faces.

W E now approach the last period of the joint reign at Devonshire House. The Fall of the Bastille had been greeted by the Whigs almost as a party triumph. The execution of Louis XVI. and his Queen had an immediate effect upon English feeling. The emigrants who crowded the Whig salons belonged naturally to the royalist party. Many of the French noblemen who had been welcomed in Mayfair were now languishing in the prisons of France or giving up their lives on the guillotine. Great Britain was engaged in a seemingly interminable war, and beset by troubles at home.

There was much outward gaiety in London. The Duchess and Lady Elizabeth entertained lavishly, and Devonshire House remained a centre of political influence. They still travelled abroad—but not by way of Paris—to Switzerland and Italy. But the old life had ended, and the old friends were one by one bidding adieu and slipping out of the conflict. It would be absurd to say that Devonshire House was gloomy. That condition did ultimately arrive, but not until after the beginning of the nineteenth century. There was however an acute tension, a feeling of dread for the future which did not relax for over twenty years.

How real that strain was amongst the " governing classes " can be illustrated by a short anecdote concerning the second Earl Spencer, brother to the Duchess. Gibbon said he was " a valuable man, and, when familiar, a pleasant companion."

By tradition of politics he belonged to the "old Whig" school, but, in spite of the past history of the Spencers, he became a close adherent of Pitt, and was appointed First Lord of the Admiralty. Lady Lyttelton, his daughter, used to relate that one day she rushed with her mother into Lord Spencer's room at the Admiralty, having heard rumours of a great victory, and that they found him in a dead faint on the floor, with the despatches from Nelson announcing the Battle of the Nile clasped in his hand.

The Whig party had split, and the feeling between the two sections, or at least between the wives of the leaders, was bitter. Lady Lyttelton tells us that in later life Lady Spencer, a daughter of the Earl of Lucan, hated a Tory with a deep hate. But in the days when her husband was a member of a Tory Government she received the Tory clans, and held no intercourse with the "New Whigs," of which party Sheridan and Fox were the leaders and Duchess Georgiana, her sister-in-law, the leading goddess. "So keen was the party feeling that for some years the two ladies never visited each other." [1]

After the birth of her son the Duchess slowly altered into a more sedate woman. She was a good mother, and took those duties of her household with a proper seriousness. Dutens, in his *Memoirs of a Traveller*, notes that in 1791, "at the age when women are most attached to the world, having lost nothing of her beauty and attractions, she withdrew from it, to give herself up entirely to a family and to a small circle of friends." This is slightly exaggerated, for the same contemporary in another chapter of his book adds that as her daughters grew into womanhood the Duchess mixed again in society. Frances, Lady Shelley, writing at second-hand, says that the Duchess of Devonshire left

---

[1] Lavinia, Lady Spencer, has been described as haughty, exclusive, intolerant, and a fiery partisan. Gibbon found her charming, with sense and spirit, and the wit and simplicity of a child. Dr. Burney said she was "a pleasant, lively, and comical creature, with more talents and discernment than are expected from a character so *folâtre*." As she grew older her temper became exceedingly tyrannical, and when put out she could swear in a most disconcerting fashion.

the gay world. " Her admirable daughters had never mixed in her evening coterie, and were brought up in that strict propriety which characterised the daughters of our Grandees in those days. Children were never admitted to hear the gossip of their elders, and knew nothing of the world until they married." So much the worse for the children, and also for the world in which they had to act the parts of men and women.

The Duchess and her doings were always subjects of exaggerated censure. Prim Mrs. Ord warned Fanny Burney not to have anything to do with such a set. Whenever the name of Devonshire was mentioned there was an opportunity for what Horace Walpole calls " licentiousness of abuse." Lady Shelley with a certain felinity compares the Mexborough family with the mansion in Piccadilly. Lady Mexborough's invitations could not be accepted. " There never was a house where such profligacy reigned ! Devonshire House, at all events, wore the garb of the greatest refinement and delicacy. It enshrined all the charms of talent, beauty, and those *agréments*, imported from the Court of Marie Antoinette, which veiled the inveterate profligacy of that set with elegance and outward propriety. In that fascinating coterie the most sensitive natures would become demoralised, before discovering that they had unwittingly entered the very precincts of Circe's court."

Much of this criticism is the rankest nonsense. There was an unfortunate blot on the Devonshire House circle, but it was not an error to which undue importance was attached in the eighteenth century. The most dissolute member of the circle was George, Prince of Wales. Fox was living in conjugal happiness with his wife at St. Anne's Hill, a pattern of all the virtues. The only oversight on his certificate of marriage and morality was the date—which should have been antedated by ten or twelve years. Sheridan had, it was true, once fallen in love with Mrs. Crewe. But that was an old story which had never developed into scandal. During the period to which Lady Shelley refers the worst one could say of " Sherry " was the lamentable fact that he was drinking his brilliant intellect into a condition of maudlin waste.

The Duchess of Devonshire was always gay, and that, with a certain section of English opinion, is too often accounted a crime. Fanny Burney aptly describes her personality at the time of the birth of the long-awaited heir.

" I now saw the Duchess far more easy and lively in her spirits, and consequently, far more lovely in her person. Vivacity is so much her characteristic, that her style of beauty requires it indispensably ; the beauty, indeed, dies away without it. I now saw how her fame for personal charms had been obtained ; the expression of her smiles is so very sweet, and has an ingenuousness and openness so singular, that, taken in those moments, not the most rigid critic could deny the justice of her personal celebrity. She was quite gay, easy, and charming : indeed, that last epithet might have been coined for her."

Yet, behind the mask, this lady had many secret troubles, and the chief was one she should never have been troubled with. She suffered from a continual lack of pence.

This worry was largely of her own making. Everything Ferdinand Christin said of her love of play was strictly true. She was, and had been from the early days of her married life, a confirmed and rash gambler.

Perhaps Lady Shelley when she spoke of the profligacy of Devonshire House intended her indictment to include card playing. At the house itself there does not appear to have been any outrageous exploits on the green tables. But most of the women and practically all the men of that circle spent half their lives " dealing and punting." There is this excuse for the women : they copied the men.

Dr. Johnson regretted that he had never learned to play at cards. " It is very useful in life ; it generates kindness and consolidates society." Dr. Johnson was generally correct in his judgments, but when he was wrong he was foolish. Card playing does not generate kindness,[1] and instead of con-

---

[1] There is more friendliness amongst the prisoners of a menagerie than between the partners at a rubber of whist. " I have known,"

solidating society it speedily disintegrates it. The gambling in Mayfair during the first thirty years of the reign of George III. was the curse of the English aristocracy, only ceasing when the rage burnt itself out. Fox, and we could have no better authority, says the highest play was between 1772 and the outbreak of the American War. In 1780 faro superseded loo. The next generation, although not wholly free, to a large extent escaped the plague which had ruined their fathers.

Charles James Fox was the worst offender. His gambling adventures would fill a library, and can be traced throughout all the familiar correspondence of his youth. Selwyn pictures him losing and winning great sums, " elbow deep in gold." He would play for hours, until at last, in utter weariness he would rest his huge saturnine face upon his arms and fall into a deep slumber on the edge of the baize table. At the most solemn moments his mind was conceiving fresh ventures. The night before the death of his mother he sat in the clubroom at White's, and " planned out a sort of itinerant trade, which was of going from horse race to horse race, and so, by knowing the value and speed of all the horses in England, to acquire a certain fortune." In March, 1782, when Fox had already reached parliamentary importance, and was being pestered by office-seekers, Selwyn reports to Carlisle that " Charles was closeted every instant at Brooks's by one or the other, that he can neither punt or deal for a quarter of an hour but he is obliged to give an audience." Selwyn calls it a scene " *la plus parfaitement comique que l'on puisse imaginer*, and to nobody it seems

---

writes Fielding in *Amelia*, " a stranger at Bath who has happened fortunately (I might almost say unfortunately) to have four by honours in his hand almost every time he dealt for a whole evening shunned universally by the whole company the next day." When the sixth Earl of Chesterfield was at Spa in 1775, Lady Orwell, a lady of more than fifty, found fault with his whist-playing. " He got up in a violent passion, vow'd he would not bear to be scolded by any but young and handsome women, and added many other grosièretés, till she fell into tears." The Earl left Spa the next morning, but had the decency to write and ask pardon of the lady he had so affronted.

(more) risible than to Charles himself." The scene was laughable from one point of view. Pathetic from another when we remember that these gamesters had the government of the Empire in their hands at a most critical moment with stakes of human lives rather than spades and clubs, sovereigns and I.O.U.'s.

Fox's faro bank was more than a nine days' wonder. Lady Louisa Stuart remembered it years later. "You who are used to hear of Mr. Fox only as the head of a great party, the statesman, the patriot, etc., what would you have said to this paragraph? "Brooks's is very flourishing: the *young Cub* [Fox] (an old nickname) and Co. have won a great deal of money this winter by a Faro Bank they set up just after the Eo (?) tables were put an end to." But this was from a ministerialist. Now hear one of his intimate friends: "Charles has won a good deal of money lately. He and Richard have set up a Faro Bank together." And another: "Charles has found a better thing than the Govt. of M——(Madras) in St. James's Street. He has set up a Faro Bank in conjunction with Richard (Fitzpatrick), and I verily believe he is at this moment worth £20,000; but he does not think it at all necessary to pay any of his debts with it, for there is an execution in the house almost every day." Ah! you will think this was the great man's youthful follies. No such thing; he passed his *youth* in *losing* money, and was then 40 or near it. The next year, Lord North being driven out, he became Secretary of State and Richard Secretary of War, and they made over the Faro Bank to one of their party, for whom they could not find a place in the administration. All this as openly as possible —none of them in the least ashamed of it—and now you are taught to admire them as patterns of uprightness and public virtue."

These were the recollections of a lady, who, like Frances, Lady Shelley, did not write from personal experience. The faro bank was managed by a partnership of men belonging to the Duchess of Devonshire's friends. Thomas Raikes, that well-informed man about town, gives more interesting details. Lord Cholmondeley, bosom friend of the Prince of Wales, and constant visitor to Piccadilly, was one of the four partners. Set up at Brooks's in St. James's Street the bank ruined half the members. They would not trust the waiters to be croupiers, but themselves dealt the cards alternately, being paid three guineas an hour out of the joint fund, and at this rate Lord Cholmondeley, and other noblemen of the highest rank, were seen slaving like menials till a late hour in the morning. The gains were enormous. Mr. Thompson and Lord Cholmondeley realised from £300,000 to £400,000 each. Tom Stepney had a share, but would always punt against his own partners, and lost on one side what he gained on the other. A Mr. Paul, who brought home a large fortune from India, lost £90,000 in one night. Ruined, he returned to India to make another fortune.

The mental and physical activity of these men of the late eighteenth century is amazing. They were seldom at rest, yet they had none of the time and labour saving appliances of the present day. The slightest journey was tiresome, but they were always travelling, from their country estates to London, and from London to the Continent. They spent hours in the thick atmosphere of the House of Commons, and left it in the early hours for the still more exhausting atmosphere of the St. James's gambling dens. Each man drank more bottles at a sitting than we dare touch glasses. Meals were heavy. Selwyn's friend, the Rev. John Warner, D.D., speaks of " an immense dinner and an ocean of claret.[1] Such titans, beyond conception

[1] Dr. Warner visited Devonshire House. Here is his history of a dinner with Henry Hoare, the banker, and Philip Champion Crespigny, King's Proctor and M.P. " The whim took them, as it sometimes will, to have a blackguard scheme of dining in my cabin, and ordering their dinner ; and a very good one they had : mackerel, a delicate neck of veal, a piece of Hamborough beef, cabbage and salad, and a gooseberry tart ; and when they had drunk the bottle of white wine, and of port, which accompanied the dinner, and after that the only double bottle of Harry's claret that I had left, I found in an old corner (as they could not again descend to port, or, as the boys at Eton call it, black-strap) one of the two bottles of Burgundy which I

first in pleasure as well as in duty, leaders of vice and virtue, could never have been subjugated by a foreign power.

The women followed the example of their husbands, brothers, fathers—Lord Spencer, the Duchess's father, gambled so wildly that when he died his vast estate was seriously embarrassed. Lord Chesterfield advised his son " never sit down to play with men only, but let there always be a woman or two of the party, and then the loss or the gain cannot be considerable." That advice was of little value at the end of the eighteenth century. Mrs. Hobart, known as Lady Buckinghamshire, opened a public faro bank in St. James's Square, thus rivalling the commercial instincts of Lord Cholmondeley. In 1796 the Duchess of Devonshire's sister, Lady Bessborough, was arrested and fined at Marlborough Street Police Court for gambling at Lady Buckinghamshire's house. Chief Justice Kenyon declared that nothing would prevent this frenzied gambling amongst the ladies of society until they were sent to prison. A sinister creature named Martindale moves in the background of all these transactions, raising money for his fair clients, discounting bills, acting as a go-between in a multitude of shady financial transactions.

In 1780 Walpole mentions amongst other gossip that the Duchess had won £900 by betting at lotteries. She went after the opera to the office for lottery tickets, to bet with the attendants on the numbers which would prove successful at the drawing. In one unlucky evening she lost £300. In 1791, again quoting Walpole, we are told that she is in the hands of the Jews. A letter turned up in a London sale room lately, written in French, and suggesting the pledging of her diamonds as security for a loan. Another undated letter speaks of acute financial worries.

" My dearest Therese," writes the Duchess " I have no

took from your cellar when you gave me the key of it ; and, by Jove ! how they did abuse my modesty, finding it so exquisite, that instead of two I did not take two dozen. But having no more, we closed the orifice of the stomach with a pint of Dantzic cherry-brandy, and have just parted in a tolerable state of insensibility to the ills of human life."

excuse for not writing to you but the uncertainty I am in till something or other is settled or begun.

" Mr. Heaton's illness put us terribly back, and though the Duke is positively resolved to a reform—indeed too necessary—it hurts him to set about it.

" We are alone except Bess and Lord Fred, who comes to-day ; but we are going to Hardwicke, and Bess and I hope we shall be there alone with him, when I dare say we shall get him to settle on some beginning ; till then, I confess, I shall have no peace.

" I am quite well and take a great deal of exercise, both walking and riding, for I find bodily fatigue is the way to rest my mind and makes me sleep better than all the opiates they gave me when my nerves were so bad."

Her health became indifferent.   In 1796 she suffered from a severe cold, which, according to Horace Walpole, ended in the partial loss of sight of one eye.   In November of that year, writing to Frederick Foster, Lady Elizabeth's elder son, she refers to " the dreadful complaint I have had on one eye which has occasioned my being forbid writing. . . . You must excuse this bad writing, as I am still half-blind." And to Lady Elizabeth she addressed some verses upon her apprehension of becoming blind.

> The Life of the Roebuck was mine,
>   As I bounded o'er Valley and Lawn ;
> I watched the gay Twilight decline,
>   And worshipped the day-breaking Dawn.

But " Dependance on Thee is my Choice," for——

> Ere my Sight I was doomed to resign,
>   My heart I surrendered to thee ;
> Not a Thought or an Action was mine,
>   But I saw as thou badst me to see.

Amidst all these trials, she did not lose her charm.   Dutens speaks of her at this period as affable, kind, and unreserved in society.   Her good nature, he writes, increased her embarrassments, for she was very charitable and borrowed in order to give.   She thought only of the interests of others. Her mind was quick and active.   She appeared always to act entirely from the impression of the moment. And he noted that her uncommon gracefulness was in her air rather than in her figure.

Meanwhile, despite private and domestic preoccupations, the gilded life of Devonshire House continued without change. The Duke was still engrossed in politics, a sleeping rather than an active member of his party. The Duchess and Lady Elizabeth travelled to and from Switzerland and Italy. In 1795 the Countess Bentinck met her at Hamburg. " The Duchess was dressed in the old English style, wearing a sort of hooped petticoat. She had a wonderful figure, a perfectly shaped bust, and glittered with jewels. Indeed, she outshone all, even the youngest, in the brilliance and magnificence of her appearance."

In London Gibbon reported that Devonshire House was " a constant though late resort of society." Gibbon himself, when in town, was already ready to spend an hour in the company of the " good Duchess" and " the wicked Lady Elizabeth." Once he found the ladies busily stitching together red flannel waistcoats for the British soldiers in Flanders. During his last illness he was contemplating a visit to Devonshire House. " I am going to Devonshire House on Thursday," he told Lord Sheffield, but he grew rapidly worse, and, on Wednesday, was dead.

Old faces disappeared, but new ones came to the front. We do not know if Nelson went to Devonshire House, but the Duchess met him several times at Lord Spencer's, and at Lord Abercorn's made the acquaintance of Lady Hamilton and saw those famous " Attitudes " and poses which had gained the approbation of artistic Europe.

CHAPTER XX

Lady Elizabeth Foster's troubles—the Earl of Bristol in Berlin— his dreams of a royal marriage—his behaviour; in Italy—his death—mixed regrets.

LADY Elizabeth Foster had her own troubles to bear. She had rarely seen her children, who were being educated by their father in Ireland. John Thomas Foster died in 1796. The unfortunate marriage had lasted twenty years. Lady Elizabeth was now free to marry, but she did not—was not able to—make any change in her state. But her two sons were immediately invited to Devonshire House. " I write now to assure you of the warm interest I take in everything that concerns you and my impatience to see you," wrote the Duchess to Frederick Foster in November, 1796. " Your appartements, and your brother's, are quite ready at Devonshire House. I hear you are to set out on the 20th, I do most earnestly *entreat* you to let your journey suffer no further delay. Your Dear Mother's heart is so full of anxiety and expectation that any disappointment or delay in the expected moment would be fatal to her health."

There was some little exaggeration, for Lady Elizabeth does not seem to have been particularly unwell, and there was little reason to anticipate her early demise. Her anxieties were more on account of the Herveys than the Fosters.

Her father, Bishop of Derry and Earl of Bristol,[1] had been odd from his youth. Lord Bristol was a man of

[1] He succeeded his brother to the title of Earl of Bristol, and to the family estate of Ickworth Park, near Bury St. Edmunds, in December, 1779.

considerable parts, but far more brilliant than solid. His
family was indeed famous for talents ; equally so for eccentricity, and the eccentricity of the whole race shone out
and seemed to be concentrated in him. In one respect he
was not unlike Villiers, Duke of Buckingham. " Everything
by starts and nothing long " ; generous, but uncertain ;
splendid, but fantastical ; an admirer of the fine arts, without
any just selection ; engaging, often licentious in conversation ; extremely polite, extremely violent. " His distribution of Church livings, as I have been informed among the
older and respectable clergy in his own diocese, must always
be mentioned with that warm approbation which it is justly
entitled to. It is said (how truly I know not) that he had
applied for the bishopric of Dublin, afterwards for the
lieutenancy of Ireland ; was refused both, and *hinc illæ
lacrymæ*, hence his opposition."

He rapidly added fresh pages to the many legends of
Hervey folly. Had the Herveys simply been foolish
nobody would have paid any attention to their freakish
pranks. But the disconcerting fact about the three mad
families of East Anglia, the Walpoles, the Townshends, and
the Herveys, was that through their waywardness ran a
streak of genius. Elizabeth, Lady Holland, summed up
Lord John Townshend as " like the rest of his family he
is mad ; never enough to be confined, but often very flighty."
The remark applied equally well to Lord Bristol.

In Ireland he had excited bitter animosity and also
appreciative goodwill. His efforts on behalf of Catholic
emancipation, and his active encouragement of the Irish
volunteer movement, were judged from a partisan standpoint. His actions were always exaggerated. His activity
as a leader of the Irish patriots during the American war was
never forgiven. His theatrical entry into Dublin in 1783
as a member of the Convention of Volunteer Delegates was
not easily forgotten. Escorted by a body of dragoons, he
sat in an open carriage, " full of spirits and talk, apparently
enjoying the eager gaze of the surrounding multitude, and
displaying altogether the self-complacency of a favourite

marshal of France on his way to Versailles, rather than the grave deportment of a prelate of the Church of England."

He was at once a saint and a rogue. Everything depended upon the point of view. Certainly he was a megalomaniac. Yet there must have been something good in the Protestant bishop and nobleman whose death was mourned by the Catholic bishop and Presbyterian minister of Derry. Rich, hospitable, lavishly generous, passionately fond of show and popularity, an exquisite judge of art—these were his virtues. His correspondence with his daughter Lady Elizabeth reveals the darker side of his character.

As a bishop he was a domestic man. But when he succeeded to the earldom his manners degenerated. Lady Bristol and the diocese were deserted. He spent years travelling on the Continent. In the United Kingdom his chief interest was the building of huge palaces in County Down and Suffolk. He had grandiose dreams for the family, and contemplated a royal alliance for his eldest surviving son. True the lady was the daughter of a left-handed marriage, but that was not a matter to be squeamish over. From Pyrmont, in 1796, he sent letter after letter to Lady Elizabeth, advocating the marriage of Lord Hervey to the Comtesse de la Marche, a daughter of Frederick William II. of Prussia and a lady who had probably started life in the Italian Opera at Berlin, but was now respectably known as Wilhelmina, Countess of Lichtenau.

She was "the prettiest, sweetest, most delicate, and innocent, as well as accomplished little woman I ever saw," said the would-be father-in-law. She was also endowed with £100,000, and the promise of a dukedom to her husband. The Herveys would then have "a perpetual relationship" with the Princess of Wales, who was the daughter of the Duke of Brunswick, and a still closer connection with the Duchess of York, daughter of Frederick William and half-sister to the Comtesse. The King of Prussia was "bent upon it," and the two fathers arranged that Lord Hervey should be made ambassador to Berlin, "with such an influence and preponderance in favour of dear England as no other could withstand." The scheme was fascinating, and might have succeeded had not Lord Hervey been in love with another lady.

The Earl methodically argued the advantages and disadvantages of the proposed matches. As for his son's choice : " she has little or no fortune. Your brother by the last act of settlement can make no provision for either her or her children, and if he should die within five or six years—which the perturbed state of his mind might easily produce—what must be the consequence to his widow and her orphans ?

The King of Prussia installed the Earl-Bishop at Potsdam, lending him the palace of Sans Souci with its " cooks, manors, library, gallery." What did the ghost of old Fritz think of the British intruder ? " Oh ! if I can accomplish my heart and soul's desire to join your dear brother's hand with La Comtesse de la Marche—£5,000 a year down, £5,000 more in reversion, an English Dukedom, probably the embassy to Berlin—por Dio che piacere."

Like Robinson Crusoe he set down the pros and cons in two columns.

On my side.	On his side.
£5,000 a year down.	No fortune.
£5,000 a year in reversion.	Wife and children beggars for want of settlement.
An English Dukedom which the King pledges to obtain.	No connection.
Royal connection—Princess of Wales, and Duchess of York.	A love match, like all others for four generations before him.

Or, as he put it in another communication, " poverty, famine, and omnipotent love for her " (the undesirable daughter-in-law) " and her children, compared with Peace of Mind for me and himself."

Lord Hervey remained obstinate and ill, so ill that his father asked Lady Elizabeth to see Lord Spencer (who was then First Lord of the Admiralty) and borrow a frigate to take the hope of the Herveys off to Naples. He still hankered after the Prussian alliance, telling his daughter that he was off to Potsdam and Sans Souci to spend a month " with my dear Countess, and her beautiful, elegant, decent, mild, gentle daughter. Would to God she were also mine. . . . A young woman more calculated by nature as well as by education to make a virtuous man happy, I never yet saw, and I am certain you would doat on her."

His mind was incessantly scheming and arranging. He suggested that young Frederick Foster should join him on the Continent, an arrangement he thought might prove excellent for the boy's morals and intellect. He endeavoured to inspire fresh energy in the breast of King Frederick William, but to no purpose. " One hour in the lap of his Danseuse, and he lies there, the shadow of a king." If his son were ambassador at Berlin they might be able to " warm this lump of inert matter and breathe into it a permanent fire with 233,000 men at his back." At Potsdam he is perfectly happy. " Here I am truly worthy of this Philosophic Mansion, without care, and almost without thought, so consummately am I Germanized." And he amiably referred to the French as ourang-outangs and tiger-monkeys. He wished to see France crushed for ever, but he warned his daughter that the energy of the French was so great that, despite all defeats, France could easily recruit her strength, and regain her old place amongst the nations.

His anxiety for a wealthy daughter-in-law is probably explained by the state of his own pocket. At one time he had set aside £12,000 a year for the buildings in progress at Ickworth. Early in 1798 he found himself in Rome and exceedingly short of cash. He had taken a balance of his account at Messrs. Gosling's, and found that they held only £100. " Several of my own drafts from Italy have been protested, which is both expensive and disgraceful." Within six months he was imploring Lady Elizabeth to persuade Mr. Pitt to appoint him British Minister at Rome—although Lady Elizabeth had always been one of Pitt's most implacable political opponents. " All my effects at Rome are under sequestration to the amount of £20,000 at the very least, all that immense, valuable, and beautiful property of large mosaick pavement, sumptuous chimney-pieces for my new house, and pictures, statues, busts, and marbles without end, first-rate Titians and Raphaels, dear Guidos, and three old Carraccis—gran Dio! che tesoro." Despairingly he implores his daughter to invite Lord Spencer, " or, above all your greater friend the Duke of Devonshire, or the Duchess," to aid in the salvage of these unparalleled art treasures.

The old pagan had no thoughts beyond his antiques. In Lord Cloncurry's memoirs are some extraordinary stories. " He received £5,000 a quarter which he immediately expended in the purchase of every article of vertu that came within his reach. In this, as in most other cases, however, the proverb came true—wilful waste made woeful want ; and towards the end of the quarter the noble prelate used to find his purse absolutely empty, and his credit so low as to be insufficient to procure him a bottle of orvieto. Then followed a dispersion of his collection, as rapidly as it was gathered, but as might be expected, at a heavy discount."

In Ireland he had been notorious for his love of show. In Rome he became one of the sights of the city. Lord Cloncurry writes : " I have seen the eccentric Earl-Bishop ride about the streets of Rome, dressed in red plush breeches and a broad brimmed white or straw hat, and was often asked if that was the canonical costume of an Irish prelate.[1] His irregularities were so strange, as to render any story that might be told about him credible, and, of course, to cause the invention of many, that in reference to any other person would be incredible. I recollect Colonel Plunkett making a bargain with a carriage-keeper for the services of a vehicle, and upon his remonstrating against a demand of fourteen instead of twelve crowns a month asked by another, being told that it was easy for the competitor to work cheap, as

---

[1] Another contemporary writes that in Italy the Earl wore a white hat edged with purple, a coat of crimson silk or velvet (according to the season), a black sash spangled with silver, and purple stockings.

his wife had an *amico* who was a farmer, and sold the complaisant husband oats and hay cheap ; while he himself was, on the contrary, obliged to raise his charges in consequence of his wife being thrown back upon his hands by the death of Milor il Vescovo."

The end came very suddenly in July, 1803. He was now an old and worn man, hardly a credit to his name, certainly not a credit to his bishopric. Taken ill without warning on a journey from Albano to Rome he was carried into the outhouse of a cottage, where he expired. The peasants refused to allow a heretic-bishop to die under their roof. And so the owner of Ickworth died in an open barn.

He was a true type of nobleman almost extinct at the present day. He neglected his family and his bishopric ; lived an absentee from his country. After all, one may pardon a man who runs after flesh and blood, but it is not so easy to understand the character of a man whose only interest in life is marble mantelpieces or classical statuary. The obituary of Lord Bristol published in the *Gentleman's Magazine* was possibly written by the family.

" As an amateur, connoisseur, and indefatigable protector of the fine arts he died at his post surrounded by artists, whose talents his judgment had directed and whose wants his liberality had relieved. . . . He may truly be said to have clothed the naked and fed the hungry, and, as ostentation never constituted real charity, his left hand did not know what his right had distributed. The tears and lamentations of widows and orphans have discovered his philanthropy when he is no more. . . . But, as no man is without his enemies, and envy is most busy about the most deserving, some of his lordship's singularities have been the object of calumny, and his peculiarities ridiculed as affected ; when the former were only the effect of pure conduct, unrestrained by ceremony, because it meant no harm, and the latter the consequence of an entire independence, long enjoyed, serviceable to many, baneful to none."

These grandiloquent sentences sound like an echoing oration over the body of a dead hero. As a corrective we must turn to the intimate family correspondence of the Herveys. In August, 1799, Lady Elizabeth wrote to her son Augustus, " We left Ickworth yesterday a little after twelve and arrived at six ; we travelled rather with heavy hearts, for there had been unpleasant letters from my father, and my dear mother was low and unwell. I cannot tell you at present what they were, but most certainly he is a cruel man."

Lady Bristol had already expressed herself in fewer and simpler words. " I leave him to Heaven and to those thorns that in his bosom lodge to prick and sting him." That was written in 1783. She never had reason to alter her opinion of this protector of the fine arts, this guardian of widows and orphans.

CHAPTER XXI

A garden party at Chiswick—happy days—Madame Récamier and
the Duchess of Devonshire—advice to a son—family marriages
—illness of the Duchess—an interminable war—Trafalgar and
Austerlitz—general gloom—sudden death of the Duchess—
her children's love—Lady Bessborough.

"I AM returned living from *the Breakfast*. I must even
own that I found it extremely pleasant and was very
much amused.

"We got there a little after Three, and were told the
Duchess was in the Pleasure Ground. We according found
her sitting with Mrs. Fitzherbert by an urn. Several Bands
of Musick were very well placed in the garden, so that as soon
as you were out of the hearing of one Band, you began to
catch the notes of another ; thus Harmony always met your
ears. This sort of continued concert has always a pleasant
effect upon my nerves. There is a Temple which was destin'd
to the Prince's Entertainment and was very prettily decorated with flowers.

"There were about 20 Covers, and when we understood
that the Duchess and all these fine People were in their
Temple, we Goths we took possession of the House, where we
found in every room a table spread, with cold meat, fruit,
ice, and all sorts of Wine. It is a fine House, and there are
most delightful pictures in it. After the eating and quaffing
was over, the young ladies danced on the Green. Lady
Georgina Cavendish (a tall, Gawkey, fair Girl, with her head
poked out and her mouth open) dances however very well,
she has learned of Hillisbery. Lord Hartington (like the
Duke) danced also. . . . There were a great many French,

both men and women, among the number, Mde. de Boële, the Viscountess de Vaudreuil . . . Eugene Montmorency.

"We left Chiswick between seven and eight. People returned for the Opera." Lady Jerningham, who wrote this entertaining account of a garden party at Chiswick in the summer of 1800, went to bed thoroughly tired. Before finishing her letter she added some bright details of Lady Jersey hunting the Prince of Wales, who had many good reasons for keeping out of her way. "The Prince was *en Polisson*, a Brown Dress, round Hat, and a Brown Wig. He stood almost the whole time by his band, with Dr. Burney, ordering different pieces of Musick."

Devonshire House was still the scenes of entertainment no other great house in London could rival. In June, 1800, an immense ball was given. Eight hundred guests were invited, including many French. The cost was said to be over £1000. The garden parties at Chiswick were famous. "There is an indescribable charm in Lord Burlington's house that no other place possesses," wrote Lord Ronald Gower many years ago. Chiswick was a place of peace after the restless world of Piccadilly. "Happy days at Chiswick, which no crossness of our governess could spoil—the country in the spring—the smell of the jessamines after the rain—the cedars with their cones sitting so grandly upon them—the birds' nests, which we never took—the wild strawberries, which have disappeared—the lilacs breaking with their load—the vision of the duke walking amongst the trees with my mother, he bending towards her, for this dear uncle was deaf. Well, too, I recollect his coming to the foot of the old stairs at the old house at Chiswick, and telling us of Napoleon's escape from Elba, and our excitement." [1] Lord Burlington's palladian villa was classic ground. Pope was ferried from Twickenham to visit his patron. Gay sang of the wonderful gardens :

The purple vine, blue plum, and blushing peach.

---

[1] Quoted by Lord Ronald Gower from a letter written by his mother. She was a grand-daughter of the Duchess. The "deaf duke" was the Duchess's son.

Thomson came from Hampstead to

> Sylvan scenes, where art alone pretends
> To dress her mistress and disclose her charms.

To this abode of peace Georgiana Cavendish fled from a world which had lost its charms.

There were many duties to be performed. " Aunt Devonshire goes with her nieces to court," is a diary entry for May 17, 1805. She entertained lavishly. No distinguished foreigner visited London without passing through her drawing-room. During the short peace of Amiens (March 27, 1802, to May 18, 1803) Madame Récamier came to London with her mother, bringing letters of introduction from the Duc de Guines, who had been French ambassador thirty years earlier. De Guines and the Duchess had never ceased to correspond, and Madame Récamier was at once received at Devonshire House. Chateaubriand mentions in his *Memoires d'Outre Tombe* that in English society at that moment the most remarkable person was the Duchess of Devonshire, then between forty-five and fifty. She was still in vogue and beautiful, although she had lost an eye, which she concealed behind a lock of her hair. The first time that Madame Récamier appeared in public, it was in her company. The Duchess took her to the opera in her box, in which were the Prince of Wales, the Duc d'Orléans, and his brothers, the Duc de Montpensier, and the Comte de Beaujolais. The beautiful Frenchwoman excited so much interest that she had to leave by a private door before the curtain fell.

She still wrote verses, and—unhappily—she still tempted fortune. Her gambling losses were immense. Her great-grandson is responsible for the statement that she was reduced to such a pitch that even when living in Devonshire House she had to make a dash across the hall to her carriage, for fear of being seized under her own doorway by the bailiffs.

In a letter to Augustus Foster (December, 1804) Lady Elizabeth told her son that she was nervous and troubled about the arrangements for paying the Duchess's debts.

" There never was anything so angelic as the Duke of Devonshire's conduct, and the many conversations I had with him on the subject, though it made me so nervous at the time, have made me happier now, and, if possible, increased my admiration and attachment to him. I feel secure now that she will avoid things of this kind for the future, and though the sum is great, yet it will end well I am convinced." There is a peculiar ring about these sentences. Lady Elizabeth had become the actual mistress, with a tendency to preach morality to all her friends and relations. On her son's eighteenth birthday she addressed him a letter which would have been admirable from any other mother.

" Be firm," she told him, though admitting that " an unyielding disposition is still less amiable." The great fundamental qualities of his character were right. " I have never known you fail in them ; strict inviolable truth, a religious observance of one's promise, a sacred observance of another's secret and prudence for one's own ; as your situation and connections in life enlarge duties increase also, and amongst the foremost I hope you will ever feel the purest regard towards women, and never risk their happiness to gratify your vanity or even passions. I was pleased to hear W. Lamb say with earnestness that if he felt a growing passion for his friend's wife he would fly to the further end of the earth to resist the danger." [1]

The young Earl of Aberdeen, Augustus Foster's closest friend, was the first to notice the failing strength of the Duchess. " He really seems quite anxious," commented Lady Elizabeth. Sir Walter Farquhar was in attendance, and pronounced his patient better. Then the former round of fashion recommenced. In April, 1805, Aberdeen writes from Watier's Club, that "the Duchess has been very ill, but is now much recovered."

Lady Elizabeth's correspondence with her son, now British Minister at Washington, covers the many interests of the household in Piccadilly. " I ought to talk of politicks to

[1] W. Lamb, better known as Viscount Melbourne, and first Prime Minister.

you, but all conversation begins and ends with Roscius."
Augustus had fallen in love with Corisande de Grammont,
the French girl who had been placed under the Duchess's
protection at the outbreak of the Revolution. But the
elder Foster was unfortunate in his choice, for the lady and
Lord Ossulston had arranged matters and were only waiting
for the consent of a hard-hearted father, the Earl of Tanker-
ville. Lady Elizabeth was afraid her son might in despair
seek for a wife in the States : " Pray don't marry an
American, or, if you must, let her be rich—for really the more
I see of poverty the more detestable it appears to me."

There is much family news, the most important being the
marriage of Caroline Ponsonby to William Lamb. " We
were in great joy at hearing of Nelson's arrival in the West
Indies, and now all is despondency again because he has not
overtaken and beat the French and Spaniards, but he drove
them away."

Towards the autumn of 1805 the atmosphere became
generally despondent. The war was interminable. The
Duchess was ill. Young life had vanished from Devonshire House. " Her Grace's parties were terribly dull,"
said " Poodle " Byng many years after. " One sat playing
cards at little round tables, and spoke always in a whisper."
In the old days Devonshire House had every reputation save
that of dullness.

There were too many anxieties for comfort. Lady Elizabeth's son, Augustus Clifford, was with Nelson's squadron
in the West Indies. In August she wrote from Chiswick ;
" we are at present all impatience and expectation and some
anxiety about the fleet." The public situation was so
dangerous that the Whigs were ready to co-operate with
their old enemy Pitt if that could save the nation. " It is
an awful moment," wrote Lady Elizabeth at the end of
September, " yet certainly the war seems to begin with
better prospect of success than usual. . . . Everything
seems now drawing to a crisis on the continent, and it makes
one tremble to think what events may happen before this
time twelvemonth."

The tension becomes more and more unbearable. " Every thing is, if possible, worse than was reported. . . . I have seen nothing like the present moment. You hear nothing else from the drawing-room to the steward's room, in every street, and road, and lane : as you walk you hear Bonaparte's name in every mouth." Lady Elizabeth feared that the Allies were acting too slowly, that " a tardy confederacy will enable Bonaparte to beat his enemies one by one." Europe is becoming worn and senile. There is only one vigorous limb, and that the enemy.

The crisis came before these letters were delivered in Washington. General Mack capitulated to the French at Ulm on October 17. Trafalgar was fought October 21. Londoners wore silver favours with black in the centre as mourning. The younger people refused to be downhearted. Lord Aberdeen, recently married, was contemplating a series of private theatricals in conjunction with William Lamb. They were both in training for the highest positions the political world could offer, their country was on the verge of the most frightful catastrophe—and they were studying the script of *Oroonoko*, Falkland in *The Rivals*, etc., etc. Neither were their fellow-citizens depressed. " The Theatre is in great glory. Kemble and Mrs. Siddons every night," writes Aberdeen.

The Duke and Duchess wrote poetic odes upon the Battle of Trafalgar. Nelson had been with them before he left on his last voyage. " When I dined with him in London " (wrote Lady Elizabeth) " he said to us, ' in about two months I hope to have done my duty and to return to England.' He is returned in little more than two months. . . . The Victory is arrived with the remains of our beloved Nelson." Before the hero had been buried, Austerlitz was fought, and Pitt was on his death-bed.

" It is a campaign which one can compare to nothing. They have fallen before Bonaparte like card soldiers, and he does not seem to have lost an officer of note. My brother still says that the game is not up ; but what can they look to ? What has war done but make Bonaparte greater and more powerful each campaign." This was written on December 1, after the story of Ulm reached London. In the middle of the month the bad news of Austerlitz was known. " It is indeed over with the Continent," was Lady Elizabeth's verdict. " War is Bonaparte's element, and we play his cards for him when we give him an opportunity of making it. Where it will end, God knows."

The death of Pitt profoundly affected the political situation. Devonshire House was soon in the thick of Cabinet making, for Charles James Fox was a member of Lord Grenville's administration. The Duchess had not lost her early interest in political excitement. She wrote to Augustus Foster in March telling him of the progress of events, and sending " a remembrance—a memorial " of Lord Nelson. At the same time Lady Elizabeth explained a break in her correspondence. She had delayed writing, for " really there is such a gloom over everything."

The gloom became deeper. The two friends visited, went to the opera, and entertained. Suddenly the Duchess was taken ill. She had been ill before. No danger was expected, and the patient was in good spirits. Only at the last moment was there any alarm. She died on March 30.

" The physicians entirely mistook her case," wrote Lady Jerningham to Lady Bedingfeld, in one of the Jerningham letters. " Edward says that he heard in London that the poor Duchess of Devonshire had applied to the Duke for succour in her pecuniary state of affairs, and that the Duke told her in so positive a manner that he had engaged himself never to do more in the business, having paid enormous sums, that the Duchess in despair of ever prevailing in this her last and only resource fell ill ; that the first days the Duke supposed the illness a little put on, but when he understood that she was so bad and in danger of her life, he entreated the doctor who sat up with her, if she had a lucid interval to assure her that every wish she had should be complied with, and that he would purchase her health with anything she could command. But, poor thing, I suppose it was then too late.

I pity the Duke who, they say, is very much affected. And well he may ! ''

Her death left a vacant place in fashionable society which even her rivals could not fill. When the Prince of Wales heard of the death of his old friend he said, '' Then the best natured and best bred woman in England is gone.''

'' She was the only female friend I ever had,'' wrote Lady Elizabeth to her son. There is no need to quote her highflown panegyrics, her exaggerated emotionalism at the death of her life-long companion. '' I have had no heart, no courage, to do anything, nor will you be surprised at it. . . . Her society had an attraction I never met with in any other being.''

These words were true. We can only attempt to estimate the charm of the Duchess by reading the letters of those who surrounded her. In the correspondence of Harriet, Countess Granville, are two letters the Duchess received from her daughter shortly before her death. '' You would be tired of the endless repetition if I were to tell you how constantly I wish to be with you. I must be very different from what I am before I could feel worthy of belonging to you ; but if to love and admire you, not only as the most indulgent of mothers, but as superior to any human being I ever met with, is to deserve it, you must scarcely find any that would deserve it as much.''

In the second letter Lady Harriet wrote to her mother : '' I never knew thoroughly what I felt for you till I left you, and when I think of the happiness of seeing your dear smile, of hearing your beloved voice, I am almost mad with joy. I am sure you alone could inspire what I feel for you : it is enthusiasm and admiration that for anybody else would be ridiculous, but to deny it to you would be unnatural.''

The Duchess Georgiana was buried in the family vault in All Saints' Church, Derby. In July, 1811, Sir Nathaniel Wraxall visited the tomb. On the coffin lay the shreds of a bouquet. '' That nosegay,'' said the woman who accompanied him, '' was brought here by the Countess of Bessborough, who had intended to place it herself upon the coffin

x

of her sister.   But as she approached the steps of the vault, her agony became too great to permit her to proceed.   She knelt down on the stones of the church, as nearly over the place where the coffin stood in the vault below as I could direct, and there deposited the flowers, enjoining me to perform an office to which she was unequal.   I fulfilled her wishes."

CHAPTER XXII

The Duke marries Lady Elizabeth Foster—Sheridan and Lady
Elizabeth—the Cavendish children—" Caro George "—com-
ments on the Duke's marriage—Henry Cavendish—Augustus
Foster and a diplomatic appointment—death of the Duke—
Duchess Elizabeth's removal from Devonshire House—the
sixth Duke—Lord Byron's marriage.

THREE years after the death of " the beautiful
Duchess," his Grace of Devonshire married her
still more beautiful friend. Lady Elizabeth Foster
had been living in the meanwhile at Devonshire
House and Burlington Villa at Chiswick.

The children of the first marriage did not remain under
her care. Lord Hartington was only sixteen at the time
of his mother's death. The eldest daughter had already
married Lord Morpeth, afterwards sixth Earl of Carlisle.
Lady Harriet Elizabeth went to live with her grandmother,
the dowager Lady Spencer. Years later her son, the Hon.
F. Leveson-Gower, published a collection of her letters,
and of this period the editor offers an explanation. " Upon
the death of her mother in 1806, Lady Harriet was left in a
painful and isolated position. She was fond of her father,
but, owing to circumstances it is needless to relate, his home
was not congenial to her. . . . The dowager Lady Spencer
loved her and gave her good advice, but although Lady
Harriet esteemed and was grateful to her, there was not much
sympathy between them. Lady Harriet however lived a
good deal with her sister, and on all occasions turned to her
for advice and support. This strengthened the tie of
sisterly affection which bound them together during the
whole of their joint lives."

Their father was a man of sluggish thought, and his marriage to Lady Elizabeth was the result of no sudden flash of energy. They were old friends rather than young lovers. Their sons and daughters were no longer children, but men and women beginning to take their due position in society. Lady Elizabeth was awkwardly placed, and the Fosters could not have been happy when they considered the tangle. These difficulties evidently did not trouble the Duke, but Creevey's memoirs give us a glimpse of the uneasy feelings of the lady.

Six months after the death of Duchess Georgiana Mrs. Creevey visited Sheridan, who was exceedingly unwell. There is a graphic picture in the memoirs of the ruined and dying politician, who was not only ill but low-spirited. " Then we sent for some wine, of which he was so frightened it required persuasion to make him drink six small glasses, of which the effect was immediate in making him not only happier, but composing his pulse." The prescription was repeated with excellent results. " Sherry " speedily recovered from " the dismals," and, under the influence of the grape, became reminiscent. He commenced to tell the ladies anecdotes of his friends, the men and women he used to meet at Devonshire House. He mentioned the name of Hare, the witty " Hare of many friends," who wasted his life and his fortune, and died almost a beggar in 1804. Hare had been one of the brightest members of the Devonshire House circle, and it was quite an easy transition to the other goddess of Piccadilly, Lady Elizabeth Foster. Sheridan told Mrs. Creevey that he had recently received a letter from her giving news of Fox. He was annoyed at it, for the concluding line was, " try to drink less, and speak the truth."

" He was very funny about it," reported Mrs. Creevey. " He cried : ' By——! I speak more truth than *she* does, however.' " He added that Lady Elizabeth had come to him the night before, crying, because " she felt it her severe duty to be Duchess of Devonshire."

The thought tickled Sheridan's fancy. He was not the

only person who awaited the last act in the little drama. That was delayed for three years. The Duke was not a man of duty, he was selfish, and without a conscience. Lady Elizabeth had altered but little since the days when Gibbon, comparing her with Duchess Georgiana, said that " Bess is much nearer the level of a mortal, but a mortal for whom the wisest man, historic or medical, would throw away two or three worlds if he had them in possession." A few seasons ago a full-length portrait of Lady Elizabeth, painted about 1806 by Sir Thomas Lawrence, appeared in the sale-room of Christie's. Although approaching middle-age she was still strikingly beautiful. The girlish pertness of Sir Joshua's canvas had completely vanished. In its stead was a new dignity and grace which Lawrence reproduced with complete success. Walpole had called her grandmother " majestic Juno," and the description applied with equal truth to Lady Elizabeth.

> Old Orpheus, that husband so civil,
> He followed his wife down to hell ;
> And who would not go to the devil,
> For the sake of dear Molly Lepel.

There was a fascination about Molly Lepel and her grand-daughter to which two generations submitted without hesitation, only too happy to live in the sunshine of such bright souls. Stendhal has said that a woman of forty is only beautiful to those who have loved her in her youth. Lawrence's portrait gives the Frenchman the lie. The habitués of the Devonshire House circle would rather have agreed with Anatole France's statement that the passing glimpse of a beautiful woman is a piece of gratuitous good luck for which every man should return thanks.

The difficulties of the various children in dealing with the odd situation their parents had created became greater every day. In 1808 Lord Hartington made his early appearances in society, attending a *bal masquerade*, and dancing in a " deliberate Cavendish way." His half-brother, Augustus Clifford, had also left Harrow. The influence of the Spencers was sought, Earl Spencer was First Lord of the Admiralty, and Clifford was sent to sea. He entered upon his naval career as a midshipman in the same ship as one of the younger Spencers. He was loved by all his cousins. " Poor Clifford ! " wrote Lady Sarah Spencer. " How I felt for him when Lady D. made that unlucky blunder "—an indiscreet enquiry as to Clifford's family and the names of his parents. " But I fear his life must be expected to afford him many such mortifications. All I can say is, that I don't envy his mother's feelings, when she thinks of all the miseries her conduct has entailed on so deserving a young man, and so amiable a young woman, as her two unlucky children are. Poor Clifford, it speaks very well of him to have felt it so much."

This feeling of commiseration was not confined to the Spencers. Even the Duke must have been aware of it. Probably he realised that if he neglected his duty towards the mother of his children he still owed a duty to the children themselves.

" The deserving young man " entered the Navy at the age of twelve, served at the reduction of St. Lucia and Tobago in 1803, was made lieutenant in 1806, and took part in the Egyptian operations of 1807. The " amiable young wo-man," known under the romantic name of Caroline St. Jules, was married in 1809, at the age of twenty-three, to the Hon. George Lamb, third son of the first Viscount Mel-bourne. In the family correspondence she is henceforth called " Caro George," to distinguish her from that other " Caro," her sister-in-law, the eccentric Lady Caroline Lamb, daughter of Lady Bessborough, and niece to Duchess Georgiana.

Mrs. Caroline Lamb was the homely wife of a man whose endearing personality made him a general favourite. George Lamb was " a clever amateur actor," a contributor to the " Edinburgh Review," the author of a comic opera, " Whistle for it," which was damned at Covent Garden, and officially an efficient wheel in the intricate machinery of government. His brother's wife became infatuated with Byron. His mother being a Milbanke, he was first cousin to the girl who became

LADY DUNCANNON

the poet's wife. Byron liked George Lamb. " He's a very good fellow, and, except his mother and sister, the best of the set to my mind." [1]

The marriage took place May 17, 1809. In the letters of Sarah, Lady Lyttelton (who, as elder daughter of the second Earl Spencer, could claim kinship with any child of the house of Cavendish), there is a patronising reference to the bride. " Of course you know all about the match of Mrs. Lamb at Devonshire House. She has taken a house somewhere near Lincoln's Inn Fields, and is already behaving so well, and so judiciously, that it gratifies the good opinion I had of her always, and makes one hope she will be very happy." The wish was gratified. During the twenty-four years of her married life the Hon. Mrs. George Lamb was far happier than many of her more exalted cousins.

Having satisfactorily disposed of one daughter the Duke turned to his other. Lady Harriet Elizabeth, the younger daughter of Duchess Georgiana, was one year older than Caroline Rosalie. She was betrothed to Granville Leveson-Gower, the youngest son of the first Marquis of Stafford. There was already a family connection between the Gowers and the Cavendishes. Lady Harriet's elder sister, by her marriage to Lord Morpeth, was already a granddaughter to the Marquis of Stafford, who now became father-in-law to the second daughter of Duchess Georgiana. Leveson-Gower, a mature statesman of thirty-four, had formed a close friendship at Oxford with Canning. Introduced by that politician to Pitt, he soon became a favourite of the minister, and was appointed ambassador to Russia. The engagement created considerable interest. Ward, who later was created first Earl of Dudley, mentioned it in one of his letters. " Canning's friend, Lord Granville Leveson, is going to marry Lady Harriet Cavendish. Lady Bessborough

[1] George Lamb was a member of the committee of management of Drury Lane Theatre, and, in addition to his other literary labours, translated Catullus. In 1819 he was the successful Whig candidate for Westminster, but was defeated at the election in 1820. He died in 1834 during the prime ministership of his brother, the second Viscount Melbourne.

resigns, I presume, in favour of her niece. I have not heard what are supposed to be the secret articles of the treaty, but it must be a curious domestic document. Lady H. has neither beauty nor wealth, but she has rank and talents. People that know her say she is very clever, and makes better verses than the late Duchess —which, Lord knows, may very well be."

This marriage was appointed to take place on Christmas Eve, 1809. Before the arrangements were actually complete the Duke himself married, and Lady Elizabeth Foster became Duchess of Devonshire. His resolution seems to have been suddenly taken, but the reason is not easy to find. Nobody in the world of fashion would have been shocked had the marriage taken place in 1807 or 1808. Everyone who had visited Devonshire House, and a number who had never crossed its threshold, were aware of the truth. There had been no family protests. The Spencers advanced the career of Augustus Clifford. The two Fosters were commencing brilliant official careers. the younger, Augustus Foster, being in the diplomatic service. The only explanation, fantastic but not improbable, is that the Duke had never contemplated the possibility of a second marriage, and that Lady Elizabeth, though often dreaming of her " duty," had not dared openly to suggest it to the only man who could carry it through.

Had the marriage taken place in 1807 the Duke might have been praised for an act of justice. In 1809, sandwiched between the marriages of his daughter by Lady Elizabeth and his daughter by Duchess Georgiana, it excited some little resentment. This feeling is clearly noticeable in Lady Lyttelton's letter to the Hon. Robert Spencer.[1] " My Grandmother S. has not been here after all ; she is not quite well, and not very happy just now. A marriage is said to have taken place which shocks her very much ;

[1] Lady Sarah Spencer, afterwards Lady Lyttelton, was the elder daughter of the second Earl Spencer, and niece to Duchess Georgiana. She married the third Lord Lyttelton, and, in 1838, became Lady-in-Waiting to Queen Victoria, and, in 1842, governess to the royal children. Her brother, Lord Robert, was in the Navy.

it is a dead secret, only told in whispers by everybody to everybody as yet. But, my Bob, you are so far, so very far away from us all, that before it reaches you it will have been publickly declared; besides, you know it already, I dare say. It is not an interesting union *de deux jeunes cœurs,* I must say, but rather the crowning of a perseverance in vice and artfulness, which is I fancy unheard of; Clifford of course knows it, as it is no other than the long-expected wedding of his venerable parents. I can't say I understand why my Grandmother takes it so to heart; it is a mortifying thing to poor Harriet to be sure, as it gives Lady Elizabeth a sort of legal right of domineering over her; but besides this I must say it seems to me the most uninteresting of events. No *ostensible* change is said to be intended yet awhile. That is, the lovely bride is not to have "in soft sound '*your grace*' salute her ear." How long her humility will dispense with the honour is difficult to calculate; but I dare say before you can answer this letter the Duchess of Devonshire's parties, and the Duchess of Devonshire's perfections, will be talked of in London. So much for this marriage."

There is little other written comment upon an event which gave rise to much gossip. The marriage took place very quietly at Chiswick. On September 25, Lady Elizabeth wrote one of her usual chronicles of current politics to her son Augustus Foster, who was with the British legation at Stockholm. Evidently but part of the letter is reprinted in the correspondence published by the late Vere Foster. "The strangeness of the times continues," is the opening sentence. The strange doings are Canning's resignation and Castlereagh's duel—not the preparations at Chiswick. On September 28, Elizabeth, Duchess of Devonshire, takes up the pen. "Since I wrote you nothing more has occurred." There are references to Lord Grey and Lord Granville, the union of Canning and the Opposition, the progress of the war, Lord Wellington's defensive measures, Perceval's offer to share the Cabinet. "They say Lord Grenville don't accept and that Lord Grey won't come to town. This is very odd indeed." Yet the still odder domestic incident is not touched upon.

At the close of 1809 Elizabeth the Duchess was left the only woman in Devonshire House. Gibbon's "bewitching animal" was now a woman of fifty. She was still a goddess, but, judging from the letters which cover the short period of her reign, rather a frigid and unsympathetic goddess to the young world around her. The interests of her life were entirely political. In her correspondence, as published, there is not a reference to literature or art. In March 1810 she writes : " Mr. Cavendish, the philosopher, has died worth £1,075,000, and though it is a week ago we are still ignorant how he left his property. The Duke and I, however, are quite convinced that he has left him nothing, so the question is how much he has left to Lord George (Cavendish), and what to men of science and for charities." Before long the Duchess knew that the vast accumulations of the old bachelor had gone to Lord George, better known by his later creation of Earl of Burlington. The philosopher was too engrossed in his laboratories at Clapham to care for the gaieties of Devonshire House. Duchess Georgiana visited Clapham, and even fitted up a room for scientific experiments of her own. But the Duke disliked the intimacy, with the words, " He is not a gentleman—*he works* "[1]

---

[1] Henry Cavendish (1731-1810) was a grandson of the second Duke of Devonshire. Famous throughout Europe as a scientist, he was most celebrated in London for the old-fashioned cut of his clothes, and the eccentricities of his character. Like many other members of his house he did not mix freely in the world, but lived in the greatest seclusion at Clapham or Gower Street. Lord Brougham tells the following story of his odd manner :—" The bankers with whom he kept his account, finding that his balance had accumulated to upwards of £80,000, commissioned one of the partners to wait on him, and to ask him what he wished done with it. On reaching Clapham, and finding Mr. Cavendish's house, he rang the bell, but had the greatest difficulty in obtaining admission. ' You must wait,' said the servant, ' till my master rings his bell, and then I will let him know that you are here.' In about a quarter of an hour the bell rang, and the fact of the banker's arrival was duly communicated to the abstracted chemist. Mr. Cavendish, in great agitation, desired that the banker might be shown up, and, as he entered the room,

Lady Sarah Spencer suggests in a letter that this dislike was
mutual. "It was expected this enormous fortune would
have gone to the Duke of Devonshire, as the old man was very
proud of his family name ; but whether he forgot his grace's
existence, or perhaps thought that said existence was somewhat of a *disgrace* to the noble name of Cavendish, he has not
mentioned him once in this important will, which I can't
much regret, the Duke and Hartington both being *pretty
well* off."

The letters to Augustus the diplomatist continued without intermission. Early in January, 1811, the Duchess told
her son that she has had to return to London in order that
the Duke could take his place in Parliament. The ministers
had been beaten, "but, lo and behold, the vicissitude of
things : the king is now said to be recovering, and there is
an end of the Regency." The Duchess was active before
her great friend had lost all his power. On February 15,
1811, she sent Augustus Foster a letter with an enclosure
"which I received at the Play last night." The document
came from the Prince Regent, and nominated her son as
Minister to the United States of America. "I hope this
will meet with your approbation," wrote the Prince to
"my dearest Duchess." "Nothing can ever afford me more
pleasure than whatever I know can convey satisfaction
both to your self as well as the dear Duke."

She refused to take credit for the appointment. She told
her son that she had not mentioned his name either to the
Prince or to any other person in authority. As Augustus
was in Ireland she acknowledged the royal letter, and she
told him that the appointment, although one of exile, was

saluted him with a few words asking him the object of his visit.
' Sir, I thought proper to wait on you, as we have in hand a very
large balance of yours, and we wish for your orders respecting it.'
' Oh, if it is any trouble to you, I will take it out of your hands. Do
not come here to plague me about money.' ' It is not in the
least trouble to us, sir ; but we thought you might like some of it
turned to account, and invested.' ' Well, well ; do what you want
to do ? ' ' Perhaps you would like to have £40,000 invested ? '
' Yes, do so, if you like ; but don't come here to trouble me any
more, or I will remove my balance.' "

evidently intended as a distinction. The mission was
"important and advantageous." Then she spoke of his
courtship of Miss Milbanke. Would she care to go so far
from home as the United States ? " If she has any liking
for you, the idea of your going would make her decide in
your favour." Augustus Foster hated the thought of going
to America. He wished to enter parliament. " Pray
pause and consider how few people rise to any eminence in
it ; how very few obtain from parliamentary merit alone
either fame or emolument." On the other hand, as
Minister to the United States, " considering our connections and friendships, you are likely to receive flattering
marks of approbation. . . . Your happiness and advantage
is all I wish for, but I should be sorry to see you throw away
the means of doing yourself credit from an unfounded
pursuit of other objects."

The letter is that of a woman of sound wisdom and
practical common-sense. She had the welfare of her family
at heart. But apart from her sons and daughters she was
not loved. Lady Harriet, now a stepdaughter, speaks of
a " very dull " dinner at Devonshire House in 1810. Indeed,
whenever she speaks of her old home the word " dull "
invariably creeps in. Her mother, Duchess Georgiana,
had always routed the demon. But she was a Spencer. The
Cavendishes of that day never could escape unaided from
the dullness of their surroundings, the utter weariness of
a magnificence they had created almost unconsciously.
There was a certain distinction in this complete lack of
interest. During the reign of the second Duchess, as under
that of the first, an invitation to the mansion was coveted
and struggled for. But the old circle had almost entirely
disappeared. Gibbon, Johnson, Reynolds, Fox,—to men-
only the brighter names—were dead. Sheridan's star had
paled. James Hare and his fellow wits had cracked their
last jest. The " blue-stockings " had vanished. Old Lady
Spencer, the mother of Duchess Georgiana, still lingered on.
Gossip said she had become a Methodist. She certainly
was very actively engaged in the establishment of Sunday
Schools. She had enjoyed the whole play. Perhaps she

did not comprehend all its phases. " She was a woman who did not possess naturally any quickness of understanding," Lord Althorp, her grandson, was pleased to observe, " nor do I think that she possessed sterling good sense." [1]

Before a new salon could be formed at Devonshire House the blow fell. In August, 1811, the Duke died. " The poor Duke of Devonshire adds another to the list of Farquhar's victims," wrote William Henry Ward. " He utterly mistook his case. I am very sorry for his death, though I hardly knew him, for it is a distressing event to many people whom I know and like. . . . It is a sad blow to the party."

The " party " paid a decorous tribute, but there was little comment in the press. The Duke had always disliked show, and there was no display of ostentation in the procession which left the gates of Devonshire House for the Cavendish tomb at All Saints,' Derby. The funeral train, reported one of the morning newspapers, consisted of eight outriders." The ducal coronet supported by a person on horseback, bareheaded. The hearse unadorned. The carriage of the deceased with six horses, and servants in mourning. The Prince Regent's state carriage." Then followed sixteen carriages belonging to the Whig nobility. These empty carriages followed the hearse as far as Oxford Street, and the ceremony was over as far as London was concerned.

Robert Adair, M.P., published a small memorial volume at the request of the Duchess. The eulogy was exaggerated. Mr. Adair, after enriching the late Duke with every virtue, was not quite sure how the world could continue after the loss of such a paragon. " In 1806," he wrote, "the

[1] Lady Harriet Cavendish spoke more kindly of her. In 1810, after her marriage, when staying with her sister-in-law, the Duchess of Beaufort, at Badminton, Lady Spencer joined them. " My grandmother arrived here yesterday morning. She has been quite delightful, and it is so to me to see her so much pleased and at her ease with Granville and the Duchess. I should imagine that she had passed half her life here, and her perfectly good and *dans son assiette* manner in whatever society she falls into always excites my surprise and admiration. Very early hours, very good books, and most unwearied chess-playing are just what suit her. She is all kindness to me, pleased with our having wished to have her here so intimately."

world was deprived of Mr. Fox, and our tears are yet flowing for Mr. Windham. Short indeed is the space within which the grave has been heaped with everything great and excellent in the country! but we must look forward still; and since it is not granted to us to avert the growing difficulties of our situation under the guidance of these virtuous men, we must learn by their example how to meet them."

A paragraph in the news gave a short digest of the Duke's will. The value of his effects was proved at above £250,000 and under £300,000, the duty paid upon the probate being £3,000. The duty at the present day would be more than the total value of the effects a century ago. The Duchess Elizabeth had a jointure of £4,000, to which the new Duke immediately added an additional £2,000.

The Duchess was inconsolable. Elizabeth Foster loved this cold, passive, taciturn man. And with his death she recognised the end of her career as an active force in the political life of her time. She had ambitions not only for herself, but also for her children, particularly those sons, the Fosters, to whom she had been but an incidental mother. As a Dowager Duchess her reign was shorn of all its glory.

Had the Duke ever loved in quite the same degree? It is improbable that he ever fully reciprocated her affection since those early days of transport in 1784. The whole history of their passion can be summed up in the words of an old couplet.

Much ado was there, God wot;
She would love, but he would not.

Her first letter to her son Augustus Foster was a cry of utter despair. She wrote from Chiswick on August 30, telling him of her " dreadful misfortune. . . Calmer now but as wretched. . . . I can only wonder that my life and intellect have lasted. . . . The husband whom I have lost was the creature of my adoration, and long had been so. He was so eminent in all that is good, amiable, noble, and praiseworthy. I almost wondered at my own happiness in being united to him, and when you was with us here, scarce more than three short months ago, there was not a day, scarcely an hour, I did not thank Heaven for the happiness of belonging to such a man. Oh, God, it is too, too much. . . Thankful I am, though that moment of misery never can be effaced from my heart, that I had strength to be with him to the last, and that it was in my arms that he expired; yes, expired, and I live to write it."

The Duchess's emotion was heartfelt. But, without wishing to cast any doubt upon the poignancy of her grief, it may be noted that even in this moment of affliction she wrote in the style of one of Rousseau's heroines.

In November another letter followed in the same strain. " such a being as *him* surely never existed." She is happy only in her children, Augustus and Frederick Foster, Caro George and Clifford. " But life has lost its charm, and the world the noblest creature that ever adorned it. To have been his ; to bear his name, is still my pride and comfort."

The brothers and sisters of the different families met upon equal terms of friendship. The young Marquis, now the sixth Duke, inherited a distinct Spencer personality. For example the Cavendishes disliked show. It was a mark of the race. Henry Cavendish, the philosopher, was economical, not through parsimony but because he essentially disliked waste or outward pomp. The late Duke endeavoured to live as a private gentleman, and seems to have spent little upon his own needs. When told that he had been created a Knight of the Garter, and was to have the coveted blue ribbon, he replied that he should prefer a blue great-coat. But the Spencers had always enjoyed ostentation, and the young Duke soon proved that he was of the same blood. Ward (afterwards Lord Dudley), in referring to the death of the fifth duke, added : " the present Duke is gentle and amiable in his disposition, but quite a boy in understanding and acquirements. Luckily he is very much attached to his sisters, who are very good and sensible, as well as very agreeable women. I hope they will manage him till he has acquired knowledge and experience enough to manage himself. Hitherto he has behaved admirably." This judgment agrees with an earlier one. In 1804 Byron and the young Marquis were schoolboys at Harrow and the poet wrote to his sister Augusta : " Hartington is on very good terms with me, nothing more, he is of a soft milky disposition, and of a happy apathy of temper which defies the softer emotions and is insensible of ill-treatment."

He was interested in politics, although the obstinate deafness from which he suffered throughout life must have hindered his intercourse with other men.   But as early as 1806 he was canvassing in Yorkshire on behalf of his friend Lord Milton, in that terrific election contest which is said to have cost the Fitzwilliam and Harewood families £100,000 apiece.   In 1821, according to Creevey, he declared for the party of Reform, and agreed with other members of the nobility to raise £200,000 to £300,000 for the unfortunate Queen, wife of the prince who had been on such intimate terms with his mother and the Duchess Elizabeth.

In no way did the young Duke disappoint his friends' expectations.   He made handsome provision for Augustus Clifford.   The Margravine of Anspach, not exactly a saint if all stories are true, told C. K. Sharpe in 1802 that there was no religion of any description amongst Protestants. " I except the Duke of Devonshire, who, for the last trait of generosity amongst a thousand, has just given £2,000 a year to a bastard of his father's ; who, having been kept and educated by the bounty of his father, was forgot in the will : his name is Macdonnell."   Such children were not always forgotten.   Lord Egremont gave his brother's natural daughters £40,000 each on their marriage.

After her husband's death Duchess Elizabeth had to leave the house which had been her home for nearly thirty years. She was no longer the mistress of Devonshire House, which, indeed, was not to have a mistress for half-a-century.   Caro George told Augustus Foster of the troubles of packing. " I am now writing at a very melancholy moment.   The Duchess is come to town to pack up all her things and to leave this house for ever.   It is a moment I have always dreaded for her.   I think a widow's situation at all times a most dreadful one ; at the time that she wants most comfort and care she is obliged to leave her home and the comforts she has been used to all her life. There are a thousand little things, too, which have annoyed and worried her. It grieves me to the heart to see her unhappy. We are going to the seaside for a little while. The Liverpools [1] have, I believe, lent her Walmer, and we shall go there till she has got a house in town, and she will then settle in London. I think it is the best place for her, for she is not very fond of the country, and, so used to Society as she has been all her life, I am sure that great retirement would be the worst thing for her." The letter is very charmingly written, and gives much information. Mrs. Lamb refers to the Milbankes. She has just left Brocket Hall. "They are all going on very jollily there." Her sister-in-law, and namesake, Caro, " is a little less mad than usual."

In January, 1812, the Duchess took up her broken correspondence with her son. " I as yet see nobody but the friends, the immediate friends of him I know not how to live without, nor do I feel as if I ever could." Her interest in the family was unabated. " You will see that the Catholick question has been brought on ; dear Hartington seconded. Lord Fitzwilliam was very much frightened, but did it well, and ended with a true Cavendish sentiment that, thinking this measure right, he supported it, and always would . . . Hartington is affectionate and kind, but very young and surrounded." The reputation of Augustus is rising. " Oh ! the comfort of that. I thank God for the children he has given me."

A month later she had taken up her residence in her new house in Piccadilly, numbered as 13, Piccadilly Terrace. Augustus Foster was wooing Miss Milbanke. " I am afraid my chance is small with Miss Milbanke," he told his mother. " I shall almost hate her if she is blind to the merits of one who would make her so happy," wrote the Duchess. In May it is evident that Foster must give up all desires in that quarter. "Letters have passed," wrote the Duchess,

[1] Lady Louisa Hervey, sister to Duchess Elizabeth, married the Earl of Liverpool.

" which will have, to our great regret, put an end to all our hopes on that subject. . . . She is so odd a girl. . . . In short, she is good, amiable, and sensible, but cold, prudent, and reflecting. . . . Lord Byron makes up to her a little, but she don't seem to admire him except as a poet, nor he her, except for a wife."

As Augustus was still detained at Washington he was not able to court in person, and the negotiations continued during the whole of the summer in a cold-blooded way. " She is certainly rather too cold in her manners," he wrote," and gives to reason too much empire over her mind, but she has good eyes, is fair, has right ideas, and sense, and mildness." In June the Duchess replied : " Your Annabella is a mystery ; liking, not liking ; generous minded, yet afraid of poverty ; there is no making her out. I hope you don't make yourself unhappy about her ; she is really an icicle." In July : " I hear of no one likely to be favoured by her, so I shall still live in hope for you." Caro George told her half-brother to have confidence. Miss Milbanke had asked about him. " Another thing which speaks very well for you is that Sir Ralph (her father), whose judgment is, I believe, entirely formed upon that of the female part of his family, praises you, I hear, beyond anything." But the heiress of Wentworth was not destined to become the wife of Augustus Foster. To the intense surprise of all who knew her, Miss Milbanke married Lord Byron, January 2, 1815, and her future career became history itself.

CHAPTER XXIII

Lady " Caro " Lamb—Byron as a tenant—the Duchess Elizabeth
in Paris—foreign society in Rome—the Devonshire circle—
Cardinal Gonsalvi—archæologists—excavations and publishing—the Duchess as an editor of the classics—her interest in
politics—last illness and death—curious action of the sixth
Duke.

DUCHESS Elizabeth did not remain long in London
at Piccadilly Terrace. She entertained largely,
but the young life had disappeared from her circle.
Amongst those who visited her were Madame de
Staël, Lady Bessborough, Mrs. Siddons, Kemble, Thomas
Moore, Ward, afterwards Earl of Dudley, Lord Dillon,
Lord Harrowby, and several of the foreign ministers. This
list suggests a drawing-room of appalling solemnity, an
atmosphere of priggishness which not even the light-hearted
eccentricities of Lady Caroline Lamb could dissipate.

Lady " Caro," niece of Duchess Georgiana, married to
William Lamb (Lord Melbourne) in 1805, was now engaged
in that extraordinary flirtation with Lord Byron which
commenced in the spring in 1812. Duchess Elizabeth
described her as a " wild, delicate, odd, delightful person,
unlike everything." Her relations were never able to
determine if she was a genius or a madwoman. But when
she wrote novels in which she caricatured all the people she
knew and disliked the family decided that she ought to be
placed under restraint.

" I am ordered peremptorily by my own family not to
write," she told Lady Morgan in 1818. " I ask you, my
dear Lady Morgan, if one descended in a right line from
Spenser, not to speak of the Duke of Marlborough, with all

323

the Cavendish and Ponsonby blood to boot, who you know were always rebellious, should feel a little strongly upon any occasion, and burst forth, and yet be told to hold their tongues and not write, by all their relations united—what is to happen ? "

The friendship of Lady " Caro " and Byron provoked much gossip in the Duchess's circle. The name of Byron came to the front again when the poet married Miss Milbanke, the lady Augustus Foster had wooed so long and in vain. By a coincidence Byron became the tenant of the Duchess's house at 13, Piccadilly Terrace, when she decided to settle abroad. It had already been inhabited by Lord Yarmouth, (afterwards second Marquis of Hertford), Thackeray's Marquis of Steyne in *Vanity Fair*, and Disraeli's Monmouth in *Coningsby*. When Lord and Lady Byron took up residence the house became the scene of a conjugal drama which finally wrecked the poet's hopes of domestic happiness.

Byron was not an ideal tenant. He had as strong a disinclination to pay a ducal rent as any Scottish crofter. Hobhouse hired the mansion for him at a rent of £700 a year. In March, 1815, Byron wrote to Thomas Moore: " We mean to metropolize to-morrow, and you will address your next to Piccadilly. We have got the Duchess of Devonshire's house there, she being in France." In April, 1816, the tragedy was played to the end. He had told Lady Byron, " you and I can never meet in this world nor in the next." The house opposite the Green Park had already lost its mistress. The rent had not been paid, and the Duchess of Devonshire distrained upon the furniture. " They have seized all the servants' things," wrote the distracted poet. " I hope you will see to these poor creatures having *their* property secured ; as for *mine* it must be sold . . . I sail to-night for Ostend." The Duchess's house was Byron's last home in England. Hobhouse, writing to Hanson, said : " It is really a thousand pities that the Duchess of Devonshire should not be paid ; but if his lordship's orders are precise, there is no help for it."

Duchess Elizabeth possibly made a personal application, for

Byron wrote to her from Venice in November, 1817, acknow-
ledging a letter. " Amongst the many unpleasant consequences of my residence in Piccadilly, or rather, of the cause
of that residence, I can assure your Grace that I by no means
look upon it as the least painful that my inconveniences
should have contributed to your's. Whatever measures Mr.
Denen might find it proper to take were probably what he
deemed his duty, and, though I regret that they were necessary, I am still more sorry to find that they seem to have been
inefficacious. Indeed, till very lately I was not aware that
your Grace was so unlucky as to have me still amongst the
number of your debtors. I shall write to the person who has
the management of my affairs in England, and although
I have but little control over either at present, I will do the
best I can to have the remaining balance liquidated."
There is no record that it ever was.

This Byronic episode was an unpleasant interlude in an
otherwise untroubled existence. The Duchess spent most of
her time in Paris, on the friendliest terms with Madame de
Staël, and more particularly with Madame Récamier.
Her French circle included Benjamin Constant, Dénon, the
Comte de Ségur, Gérard, Sismondi, Auguste de Staël, Humboldt, Talma, and Cuvier. Amongst the English were the
Leitrims, and Lady Morgan, the Irish novelist. There were
many foreign residents in Paris in the early days of the
Restoration who believed in the dictum of Quintin Craufurd.
" Make your fortune where you like but enjoy it in Paris."
Another visitor was the Princess Jablonowski, name forgotten in the twentieth century. According to Lady Morgan
she was celebrated in Restoration circles as being the only
woman who was ever the intimate friend of Napoleon
without being his mistress.

In 1818 Lady Morgan wrote : " Everybody seems bound
for Italy ; the papers announce the Duke of Devonshire's
departure today ; Duchess Elizabeth is already off." In
Italy the Duchess passed the remainder of her life. Occasionally she journeyed to Paris and Spa. London she does
not appear to have revisited. In Italy she was able to

retain a social importance which as a Dowager Duchess she had lost in England.

In many respects Italy was more attractive for the foreigner even than France. Ticknor, the American, discovered that society in Rome was different from society in any other part of the world, and the Romans themselves were not the most prominent section of their city. French was the universal language in the drawing-rooms, which were crowded with strangers from every capital of Europe.

Every nation had its own circle. " Thus the Germans, the English, and French have their separate societies,—preserving in the forms of their intercourse, and in their general tone the national character that marks them at home ; except when, perhaps, two or three times in the week all the strangers in Rome, with a few of the best of the Italians, a quantity of cardinals, bishops, and ecclesiastics of all names and ranks, are brought together at a kind of grand rout, called a *conversazione* or *accademia*. . . . Nothing can be more amusing than one of these farrago societies which I have seen at the Duchess of Devonshire's and Count Funchal's, the Portuguese Ambassador—the east and west, the north and south. . . . All brought together to be pushed about a couple of hours or more in an endless suite of enormous rooms, and then wait for their carriages in a comfortless antechamber—all national distinctions half-broken down by the universal use of French, even among persons of the same country, and more than half preserved by the bad accent with which it is spoken—the confusion of the Tower of Babel produced without a miracle or an object."

Yet these gatherings included too many notable men to be wholly dull. Amongst the Germans were Bunsen and his English wife, Madame de Humboldt, Niebuhr, and the Crown Prince of Bavaria. Thorwaldsen, Lund, and Schadow represented the northern nations. There were a few Frenchmen, many Russians and Swedes. " The English everywhere and in all great collections, formed a substantial part of society in Rome during the whole winter. The greatest gaiety was among them, and the greatest show, except

that made by the diplomatic part of the *beau monde.* . . .
I went to the Duchess of Devonshire's conversaziones, as
to a great exchange, to see who was in Rome, and to meet
the world. The Duchess is a good, respectable woman in
her way. She attempts to play the Mæcenas a little too
much, it is true ; but after all, she does a good deal that
should be praised, and will not I hope be forgotten. Her
excavations in the Forum, if neither so judicious nor so
fortunate as Count Funchal's, are satisfactory and a fair
beginning. . . . Her *Horace's Journey to Brundusium*
is a beautiful book, and her Virgil with the best plates she
can get of the present condition of Latium will be a monu-
ment of her taste and generosity."

Duchess Elizabeth was now settled in Rome " in almost
regal splendour." Her most intimate friends were Madame
Récamier and Cardinal Gonsalvi, the Papal Secretary of
State. Undoubtedly she possessed much influence. In
1821 Byron—forgetting the incident of the rent and Piccadilly
Terrace—asked her to exert her power in the holy city to
obtain the repeal of a decree of exile issued against the two
Counts Gambia of Ravenna. Byron's letter is very tact-
fully worded. " If my acquaintance with your Grace's
character were even slighter than it is through the medium
of some of our English friends, I had only to turn to the
letters of Gibbon (now on my table) for a full testimony to
its high and amiable qualities." This reference to her old
admirer, dead nearly thirty years, must have touched the
heart of Duchess Elizabeth. Her reply, from Spa, was more
than gracious. " I always wish to do any good I can, and
in that poor Gibbon and my other friends have but done me
justice ; but believe me also, that there is a character of
justice, goodness, and benevolence in the present Government of Rome, which, if they are convinced of the just
claim of the Comtes de Gamba, will make them grant their
request. Of Cardinal Gonsalvi it is truly said, ' Il a établi
une nouvelle politique formée sur la verité et la franchise ;
l'estime de toute l'Europe le paye de ses fatigues.' "

Gonsalvi was a constant visitor to her salon. Ticknor

wrote : " The most important and interesting man who went there was undoubtedly Cardinal Gonsalvi, the Pope's Prime Minister, and certainly a thorough gentleman, and a man of elegant conversation." Thomas Moore, who was in Rome at this time, described the Cardinal as " a very fine looking fellow," a statement Lawrence's portrait fully substantiates. Gell, the antiquary, told him " some ludicrous things about the Duchess of Devonshire's sway at Rome ; her passion for Gonsalvi, her admiration for the purity of the Roman Government." This admiration she did not attempt to disguise. " I know not any capital so adorned by its sovereign as this is," she wrote to Lady Morgan.

From her father the Earl-Bishop the Duchess inherited a passion for classical antiquities. In Rome and Naples was a large circle of connoisseurs whose chief interest was centred in the past. At Naples the Archbishop of Tarentum gave literary receptions which the English colony of Rome often attended. The patriarch belonged to one of the oldest and richest families of the south of Italy. He had been minister of State as well as archbishop of the Church. At the age of seventy-six, refusing to accept further honours, he lived a life of simplicity, dignity, and purity of character. Every evening he received a dozen of his friends between six and seven o'clock, and one read aloud from a classical author, a tragedy of Alfieri, a verse of Poliziano, a new pamphlet on Pompeii. Another room was set aside for conversation. In such society the Duchess found her true expression and individuality.

Another intimate of her circle, Sir William Gell, divided his time between Naples and Rome. This classical arch-æologist was a Derbyshire man, a consummate fop, and a trained courtier, for he had been one of Queen Caroline's Chamberlains. Gell lived in a small house in Rome, which he decorated " in all the bright, staring colours I could get, a sort of thing between Etruscan and Pompeii." At Rome he went much into society. In his rooms he was " sur-rounded by books, drawings, and maps, with a guitar, and two or three dogs." He delighted in " lionizing," and was

" always hankering after patricians," according to ill-natured report. Amongst his associates, who met on the common ground of the Duchess's salon, were Lord North, Randohr, the Prussian minister, Mr. Benjamin Smith, son of the member for Norwich, Sir William Cumming, and that society favourite, Miss Lydia White.

The Duchess became an enthusiastic classical archæologist. In a letter to Lady Morgan, dated May 22, 1823, she reveals her supreme interests. " We have had a severe winter for Rome ; and even today though very fine here we saw snow on the Alban Hill. A Marchesa Farra Cuppa has begun an excavation at Torneto, ancient Tarquinia, which has excited a great degree of interest. A warrior with his lance and shield was discovered entire, but the first blast of air reduced it to dust. She gave me part of her shield. A small vase of a beautiful form and two very large oxen are, I believe, coming to the Vatican Museum. The antiquity of them is calculated at three thousand years. Other excavations are making by some proprietors at Rome Vecchia. The first *fouille* produced a beautiful mosaic statue of a fine stag, in black marble. I feel gratified that my Horace's satire is approved of."
And am, dear Madam
Your ladyship's very sincerely,
ELIZABETH DEVONSHIRE.

P.S.—A fine statue of a Bacchus has been discovered, about four days ago, not far from Cecilia Metella's tomb."

Such a letter would have delighted the heart of her father, the Earl of Bristol. She pursued her hobby with all the restless energy of the Herveys, backed by the immense wealth of the Cavendishes. She not only conducted excavations in the Forum, but she issued editions of the classics in the most magnificent form.
The first book thus prepared was Horace's *Iter ad Brundusium*, published in folio at Rome in 1818, and illustrated by two Prussian artists, the brothers Ripen-

hausen. One hundred and fifty copies were prepared for presentation. When some sixty had been distributed the Duchess noticed some defects, " real or ideal," destroyed the remaining ninety, and commenced to work upon a new edition with improvements. This was issued, condemned, and a third was put in hand under the patronage and with the help of Cardinal Gonsalvi. On each presentation copy of this superb volume is written, in the Duchess's own hand, the inscription, " De la part d'Elizabeth Duchesse de Dévonshire, née Hervey."

Then followed *L' Eneide di Virgilio recata in Versi Italiani da Annibal Caro*, in two folio volumes. One hundred and fifty copies were printed for presentation to crowned or sovereign princes. The volumes include fifty plates illustrating the various sites referred to in the epic, together with a portrait of the Duchess after Lawrence. Cardinal Mezzofanti was of assistance in this publication. " This edition has won the admiration of all our artists," he wrote. " And the Duchess, not content with its present illustrations, has gone to Mantua, taking with her another excellent landscape painter to make a sketch of Pietole to be added to the other plates which already adorn this splendid work of art."

Lastly she arranged an edition of the *Divine Comedy*, in the French version of her friend Artaud, to be illustrated with one hundred plates. This was never completed.

Her interest in politics remained unabated. The liberation of Greece excited her warmest sympathies. " Events of the day are passing which may deserve blame," she wrote to Lady Morgan. " But the efforts—the heroic efforts which the Greeks have made, and are making, are worthy of all our admiration, and will end, I hope, by restoring that interesting country to its situation in Europe." She pressed upon the British Government the Papal view of the Catholic claims, here, in fact, carrying on the work of her father the Earl-Bishop. " How far," said a friend, " the question was in consequence advanced is not very discoverable, for not only the successive monarchs of England, during her life, continued opposed to it, but her brother-in-law, Lord Liverpool, so long our prime minister, while she lived was its decided adversary ; nor did the measure pass into law for above five years after her decease."

Louisa de Stolberg, widow of the younger Pretender, wrote to the Duchess from Florence, " Ma belle amie, on dit ici que vous régnez à Rome. Permettez moi d'aller vous visiter dans vos états.' Thomas Moore found the Duchess and Lady Humphrey Davy " the rival *cicerones* of Rome." Moore " went in the evening to the Duchess of Devonshire's assembly, dull enough ; but that beautiful creature, Mrs. Dodwell, was there : asked the Abbé Taylor to introduce me to her, but he would not, said it would not be proper." He went again, perhaps to have another glimpse of the beauty, for she was present. Madame Renaudin was singing, " the most celebrated musical person they have." On a third occasion he himself was the vocalist, and the Duchess had invited Canova and Lawrence to meet him.

Duchess Elizabeth was now in her sixty-third year. One who met her in Rome at the end of her life writes that she became " so emaciated as to resemble a living spectre ; but the lines of a rare and commanding beauty still remained. Her features were regular and noble, her eyes magnificent, and her attenuated figure was upright and dignified, with the step of an empress. Her complexion of marble paleness completed this portrait. Her beautiful arms and hands were still as white as ivory, though almost like a skeleton's from their thinness. She used in vain to attempt to disguise their emaciation by wearing bracelets and rings."

When her illness was known to be fatal the Duke of Devonshire, her stepson, journeyed to Rome. " He treated her with respect and even affection, but there was an evident reserve between them. At her death he carefully excluded all friends to whom she could in her last moments confide what might, perhaps, at that hour, trouble her conscience. Her friends Madame Récamier and the Duc de Laval were only admitted to bid her farewell when she was speechless, and a few minutes before she breathed her last."

This action aroused much comment, and was received as certain proof of the legend respecting the young duke's birth. A suggestion, which may be accepted as probable, has been made that the Duchess Elizabeth was inclined towards the Church of Rome, and that the Duke feared a conversion upon her death-bed. But, as the same writer added, " the point is one that cannot be settled." Had Elizabeth Devonshire turned from Church of England to Church of Rome the fact would have made no difference to her family or fortune. Her death took place March 30, 1824.

CONCLUSION

THE Devonshire House Circle existed for exactly fifty years. When Duchess Georgiana married in 1774 there had not been a mistress of the old house for many years. With the death of Duchess Elizabeth in 1824 there followed another long interregnum. For the sixth duke remained a bachelor until his death in 1858, when, in the words of the peerage, the barony of Clifford fell into abeyance between his sisters and co-heiresses, the Countesses of Carlisle and Granville, and the dukedom devolved on his grace's cousin, the second Earl of Burlingtou.

Of the sixth Duke it can be said that he was loved by his family and loved by those who served him. No finer epitaph can be pronounced upon any man. In his younger days he had been a true Cavendish in his encouragement of learning and science, and in his lavish magnificence which culminated in the famous embassy to Petrograd. But his extreme deafness was a bar against much public activity, although, according to Creevey, he was a zealous supporter of the movement for reform.

His closest associate remained the half-brother with whom he had been educated, Augustus Clifford. The young midshipman had influential friends, and made rapid progress in his profession. He was noted for great courage in the operations which concluded in 1812, and was afterwards attached to the Lord High Admiral, the Duke of Clarence, afterwards William IV. For several years he served as a member of Parliament, was given the C.B. in 1815, knighted in 1830, and created a baronet by Queen

Victoria in 1838. In 1832 his brother the Duke of Devonshire, then Lord Chamberlain, appointed him Gentleman Usher of the Black Rod, a post he held until his death in 1877 at the age of eighty-nine. Like all the members of his family he was an enthusiastic patron of the fine arts, and formed a unique collection of paintings, sculpture, etchings, engravings, and bijouterie.

" I knew Sir Augustus Clifford well, and had a very high opinion of him," wrote Sir W. Fraser in *Hic et Ubique.* " The position which he filled for many years as Serjeant-at-Arms of the Queen's Household, lent by Her Majesty to the House of Lords, was one requiring great personal dignity. This Sir Augustus had in a greater degree than anyone I have seen. It is no easy thing to advance at a slow pace up the centre of a highly sarcastic body such as the House of Commons, to announce the formal ' desire ' of the Sovereign."

Had Sir Augustus left any memoirs—his only literary exercise was a privately issued life of his half-brother, the Duke—he could have noted many extraordinary changes in England and the higher circles of English society. And he could have cited a few of the extraordinary parallels which history is always able to present. Great nations are ever in transition and evolution, although the essential character of a race does not appear to alter to any large extent.

During the American War of Independence the Home Government was severely criticised for its lack of energy. Sir Augustus was but a child when George Selwyn died, but he knew many of the men who were responsible for that disastrous campaign. George Selwyn wrote to Lord Carlisle at Castle Howard. " We are quite undone. A civil war in England is expected. We are privately, I don't know how, at a greater expense, that is, in contracts, than during the war. Nobody knows where it will end, or how. *Je le crois.* I wish I could stuff my ears with cotton till the hurly-burly was done ; for if I was disposed to be vapourish, I should expect, when I went to bed, that in the morning I should (not) know where to find bread.'" Seven days later he wrote : " America is to have all our force opposed to it, but I think it is so, by degrees, that they are continually getting advantages, for want of our sending sufficient force, and our foolish moderation being imputed to the timidity or fluctuation of our counsels. If I was to give my sentiments in the House, they would not complain of my prolixity ; for all I have to say upon this matter is, what Queen Elizabeth told her Council in relation to the Queen of Scots, " *Aut fer, aut feri.*" More cannot be expressed in so few words. I am confident that every *moyen parti* will be infructuous."

How strangely modern it all reads. Yet the date is 1775. " All is lost ! " cried England when Byng was defeated at Minorca, yet never once was public energy affected by private pessimism.

After 1815 this pessimism took another form. No longer fearing foreign enemies the legislators of Great Britain began to dread internal revolution. " I don't believe there will be a king in Europe in two years' time," wrote the Earl of Sefton to Mr. Creevey in 1830, " or that property of any kind is worth five years' purchase." Four years later Queen Adelaide was still gloomier, having " a fix'd impression that an English revolution is rapidly approaching, and that her own fate is to be that of Marie Antoinette, and she trusts she shall be able to act her part with more courage."

This pessimism not only coloured the criticism of public affairs. The race itself was always in a state of rapid degeneration. Mrs. Thicknesse, in her *School for Fashion,* published in 1800, quotes Dr. Warner, the friend of Selwyn, " on the altered disposition of the ladies of England." He had left them in 1790, the " coyest and loveliest of the female kind." They were then " as chaste and modest as the unsunn'd snow," and they came in his view " to angels nearest in this world below." When he returned to England in 1793 he was aghast at the change. They were without waist and without modesty. To-day we venerate those women as the mothers of the heroes of Waterloo.   This self-depreciation is a truly British virtue, and, like many virtues, pushed so far as to become in actuality a vice.

These hopes and fears of the past have a very real value for the present.   In the story of the Devonshire House Circle the reader may draw what morals he may desire.   But the men and women who congregated round the two Duchesses more than a century ago were beset by the same pre-occupations and cares as we of to-day.   Despite occasional despondencies they surmounted all their difficulties.   They steered the ship of State to victory.   And in this respect the story of their brave deeds is our example.

INDEX

LACROIX, PAUL, 236, 239
Lafayette, marquis de, 269
La Fontaine, 236
La Galissonière, 94
Lahoop, Mrs., 25
Lamb, Lady Caroline, 67, 248, 310, 323, 324
—— George, 310, 311
—— William, 302, 303
Lambton (see Durham, Earl of)
Landaff, Bishop of, 26
Langton, Bennet, 270
Lansdowne House, 21, 26
—— Marquess of, 216
Latimer House, 30
Lausanne, 223, 224, 230, 231, 232, 233, 256, 274
Lauzun, duc de, 264, 268, 271
Laval family, 255, 331
Lawrence, Sir Thomas, 309, 330
Lecky, W. E. H., 59 note
Lee, Miss, 277, 279
Leeds, Duke of, 256, 266
Leicester, Earl of (Coke), 9 note, 52 note, 84, 85, 85 note
Leicester Square, 3
Leinster family, 57 note
Lemaitre, Jules, 242 note
Leman, Lake, 230, 274
Lennox family, 7, 142
—— Lady Caroline, 51
—— Lady Sarah, 109, 142
Lepell, Molly, 174, 223, 309
Lichfield, Lord, 84 note
Liége, 45
Lincoln's Inn Fields, 21
Linley, Eliza Anne (Mrs. Sheridan), 129, 139, 163, 164, 217
Liverpool, Earl of, 177 note, 321 note
Locke, John, 80 note
London, Bishop of, 14
Lonsdale, Earl of, 182 note
Loughborough, Lord, 211
Louis XV., 77, 262
—— XVI., 262, 280
Lovelace, 40
Lowndes Square, 25
Lucan, Lady, 149
Ludgershall, 10
Luxembourg family, 255
Lyttelton, Lord, 2
—— Sarah, Lady, 135, 250, 281, 312, 313, 313 note

MACHEATH, CAPTAIN, 26
Mack, General, 303

M'Lean, " gentleman," 27
Mann, Sir Horace, 26, 36, 54 note, 74, 181, 183
Marble Hill, 156
March, Lord (see Queensberry, Duke of)
Marie Antoinette, 255, 262, 263, 264, 265, 266, 267, 269, 282
Maintenon, madame de, 236
Markham, Archbishop, 14
Marlborough House, 14, 21
Marlborough family (see Churchill)
—— Sarah, Duchess of, 21, 35, 38, 89 note, 152, 173, 174
Marseilles, 255
Martindale, 287
Martinique, 259
Mary I., 28
—— II., 21, 31
Marylebone, 3, 26
Mason, 154, 214
Mayfair, 19, 58, 58 note
Mazarin, duchesse de, 32
Medwin, 279
Melbourne, Lord, 204, 277
——Lady, 110 note, 159
Mexborough, Lady, 282
Mezzofanti, cardinal, 330
Michelet, 242 note
Milbank, Lady Augusta, 82 note
Milbanke family, 320–322
Milton, Lord, 157, 158
Minto, Lord, 131, 145, 163, 217, 237
Moira, Lord, 219
Monckton, Miss (see Corke, Lady)
Montagu, Mrs. Elizabeth, 2, 61, 105, 107 note, 118, 120, 124, 141 note, 145, 150, 151, 199, 239 note
—— Lady Mary Wortley, 1, 3, 14, 41 note, 44, 45, 50 note, 80, 173, 174
Montaigne, 44 note
Montmorency, 255
Montolieu, baron de, 330, 232
Montpellier, 45
Moore, Dr., 236
Moore, Thomas, 323, 324, 328, 33
Mordaunt, Anna Maria (see Poyntz, Mrs.)
—— family, 172
More, Hannah, 12, 145
Morgan, Lady, 67, 326, 328, 330
Morland, George, 152
Morley, Lord, 246
Morpeth, Lord, 256
Morris, Captain, 202
Moser, Mary, 102, 103

Lightning Source UK Ltd.
Milton Keynes UK
UKHW04f0903231018
331030UK00009B/572/P